CW01574778

Robert E. Meditz

The Dialectic of the Holy

Tillich Research

Tillich-Forschungen
Recherches sur Tillich

Edited by
Christian Danz, Marc Dumas, Werner Schüßler,
Mary Ann Stenger and Erdmann Sturm

Volume 7

Robert E. Meditz

The Dialectic of the Holy

Paul Tillich's Idea of Judaism within the History of Religion

DE GRUYTER

R E M
March 2017

ISBN 978-3-11-043997-7
e-ISBN (PDF) 978-3-11-043257-2
e-ISBN (EPUB) 978-3-11-043277-0
ISSN 2192-1938

Library of Congress Cataloging-in-Publication Data
A CIP catalog record for this book has been applied for at the Library of Congress.

Bibliographic information published by the Deutsche Nationalbibliothek
The Deutsche Nationalbibliothek lists this publication in the Deutsche Nationalbibliografie; detailed bibliographic data are available on the Internet at http://dnb.dnb.de.

© 2016 Walter de Gruyter GmbH, Berlin/Boston
Printing and binding: CPI books GmbH, Leck
♾ Printed on acid-free paper
Printed in Germany

www.degruyter.com

MIX
Papier aus verantwortungsvollen Quellen
FSC® C083411

Contents

Abbreviations and Note on the Text

In this book the following acronymns and abbreviations have been used:

1910 Dissertation	Paul Tillich, "The Construction of the History of Religion in Schelling's Positive Philosophy: Its Presuppositions and Principles." Published under the same title, in translation and with an introduction and notes by Victor David Nuovo (Lewisburg, PA: Bucknell University Press, 1974)
1912 Dissertation	Paul Tillich, "Mysticism and Guilt-Consciousness in Schelling's Philosophical Development." Published under the same title with an introduction and notes by Victor Nuovo (Lewisburg, PA: Bucknell University Press, 1974)
Earley Dissertation	Glenn David Earley, "An Everlasting Conversation: Judaism in the Life and Thought of Paul Tillich." PhD dissertation, Temple University, 1983
Earley, *Judenfrage* essay	Glenn David Earley, "Paul Tillich and Judaism: An Analysis of 'The Jewish Question' – A Christian and a German Problem," in *Theonomy and Autonomy: Studies in Paul Tillich's Engagement with Modern Culture*, ed. John J. Carey (Macon, GA: Mercer University Press, 1984), 213–241
BNAPTS	*Bulletin of the North American Paul Tillich Society*
BRSUR	*Biblical Religion and the Search for Ultimate Reality* (Chicago: University of Chicago Press, 1955)
E	*Ergänzungs- und Nachlaßbände zu den Gesammelten Werken von Paul Tillich*, 18 vols. (Stuttgart: Ev. Verlagswerk, 1971– ; Berlin: De Gruyter, 1994–2013)
GEC	German Evangelical Church
GW	Paul Tillich, *Gesammelte Werke*, 14 vols., ed. Renate Albrecht (Stuttgart: Evangelisches Verlagswerk, 1958–83)
Harvard Archives	Harvard University Archives, Cambridge, Mass. The Tillich collection is archived under bMS 649
Judenfrage lectures	"The Jewish Question: A Christian and a German Problem," four lectures delivered at Der Deutschen Hochschule für Politik in the summer of 1952 and first published in *Schriftenreihe der Deutsche Hochschule für Politik* (Berlin: Gebruder Weiss, 1953); subsequently published in *GW* vol. III, *Das religiöse Fundament des moralischen Handelns: Schriften zur Ethik und zum Menschenbild*, 128–170.
NRSV	New Revised Standard Version
Religious Situation	Paul Tillich, *The Religious Situation*, trans. and preface H. Richard Niebuhr (New York: Meridian Books and Living Age Books; London: Thames & Hudson, 1956)
RSV	Revised Standard Version
Schelling, *GW*	Manfred Schröter, ed., *Gesammelte Werke*, by F. W. J. Schelling. 14 vols. (Munich: C. H. Beck, 1927)
Schelling, *SW*	F. W. J. Schelling, *Sämmtliche Werke*, Part I, vols. 1–10 and Part II, vols. 1–4 (Stuttgart und Augsburg: J. M. Cotta Verlag, 1856–1861)

Socialist Decision	Paul Tillich, *The Socialist Decision* (New York: Harper & Row, 1977), trans. Franklin Sherman from the German *Die sozialistische Entscheidung*, as published in *GW* vol. II, *Frühe Schriften zum Religiösen Sozialismus*
ST	Paul Tillich, *Systematic Theology*, 3 volumes (Chicago: University of Chicago Press, 1951, 1957, 1963)

The footnotes employ the short title referencing system whereby a bibliographical citation provides full publication details at first mention and a shortened form thereafter.

Acknowledgements

This book is based on my doctoral dissertation, completed at the University of Exeter (UK) and Hartford Seminary (the "Hartford Joint Programme"). First, I would like to thank those who guided me through the process: Kelton Cobb, Timothy Gorringe, Najib Awad, David Tollerton and Fred Parella, the latter serving as my external examiner for the *viva voce*.

Second, I would like to thank Frances O'Donnell, Curator of Manuscripts and Archives at the Andover-Harvard Theological Library, who provided me with copies of Tillich's lectures, many of which are unpublished.

Third, I would like to thank Marie Rovero and Andrea Jones of the Hartford Seminary library, who located numerous hard-to-find books and articles, cheerfully, and in a timely fashion.

Fourth, I would like to thank Mary Ann Stenger and Christian Danz, who provided essential commentary to complete the process of converting the dissertation to a book.

Fifth, I am grateful that "at the last minute," Marion Hausner Pauck clarified some key biographical details of Tillich's life. Any factual errors are my responsibility.

Finally, I would like to thank my wife Linda S. Meditz, for her love and support. She knows first hand the challenges, and satisfactions, of scholarly work.

Preface

I first became intrigued with the topic of Christian anti-Judaism in the 1990s, upon reading R. Po Chia Hsia's *The Myth of Ritual Murder: Jews and Magic in Reformation Germany.*[1] This book alerted me to the development of a complex ideological structure that made possible the persecution of Jews for the alleged crimes of host desecration and murder of Christian children for religious purposes. This ideological structure possessed a political dimension, illustrated by rising anti-Judaism within the Holy Roman Empire and the expulsion of Jews from Imperial cities; a social and philosophical dimension, reflected in the burgeoning debate between scholastics and humanists during the late Renaissance, which was played out within the universities; and a theological dimension, which involved very complex hermeneutical issues concerning the relationship between the Old and New Testaments of the Christian Bible. After reading Hsia's book, I continued to dabble in related topics, such as the "Reuchlin affair," in which the Christian Hebraist and humanist scholar Johannes Reuchlin (1455–1522) opposed the Imperial edict to confiscate and burn Jewish sacred texts.[2] This event, too, involved a very complex set of political, social and religious factors. Common to both stories is the presence of Christian anti-Judaism, which has explicitly theological roots, and arguably has roots within the Christian New Testament itself.[3] Common to both is also a complex ideological structure, which extended the negative theological influence into society. These events left a lasting impression for two reasons. First, any thinking Christian would want to investigate the causal relation between anti-Jewish aspects of Christian theology and potential societal influence, made more urgent if it relates to the Holocaust of the twentieth century. Second, the sheer complexity of these issues is hard to believe, especially the deeply embedded nature of anti-Jewish discourse within the Western intellectual tradition.

When I enrolled in a seminar at Hartford Seminary in the fall of 2006 to read the theology of Paul Tillich, I sensed that it might be fruitful to insert Tillich's thought into the complex subject of the relationship of Christian theology to modern anti-Semitism. While Tillich was not a Christian Hebraist like Johannes

1 New Haven, CT: Yale University Press, 1988.

2 David Price, *Johannes Reuchlin and the Campaign to Destroy Jewish Books*; Oxford University Press, 2010.

3 Rosemary Radford Ruether, *Faith and Fratricide: The Theological Roots of Anti-Semitism* (Minneapolis, MN: The Seabury Press, 1974).

Reuchlin, he certainly intended to be a Christian humanist.[4] In addition, his defense of the Jews bears some similarity to Reuchlin's in the sense that both made arguments to civil authorities defending Judaism. In making this rough comparison, I seek to place Tillich within the long history of Christian-Jewish relations. This book traces the development of how Tillich understood the role of Judaism within the history of religion, and how he assigned permanent theological importance to the Jewish prophets, in the recurring struggle with idolatry.

4 For example, regarding a synthesis between Christianity and modern thought, see Tillich's "Autobiographical Reflections," in *The Theology of Paul Tillich* (revised), ed. Charles W. Kegley, New York: Pilgrim Press, 1982; 9–11; Reuchlin's humanism in part involved his adherence to the *philosophia perennis* ("perennial philosophy"), in the sense that Christianity participated in a universal system to which all rational persons could ascribe. Suzanne L. Marchand, *German Orientalism in the Age of Empire: Religion, Race and Scholarship* (Washington, D.C. and New York: German Historical Institute and Cambridge University Press, 2010), 4.

“Justice is the true power of being.” (*The Socialist Decision*, 6)

“Anti-Judaism has occurred in all of church history and represents the tragic guilt of the church.” (*Judenfrage* lectures, 428)

“It was one of the greatest moments in the history of humanity when Amos, the first of the great prophets, threatened Israel with destruction and severed the connection between God and the space with which he was associated.” (*Judenfrage* lectures, 467)

Chapter One: The Importance of Judaism for Tillich, the Context and Method

1.1 Key Biographical Details

On April 13, 1933, four months after Adolf Hitler came to power, Paul Tillich was suspended from his position as chair of the philosophy department at the University of Frankfurt for speaking out against Nazi intimidation of leftist students, and for being a "well known religious socialist."[1] Tillich was one of over 1,600 German academics that were either fired or suspended for being Jews and/or critics of the Nazi regime.[2] Enemies of the state fell into two categories. The first group included those whose political views were considered suspect, including members of the Communist and Socialist parties. The second category included those who were "racially suspect," meaning Jews.[3] Tillich's name appeared in the first category, along with his friends, philosopher Max Horkheimer, the chief administrative officer of the University of Frankfurt Kurt Riezler, and economist Adolf Löwe.[4] In addition, several other non-Jewish colleagues were dismissed as well, including the socialist pastor Günther Dehn, artist Paul Klee, social theorist Karl Mennicke, and economist Alfred Weber.[5]

1 *Manchester Guardian*, 19 May 1993; cf. Gabrielle Simon Edgcomb, *From Swastika to Jim Crow: Refugee Scholars at Black Colleges* (Malabar, FL: Krieger, 1993), 6 – 16.

2 On 7 April 1933 the newly empowered National Socialist government passed the Reich Law for the Restoration of the Professional Civil Service (the "Civil Service law"), which, among other things, prohibited non-Aryans from being employed in the civil service. Jews and the descendants of Jews were targeted in particular, although veterans of World War I and direct relatives of World War I veterans killed in action could be exempt. See Wolfgang Gerlach, *And the Witnesses were Silent: The Confessing Church and the Persecution of the Jews*, trans. and ed. Victoria J. Barnett (Lincoln, NE: University of Nebraska Press, 2000), 17 – 18. This provision, from paragraph 3 of the Civil Service law, became known as the contested "Aryan paragraph." See Larry L. Rasmussen, editor's introduction to *Dietrich Bonhoeffer: Works*, vol. XII, *Berlin: 1932 – 1933*, trans. Isabel Best and David Higgins (Minneapolis, MN: Fortress Press, 2009), 11. The German Evangelical Church attempted to adopt a similar provision in church law, in adherence to the Nazi government's policy of "synchronization," or *Gleichschaltung*, in which all dimensions of German life and culture were to be legally subject to Nazi ideology. See Gerlach, *Witnesses were Silent*, glossary, 288.

3 Wilhelm and Marion Pauck, *Paul Tillich: His Life and Thought*, (New York: Harper & Row, 1976), 130. Thereafter, "Pauck, Pauck, *Tillich.*"

4 Ibid., 130.

5 Ibid., 71, 110, 130.

In May Tillich was initially instructed by the Ministry of Education to remain in Germany until a final decision was made on his case.[6] In August of that year, Union Theological Seminary in New York, through Reinhold Niebuhr, offered him a position.[7] However, being a loyal German, Tillich hesitated, and traveled around Germany seeking advice and counsel as to whether he should leave the country. Some time in the fall of 1933, as the situation in Germany deteriorated, Tillich met with the new Nazi secretary of education,[8] who wanted to offer Tillich the chair of Theology at the University of Berlin, in exchange for retracting *The Socialist Decision*. In a 1959 interview for *Time* magazine, Tillich recalls that this interview became the pivotal moment when he decided to leave Germany and seek political asylum in the United States: "For a full hour, we discussed the Old Testament and the importance to Christianity of the Jewish tradition. At the end of the hour I knew it was over."[9] Adolf Lowe also relates that in this interview, the Nazi official also asked Tillich to retract *The Socialist Decision*,[10] in return for the prestigious chair of Theology at the University of Berlin. Tillich reportedly laughed in his face.[11] The Nazi official recommended that

---

6 The facts surrounding this are somewhat confusing, although the Paucks provide the most detailed account in English, which is partly based on personal interviews with Tillich. One confusing detail concerns which government bureau was in charge of Tillich's case, as it is either referred to as the Ministry of Education or the Ministry of Culture. The Paucks say that the May notification was by the "Ministry of Education," but that the October meeting was with Dr. Wilhelm Stuckart, age 31, from the "Ministry of Culture." Pauck, Pauck, *Tillich*, 132–136. One possible solution to this is that the Ministry of Education and the Ministry of Culture were departments within a single government bureau. For example, in April of 1934 Dr. Bernhard Rust was appointed Reich Minister of Science, Education and Culture For the People (*Volksbildung*), a year later than the Tillich incident. Erika Mann, *School for Barbarians: Education Under the Nazis*, Introduction by Thomas Mann (Mineola, New York: Dover Publications, Inc., 2014; first published by Modern Age Books in 1938), 48–49.

7 Ronald Stone observes that Horace Friess of Columbia University, along with Niebuhr, was also responsible for securing the position at Union; cf. *Paul Tillich's Radical Social Thought* (Atlanta, GA: John Knox Press, 1980), 65–66; hereafter, "Stone, *Radical Social Thought*."

8 Hannah Tillich refers to "the new Nazi secretary of education," "the secretary of culture," and "the secretary of education," in her account of Tillich's final meeting before they emigrated. See *From Time to Time* (New York: Stein & Day, 1973), 154–155. Hannah recalls that after the meeting, Tillich told her he posed two questions to the minister of education: "What about the Jews?" and "How will you deal with modern culture?" Hannah Tillich, *From Time to Time*, 154–155.

9 This incident is recounted in the feature article "A Theology for Protestants," *Time*, 16 March 1959, 48.

10 For publication details see Note on the Text above. The original German edition was published by Alfred Protte of Potsdam in 1933.

11 Related by John R. Stumme in the introduction to *Socialist Decision*, xxiv.

Tillich leave Germany for his own safety, for two years,[12] but that he expected things to ultimately improve so that Tillich could return. After agonizing over this, Tillich decided to emigrate. Aside from concern for his personal safety, this pivotal interview reveals what was most important to Tillich, what he found non-negotiable about the Nazi regime, and the importance of the Old Testament[13] and Judaism to Christian theology. It is revealing that Tillich refers to this incident in the manner that he does, since he was 73 and was being interviewed by the widely read *Time* magazine. His emigration to America at age 47 was pivotal in the sense that he went on to have another life, indeed a very successful one, but only after a very challenging beginning. However, he maintained his conviction that Judaism was vitally important for Christian theology, and that Nazism and all forms of anti-Semitism must be opposed. In fact, Tillich's choice to defy Nazi manipulation in 1933 was the first of several instances in which he displayed these convictions, which began when Hitler came to power, and continued throughout his life, emerging at critical times and places. Two additional examples in which Tillich voluntarily took a stand to combat anti-Semitism underscore this.

On 21 November 1938, just over five years after the promulgation of the first racial laws that caused Tillich to be relieved of his position at the University of Frankfurt, Tillich made a speech in Madison Square Garden to an overflow crowd, and with major press coverage, titled, "The Meaning of Anti-Semitism."[14] In this instance, Tillich clearly linked the Nazi attack on Judaism to an attack on

---

12 Hannah Tillich, *From Time to Time*, 155.

13 Throughout this book, the term "Old Testament" will be used, to be consistent with Tillich's terminology. This does necessarily not denote an endorsement of this term, and what it might imply, from a normative standpoint.

14 Oddly, in the Pauck's biography of Tillich, this event is only referred to as "a Protestant gathering protesting Hitler's persecution of the Jews," although it acknowledges that Tillich broke his self-imposed silence on public statements of a political nature since he had not yet obtained US citizenship. Pauck and Pauck, *Tillich*, 196–197, note 3. On the same day at Madison Square Garden, a mass rally protesting against the Nazis and *Kristallnacht* was staged by church, labor, literary and civic leaders from New York City, at which seventeen speeches were given, including one by Tillich. This event was one of many in America that exhibited the harshest condemnation of Nazism, and it was covered by major media outlets, including the *New York Times* and the radio station WHOM. The *Times* headline ran, "20,000 Jam Garden in Reich Protest. Varied Groups Hear Pleas to 'Smash Nazism' to End its Persecutions ...," and the story reported, "amid the variety" of the seventeen speakers, the unifying feature was the "vigor of the addresses and of the responses of the audience." I draw here from Michael Berkowitz's essay "*Kristallnacht* in Context: Jewish War Veterans in America and Britain and the Crisis of German Jewry," in *American Religious Responses to Kristallnacht*, ed. Maria Mazzenga (Houndsmills: Palgrave Macmillan, 2009), 69–70 notes 67, 82.

Christianity: "Few words are required to prove that the struggle for the eradication of Judaism is, in its profoundest meaning, a struggle to eradicate Christianity."[15] In addition, in the same speech, Tillich called for unity between Christians and Jews on the basis of a common prophetic religion, and urged solidarity with Jews and opposition to Nazism.[16] Because of his political views, Tillich had been suspended from his university position and effectively forced to leave Germany in 1933. It appears that upon arriving in America, Tillich had intended to keep his political views private, since he was a German national in an era of rising tension between the two countries. He was not yet an American citizen. However, upon learning of the *Kristallnacht* pogrom of November 9 – 10 November 1938, in which German government paramilitary groups killed 91 Jews, arrested 30,000 who were sent to concentration camps, razed over 1,000 synagogues and destroyed thousands of Jewish businesses and homes,[17] Tillich became so indignant that he felt compelled to make a speech before over 20,000 people, with newspaper and radio coverage.[18] Later, Tillich became an American citizen, on 4 March 1940,[19] fully embracing America as his new home.[20]

Three and a half years later, on 31 March 1942, a speech drafted by Tillich in German titled "The Question of the Jewish People," was broadcast into Germany.[21] This was the first of 112 weekly speeches authored in secret by Tillich and delivered from March 1942 to May 1944,[22] as part of the US government's *Voice of America* series.[23] In this speech, Tillich affirms several propositions that form the core of his understanding of the relationship between Judaism and Christianity: the Christian religion was "prepared in the womb of Jewish his-

---

15 Paul Tillich, 21 November 1938 speech entitled "The Meaning of Anti-Semitism," later published in *Radical Religion* 4/1 (Winter 1938): 34 – 36.

16 Ronald H. Stone and Matthew Lon Weaver, eds., *Against the Third Reich: Paul Tillich's Wartime Radio Broadcasts into Nazi Germany*, trans. Matthew Lon Weaver (Louisville, KY: Westminster John Knox Press, 1998), 6.

17 Mazzenga, *Kristallnacht*, introductory essay, "American Religious Groups and *Kristallnacht*," 1.

18 The Paucks say that in discussions and debates, Tillich typically remained very restrained and objective, taking seriously criticisms of his views. However, they cite several examples of Tillich being enraged at the Nazis and everything they stood for (127 – 131).

19 Ibid., 197.

20 See Paul Tillich, "I am an American," *Protestant Digest* 3 (1941): 24 – 26.

21 Stone and Weaver, *Against the Third Reich*, 1.

22 Ibid.

23 The Voice of America was part of the Radio Program Bureau of the Office of War Information (OWI). It was forbidden to use falsehood in its efforts. The Voice of America should be distinguished from "psychological warfare," as administered by the Office of Strategic Services (OSS), which was mandated to engage in subversive activities. Stone and Weaver, *Against the Third Reich*, 1 – 2.

tory;" that Jesus was of Jewish lineage; that the Old Testament is part of the Christian Bible; that the Protestant Reformation was carried out in the spirit of Paul, who was a Jew; that both Christians and Jews draw from the same law, prophets and Psalms; and that Christians cannot renounce the same religious roots out of which a religious Jew lives.[24] It appears that the Office of War Information gave Tillich considerable flexibility in preparing the content of this initial speech, and even for the entire series, since the content unmistakably reflects his unique thoughts. The speeches ultimately aim to persuade Germans in Germany to oppose Hitler, but they do not exhibit the features of crude "war propaganda;" in fact, he was asked by the Office of War Information to speak the truth as he knew it.[25] Therefore, it is very revealing that Tillich chose this topic for his first speech, because it was central to his thought, intellectually and existentially.[26] According to Stone and Weaver:

> the historic identity of the Jewish people had a significant place in Tillich's theology, as well as in his philosophy of history. Theologically, the Jews are the inspiration for his notion of the Protestant principle, that element of perpetual critique that stands against the ever-present threats of idolatry and absolutism. Historically, Jewish prophetism is the vehicle for his argument of the dominance of time over space as the necessary prerequisite for the existence of justice.[27]

These themes will be discussed in greater detail in this chapter, and in Chapters Two through Six of this book. In addition, the contributions of Stone and Weaver will be discussed further below.

---

24 Tillich, written speech titled "The Question of the Jewish People," 31 March 1942, cited in Stone and Weaver, *Against the Third Reich*, 13.

25 Stone and Weaver in their introduction to *Against the Third Reich* discuss the distinction between "propaganda studies," which focuses on the truth or falsehood of media messages, and "communication studies," which concentrates on the reception of media messages by its hearers. In this context, they assert that Tillich understood the "ambiguity" of his situation. While Tillich would have refrained from doing what the Nazis did, he understood the importance and effectiveness of mass media in a modern, technological society. Stone and Weaver, *Against the Third Reich*, 2. See also Matthew Lon Weaver, *Religious Internationalism: War and Peace in the Thought of Paul Tillich* (Macon, GA: Mercer University Press, 2010), 144–145 and notes 1–5.

26 Stone and Weaver, *Against the Third Reich*, 7. See also Ronald H. Stone, *Paul Tillich's Radical Social Thought* (Louisville, KY: Westminster John Knox Press, 1980), 102.

27 Stone and Weaver, *Against the Third Reich*, 7.

1.1.2 Select Prior Treatments of Tillich and Judaism

Tillich's critique of Nazism, his understanding of Judaism and Judaism's relationship of Judaism to Christianity, and his understanding of the Old Testament, have received prior scholarly treatment.[28] However, other than one doctoral dissertation, to be discussed below, there have been no attempts to systematically analyze how Judaism functions within Tillich's theological method. Three other Tillich scholars, Glenn David Earley, Ronald H. Stone and Matthew Lon Weaver, have each made major contributions to our understanding of Tillich and Judaism. Taken together, these three scholars present a well-rounded profile of Tillich's relation to Judaism, and in the cases of Stone and Weaver, this is done in the context of other topics. First, they all agree that Tillich has a theological understanding of Judaism as a prophetic movement, reflecting his socialist political orientation.[29] This theological understanding of Judaism is distinct from Judaism as a historical and social phenomenon. Second, Earley, Stone and Weaver agree that Tillich adopted a key metaphor for characterizing the Jews as "the people of time."[30] This led Tillich to a related idea, that the "Jewish spirit" provides a permanent critique of Christianity. Earley takes this to another level by arguing that Tillich effectively equates his concept of Jewish spirit with Tillich's more famous "Protestant principle," the critical principle he uses to identify idolatry and absolutism.[31] Third, they all discuss the importance of the thought of F. W. J.

---

28 For Tillich's critique of Nazism, see *Ten Theses*, cited in Mark Kline Taylor, Paul Tillich: Theologian of the Boundaries (London: Collins, 1987), 116 – 118. For a more detailed philosophical critique, see Franz G.M. Feige, *The Varieties of Protestantism in Nazi Germany: Five Theopolitical Positions*, Toronto Studies in Theology 50 (Lewiston, NY: Edwin Mellen Press, 1990), 395 – 443. As for the Old Testament, Tillich is quite clear about the importance of the prophetic tradition, but he has left no explicit treatment of the Old Testament. Due to his philosophical exegesis and use of ontology, he does not present an explicit doctrine of Scripture, but discusses its role in the context of other topics. For Tillich's understanding of the relationship between ontology and the Bible, see *Biblical Religion and the Search for Ultimate Reality* (Chicago: University of Chicago Press, 1955), referred to hereafter as *BRSUR*. For two rare and penetrating analyses of Tillich's hermeneutical principles, see John Charles Cooper, *The 'Spiritual Presence' in the Theology of Paul Tillich: Tillich's Use of St Paul* (Macon, GA: Mercer University Press, 1997). Also, see Courtney S. Wilder, "Existentialism and Exegesis: Being and the Bible in Bultmann and Tillich," dissertation, University of Chicago, June 2008.

29 Earley Dissertation, 240 – 259; Stone, *Radical Social Thought*, 76 – 82; Weaver, *War and Peace*, 118, 177 – 178.

30 Earley Dissertation, 388 – 403; Stone, *Radical Social Thought*, 102 and 149; Weaver, citing Tillich's *Judenfrage* lectures, refers to Tillich's view as "the people of history," 238 – 239, *War and Peace.*

31 Earley Dissertation, 378 – 412.

Schelling (1775–1854) for Tillich, although none of them see any significant relationship between Tillich's appropriation of Schelling and Tillich's view of Judaism.[32]

Despite the significant contributions of these three authors, none has fully explained how Tillich grounded his pro-Jewish views within his theological method. Earley makes a profound observation about the similarity in Tillich's mind between the "spirit of Jewish prophetism" and the Protestant principle.[33] Stone was the first scholar to provide a biographical analysis of Tillich and Judaism, and also appears to be the first to connect Tillich's adoption of socialism and his prophetic view of Judaism;[34] this has correctly remained the consensus view. Stone's work was also foundational for both Earley and Weaver; Stone was Weaver's dissertation advisor at Pittsburgh Theological Seminary. Earley was inspired by Stone.[35] Weaver astutely observes that for Tillich during World War One, the German nation possessed a salvific role within world history, analogous to the redemptive role of Schelling's second potency,[36] which will be discussed in Chapter Two. I will discuss in later chapters that Tillich deliberately singled out the prophetic feature of Judaism to play an essential role in his theological history of religions, which was identified by Earley as "Tillich's idea of Judaism."[37] My analysis will focus on this, and not on Tillich's friendships with individual Jews, or how he might have related to specific Jewish communities in his day. These topics receive substantial treatment in Earley's dissertation.[38]

---

32 Earley Dissertation, 36–37; Stone, *Radical Social Thought*, 24–31, 123, 131–132, and 152; Weaver, *War and Peace*, 32–35, it is notable that Weaver observes that Judaism and Christianity are linked together in the second potency, and are not opposed to one another, for both are revealed religions (35). Citing Erdman Sturm analysis of Tillich's "war theology," Weaver argues that Tillich's support of WWI, as manifested in his "battlefield sermons" (*Feldpredigten*), was based upon the belief that the Fatherland served as "the Second Potency," in idea inspired by Schelling; Weaver, *War and Peace*, 60.

33 Earley Dissertation, 206, 391–392.

34 Stone, *Radical Social Thought*, 77–78.

35 Earley Dissertation, xi. 13–15.

36 "Tillich believed – as do many nationalistic patriots in all periods – his nation was functioning, in Schelling's terms, as part of the second potency, as a force of selfless love and justice, against the irrationally expansive and selfish forces of the first potency, attacking it from east and west." Weaver, *War and Peace*, 06.

37 In the concluding chapter of his dissertation, Earley refers to this repeatedly, and it becomes an object of criticism. For example, he observes, "1) that Tillich's idea of Judaism is just that, and not a phenomenological description of Judaism and 2) that Tillich apparently never learned what Judaism's own questions are, but assumed that he knew what they were, thus violating his own method of correlation." Earley Dissertation, 392–393.

38 In particular, Chapters One and Two, 1–129.

The question I hope to answer is, "What was pro-Jewish about Tillich's theological method?" Tillich was pro-Jewish in four ways. First, he consistently criticized anti-Semitism. Second, he believed that Christianity could not be severed from its historical Jewish roots, as the German Christians believed. Third, he believed that the genius of Judaism within the history of religion was its "prophetic spirit," and that prophetic spirit was needed to serve as a perpetual critique of Christianity, lest Christianity lapse into paganism. For Tillich, paganism has shifting meanings, but mainly refers to the idolatry of religious nationalism. Fourth, in a less robust manner, and late in his career, Tillich argued that living Jewish communities were essential to the maintenance of this prophetic spirit.[39] This book will focus on Tillich's theological method and on how Tillich's spirit of Judaism functioned within his theological history of religion. Tillich's relationship to specific Jews and Jewish communities has been treated elsewhere, particularly in the Earley Dissertation.

In the primary source analyses in Chapters Two through Six, Tillich's dialectical history of religion will be analyzed, and the ways in which he preserves continuity between Judaism and Christianity will become evident. On the one hand, Tillich's spirit of Judaism is a theological construct in the service of Christianity. In that sense, it has limited value for current interfaith dialogue between Christianity and Judaism. On the other hand, as I hope to demonstrate, it provides theoretical support as Tillich attempts to ground a positive view of Judaism under intense anti-Semitic conditions, to be discussed in the following two sections. Section 1.2 describes the phenomenon of Aryan Christianity, a syncretistic blend of Christianity, Germanic mythology, and racial pseudo-science, which flourished in Germany during the Nazi period, with enthusiastic support from many influential members of the theological community. Section 1.3 describes the wider context of pervasive anti-Jewish sentiment that has been deeply embedded within Western thought. This briefly observes how German philosophy, expressed in the works of Kant, Fichte and Hegel, contributed to anti-Jewish sentiment. The final section (1.4) discusses Tillich's dialectical history of religion, in which two forms of dialectic are present, and serve to maintain continuity between Judaism and Christianity. These two forms are the "historical dialectic of progression" and the "ontological dialectic of balance."

---

39 For example, in 1952, Tillich writes,: "I cannot imagine that the religious socialist movements in which I myself participated could have developed without a continuous direct and indirect influence of the prophetic and critical spirit in contemporary Judaism." See "Jewish Influences on Contemporary Christian Theology;" typescript of lecture given as one of the Milton Steinberg Lectures in Jewish Theology at the Park Avenue Synagogue in New York City, published in *Cross Currents* 2/3 (1952): 35–42.

1.2 Aryan Christianity

Tillich left behind something important when he emigrated from Germany, the highly toxic phenomenon of "Aryan Christianity," which sought to eradicate the Jewish roots of Christianity. During the 1920s, a movement emerged within the German Evangelical Church led by (the) *Deutsche Christen*, or "German Christians." They embraced many of the nationalistic and racial aspects of Nazi ideology, and after Hitler came to power sought the creation of a national "Reich Church" and supported a "nazified" version of Christianity.[40] For reasons that will become evident below, I am adopting the term "Aryan Christianity" instead of "German Christianity." Aryan Christianity was a heterodox form of Christianity that in 1933 came to dominate Germany's largest Christian ecclesiastical body, the German Evangelical Church ("GEC"), which comprised nearly 70 per cent of Germany's total population.[41] The GEC sought to adhere to the new policy of *Gleichschaltung*, or "synchronization," under which all aspects of German life and culture would be legally subject to National Socialist ideology.[42] I am

---

40 See "The German Churches and the Nazi State;" cf. http://www.ushmm.org/wlc/en/article.php?ModuleId=10005206 (accessed June 28, 2015).

41 The United States Holocaust Memorial Museum determines that the Protestant population in Germany in January 1933 was 40 million, out of a total population of 60 million. Out of those 40 million, the vast majority were members of the state-supported "German Evangelical Church," which mostly included Lutheran and Reformed Protestant Christians. In addition, there were about 20 million Roman Catholics and Jews represented less than 1 % of Germany's population at that time. In January of 1933, there were 523,000 Jews in Germany, which dropped to 505,000 by June of that year, due to Germans fleeing the country. See "Germany: Jewish Population in 1933;" cf. http://www.ushmm.org/wlc/en/article.php?ModuleId=10005276 (accessed June 28, 2015). A more precise numbers of Jews was identified by the Nazis themselves, in a 1936 textbook titled, *Germany's Fall and Rise – Illustrations Taken from Arithmetic Instruction in Higher Grades of Elementary School*, which had a circulation of 715,000 copies, and asked "The Jews are aliens in Germany – In 1933 there were 66,060,000 inhabitants of the German Reich, of whom were 499,682 were Jews. What is the percentage of aliens?" Mann, *School for Barbarians*, 68.

42 According to Wolfgang Gerlach, the new National Socialist government employed a policy of "synchronization" (or in German *Gleichschaltung*), in which all dimensions of German life and culture were to be *legally* subject to Nazi ideology (*Witnesses were Silent*, glossary, 288). According to Klaus Scholder, it is important to underscore that in the spring and summer of 1933, in the wake of the Civil Service law, many in the German Evangelical Church (GEC) *voluntarily* sought to reflect and submit to the racist social policies of the Reich. At the first Reich church conference in April of 1933, supporters of Hitler within the GEC, who became known as "German Christians," supported the creation of a single Reich Church, the election of a single Reich Bishop, and the dismissal of all pastors of "alien blood," and unconditional political and social collaboration with the new Reich. Hitler appointed Ludwig Müller to the task of cre-

using the term Aryan Christianity to highlight the fundamentally anti-Jewish agenda, and to acknowledge the contribution of two works by Susannah Heschel, her 2007 book *Aryan Jesus: Christian Theologians and the Bible in Nazi Germany,*[43] and her 2009 essay "Race as Incarnational Theology: Affinities between German Protestantism and Racial Theory,"[44] both of which will provide the basis for the following discussion.

Over the past twenty-five years, there have been numerous publications in the United States that have shed new light on the role of the Christian churches in the Holocaust, including books by Robert Ericksen,[45] Doris Bergen[46] and Richard Steigmann-Gall.[47] These works, among others, complicate, or even refute, the narrative that the established Protestant Christian churches were primarily victims of Nazi persecution and were therefore unable to help the Jews. It is outside the scope of this book to provide a detailed overview of changes in the historiography surrounding this issue, but the overall thrust is that the Christian churches in Germany, especially the state supported Protestant church, either failed to oppose Nazi anti-Semitism at crucial points, or were actively complicit in undermining the status of the Jews, contributing to their de-humanization and near-extermination.[48]

---

ating an Evangelical German Reich Church, with Müller overseeing the adoption of a single Constitution of the German Evangelical Church on 11 July 1933, which was ratified by the Reich Law of 14 July 1933. Among other things, the Constitution required national church elections, which were held on 23 July 1933 and resulted in overwhelming German Christian majorities throughout the GEC. Further, the GEC held its first national synod at Wittenberg beginning on 27 September 1933. At that time, Ludwig Müller was elected first Reich Bishop of the GEC. Cf. Klaus Scholder, *A Requiem for Hitler and Other Perspectives on the German Church Struggle* (Eugene, OR: Wipf & Stock, 1989), 100. Some may object to the term "Christianity" being modified by "Aryan," due to its divergence from much of historic, Nicene Christianity. Since this aspect of the book is historical and descriptive, and not constructive, the term is appropriate given that German Christians thought of themselves as Christians.

43 Princeton, NJ: Princeton University Press, 2007.

44 Cf. *Prejudice and Christian Beginnings: Investigating Race, Gender and Ethnicity in Early Christian Studies*; editors Elisabeth Schüssler Fiorenza and Laura Nasrallah (Minneapolis, MN: Fortress Press, 2009), 211–234; "Heschel, Race as Incarnational Theology."

45 Robert P. Ericksen and Susannah Heschel, *Betrayal: German Churches and the Holocaust* (Minneapolis: Fortress Press, 1999). Also, see Ericksen's *Theologians Under Hitler: Gerhard Kittel, Paul Althaus and Emanuel Hirsch* (New Haven: Yale, 1985).

46 Doris L. Bergen, *Twisted Cross: The German Christian Movement in the Third Reich* (Chapel Hill: University of North Carolina Press, 1996).

47 Richard Steigmann-Gall, *The Holy Reich: Nazi Conceptions of Christianity 1919–1945.* (Cambridge: Cambridge University Press, 2003).

48 In addition to the works by Bergen, Ericksen and Steigmann-Gall, the failure of the Confessing Church is described at length in Gerlach's *And the Witnesses were Silent.* These failures

Heschel's book and essay add a remarkable new dimension to the already grim story of the relationship of German Protestant Christians to National Socialism. She breaks new ground by analyzing the *Institute for the Study and Eradication of Jewish Influence on German Church Life* (the "Institute").[49] The Institute was opened in May of 1939 at the historic Wartburg castle, which was "resonant with Lutheran and nationalist significance."[50] The Institute's goals were both theological and political, to create a de-judaized church, using revisionist biblical and liturgical materials, to establish that Jesus was never Jewish, that he fought against Judaism, and that he was also a victim of it.[51] For Heschel, the cumulative effect of propagating racist ideology was devastating to the status of the Jews: "Eradication of the Jews did not have to be proclaimed in order to be known as the goal."[52]

Heschel's analysis seeks to expose two myths that she observes have circulated during the post-World War II era. The first myth is that the German Evangelical Church was actively persecuted by the Nazis because it defended the historic, Protestant Christian faith of the Reformation confessions. As will be shown below, some members of the GEC, particularly members of the Institute and the faculty of the University of Jena, engaged in a systematic revision of Christian history and biblical interpretation, using anti-Semitic, racializing principles.[53]

---

should not prevent us from acknowledging the heroism of Dietrich Bonhoeffer and his associates, who opposed the Nazi government and were martyred as a result. The literature on this is voluminous. For example, *No Ordinary Men: Dietrich Bonhoeffer and Hans von Dohnanyi – Resisters Against Hitler in Church and State*; Elisabeth Sifton and Hans von Dohnanyi (New York: New York Review of Books, 2013).

49 In German, *Institut zur Erforschung und Beseitigung des judischen Einflusses auf das deutsche kirchliche Leben*; Heschel, *Aryan Jesus*, 1.

50 Ibid.

51 Ibid.

52 Ibid., 284.

53 Heschel does not define the term "racialize," although it is apparent from its use that it means to view a phenomenon through primarily racial lenses, such as viewing history through the lens of the emergence and/or disappearance of a "race." In an accompanying essay in the Fiorenza/Nasrallah collection of essays, Shawn Kelly builds an argument about racialized New Testament scholarship that sheds additional light on the concept "racialize": "I shall begin by articulating some of the argument I put forth in *Racializing Jesus*, which explores the role of race in modernity in general and in modern New Testament scholarship in particular. Throughout the course of my work, I argue that race is a social construct that functions within the discourse of modernity. I also argue that modern racial thinking is as conceptually empty as it is pervasive, and that it gains its intellectual potency by penetrating other intellectual resources. As an empty category, race tends to both protean and parasitic, infusing itself into the fabric and economy of the foundational aspects of modernity. Instead of existing alongside, say, liter-

Far from attacking Nazism, these principles actually supported it. For Heschel, the second myth is that the GEC was guilty of only promulgating theological anti-Judaism, and not pseudo-scientific, racist anti-Semitism. In this context, theological anti-Judaism fostered the view that all forms of Judaism were legalistic, preoccupied only with externalities and ritual, and devoid of true spirituality, which was delivered by Jesus and later the Christian faith. Heschel demonstrates that certain members of the GEC fostered both types of thought that were antagonistic to Judaism, with scientific racism being *the product of* modern theological revisionism. This occurred, notoriously, at the University of Jena, which since the 19th century had been at the forefront of Germany's intellectual life,[54] and became, in Heschel's view, "a stronghold of Nazism."[55]

1.2.1 The Influence of the History of Religions School

Heschel's works are the fruit of extensive archival research, and it is impossible to do them justice here. According to Heschel, Aryan Christianity emerged for political reasons to curry favor with the National Socialist political authorities.[56] What is not as well known is how the theological context facilitated the rise of anti-Semitism.[57] The basis for Heschel's argument about the logic of Aryan Christianity is that Christian theology, as "incarnational theology," since antiquity had struggled with reconciling the "fragile boundaries" between the human and divine, the carnal and spiritual, the Jewish and Christian.[58] While

ature or anthropology, racial thinking wove itself into these modern discourses. This process by which race permeates particular modern discourses can be defined as 'racialization.' " cf. Kelly, "Race, Aesthetics and Gospel Scholarship: Embracing and Subverting the Aesthetics Ideology;" in Fiorenza/Nasrallah, *Prejudice and Christian Beginnings*, 193.

54 Heschel cites Thomas Albert Howard's *Religion and the Rise of Historicism: W. J. L. De Wette, Jacob Burckhardt, and the Theological Origins of Nineteenth-Century Historical Consciousness* (Cambridge: Cambridge University Press, 27).

55 Heschel's subtitle for Chapter V, "The Faculty of Theology at the University of Jena," is "Jena as a Stronghold of Nazism," 201–241; According to Heschel, the theology students at Jena were enthusiastic supporters of the Nazis: "During the Third Reich, students at Jena, as at other universities, were in the forefront of promoting racial theory, and the theology students at Jena were no less engaged in this endeavor than their counterparts in the science and social science disciplines"; cited from Jeremy Noakes, "The Ivory Tower under Siege: German Universities in the Third Reich;" *Journal of European Studies* 23 (1993), 371–407.

56 Heschel, "Race as Incarnational Theology," for example, 214 and 222.

57 "In this, as in so many other issues, theologians anticipated and suggested anti-Jewish policy before it was formulated by the Nazi regime." Ibid., 214.

58 Ibid., 231.

these ideas themselves have a long and complicated history, she observes these vulnerabilities became exposed in light of modern historical criticism. The most important problem was the uniqueness of Jesus and his message, which had been "historicized," or made historically relative, through historical research.[59] The solution was to re-assert the uniqueness of Jesus on the basis of new research, which totally divorced him from Judaism.

This discussion will focus on how Aryan Christianity used methods of the History of Religions school to establish its anti-Jewish, pseudo-historical claims. The *Religionsgeschichtliche Schule* sought to interpret Jesus and early Christianity by referring to the beliefs and practices of late Hellenism, which was a syncretistic mixture of late Judaism, oriental eschatology, the Greek mysteries, Gnosticism and Stoicism.[60] This is the way in which Jesus and early Christianity are "relativized" by being understood as having many sources and influences from the ancient world.

Heschel develops the themes of race and historicism throughout her book and essay, and due to limitations on space, this discussion will focus on the relevant parts of Chapters I and V of her book *Aryan Jesus*. The book's introduction includes a rich discussion of Christianity and race, including an important contention that the fundamental relationship between body and soul at the heart of much modern racist discourse is a mirror of the body-soul dilemma at the heart of Christian metaphysics.[61] Chapter 1, titled, "Draining Jesus of Jewishness," explores numerous ways in which the German academic establishment collectively

---

59 Ibid., for example, 231.

60 See James C. Livingston, *Modern Christian Thought: From the Enlightenment to Vatican II* (New York: Macmillan, 1971), 304. Claude Welch claims that the terms "science of religion," "history of religion" and "study of religion" are practically interchangeable, and assigns the term *Religionswissenchaft* to the discipline as it emerged in the late 19th century. See *Protestant Thought in the Nineteenth Century. Volume I: 1799–1870* (New Haven: Yale, 1972), 69, 108–110, 123–136, and 170–171. I will also use the terms "history of religion" and "history of religions" frequently in this book, which can be more generally understood as the study of the role of world religions from a historical and comparative perspective. The analytical framework of the history of religions will recur in the primary source analysis in Chapters Two through Six of this book, with Chapter Five providing the most detailed discussion, as it analyzes Tillich's methodological use of the history of religion and the history of revelation in volume I of his *Systematic Theology.*

61 Heschel, *Aryan Jesus*, 22–23. Heschel elaborates in her essay: "The fundamental relationship between body and soul characterizing modern racist discourse is a mirror of the body-soul dilemma at the heart of Christian metaphysics, and is precisely the stamp that Christianity has placed on Western philosophy." cf. John L. Hodge, "Domination and the Will in Western Thought and Culture," in *Cultural Bases of Racism and Group Oppression*, ed. Donald K. Struckmann, John L. Hodge, and Lynn Dorland Trost (Berkeley: Two Riders, 1975); no page cited.

engaged in multi-disciplinary revisionism to establish that Jesus of Nazareth was not Jewish. In contrast to historic Christian theology, which saw Jesus as a Jew prefigured by the Old Testament, the members of the Institute transformed him into an anti-semite and proto-Nazi. According to Heschel, this argument was based on arguments that were well established long before the founding of the Institute in 1939:

> These included racial theory, as it emerged in Europe during the nineteenth century, with theories about languages and religions as manifestations of race; historicist distinctions between Jesus's teachings and those of first-century Judaism, presented by New Testament scholars; claims that Jesus's religious teachings originated in Hellenism, Buddhism, Hinduism, or Iranian culture–anything but Judaism; and assertions about the Gentile population of the Galilee in the centuries leading up to Jesus's day, given academic credence by Assyriologists. Among scholars as well as populist writers, the bases for such arguments were weak if not nonexistent, sources were read tendentiously or taken out of context, and solid data was replaced by fantasy.[62]

Two characteristic beliefs of Aryan Christianity were that Jesus of Nazareth was not a Jew but an "Aryan Galilean" who opposed Judaism, and that Judaism was a degenerate form of religion whose influence must be eradicated from the church and culture. Aryan Christianity provides an important contrast to Tillich's views in two ways. First, the remarkable claims made by Aryan Christian scholars illustrate the depth of intellectual, moral and theological failure within the church and academy. This contrasts sharply with Tillich, who consistently defended the historic Christian position of retaining the Old Testament within the Christian canon. Second, and more importantly, the proponents of Aryan Christianity and Tillich both employed a history of religions framework. However, Tillich and the Aryan Christians came to opposite conclusions concerning the role of Judaism within the history of religion, which will be demonstrated by the primary source analyses in Chapters Two through Six.

According to Heschel, the Aryan Christian belief that Jesus was not Jewish but a non-Jewish "Galilean" was supported by several assumptions that came out of the History of Religions school, and can be linked to numerous major figures within biblical studies and theology during the first half of the twentieth century. Her analysis reads like a "Who's Who" of early- to mid-twentieth century theology and Biblical studies, including major figures not typically thought of as anti-Jewish – William Wrede, Wilhelm Bousset, Walter Bauer, Rudolf Otto, and Ernst Lohmeyer. These are mainstream scholars who until now have not been tarnished with providing ideological support to an anti-Jewish, Aryan view of

62 Heschel, *Aryan Jesus*, 27.

history, unlike the those brought to light by Ericksen and Bergen, most notoriously Paul Althaus, Gerhard Kittel and Emanuel Hirsch.[63] Heschel observes in general that members of the History of Religions school rejected the authority of church doctrines, but examined them as products of the specific cultural and religious contexts of their era.[64] She also explores the methodological assumptions that were employed by the History of Religions school, two of which were shared by Tillich. The first shared assumption is that the New Testament record cannot be taken at face value in terms of historical reliability.[65] For example, if the New Testament record of Jesus's claims about himself are not historically reliable, then key Christological titles lacked a firm historical basis. The second assumption is that key Christian ideas did not derive from Judaism but were rooted in a number of religions that existed in the Hellenistic world. In Chapter Six, the discussion of Tillich's *Systematic Theology* will show that he believed certain Christological titles did have some non-Jewish roots. However, Tillich did not use the historical fact of non-Jewish influence as a justification to totally sever Christianity from its manifestly Jewish roots. Tillich believed this illustrated that the divine revelation in Jesus as the Christ did not occur in vacuum, but followed a long period of preparation. This view was not unique to Tillich, but shared widely then and since.

The first example provided by Heschel concerns William Wrede, professor of New Testament at the University of Breslau. According to Heschel, Wrede argued that the messianic claims about Jesus were theological constructs of the gospel authors, and not reliable evidence for Jesus's own beliefs about himself.[66] This had the effect of making a sharp distinction between the faith of Jesus and that of the gospel authors. Heschel astutely observes that this methodological assumption severed Biblical interpretation from church doctrine and discipline, but it also opened the door to influence by contemporary, anti-Semitic, politics: "the story of Jesus's struggle with the Jews became an allegory for Germany's so-called Jewish question."[67] For Heschel, another important claim of the History of Religions school was that Jesus was not the messiah anticipated in the Jewish

63 In particular, see Ericksen's *Theologians under Hitler.*

64 Heschel, *Aryan Jesus*, 58. Also, in a discussion of the curriculum at Jena, she writes, "History of Religions, in contrast to theology, was a discipline uninterested in the normative Christian doctrine of canonical texts, sanctioned by church authorities, instead viewing all data of an era, textual and otherwise, as historical evidence;" 202.

65 Tillich, *ST II*, 101–107.

66 Heschel, *Aryan Jesus*, 58. Cited by Heschel from Wrede's *Das Messiasgeheimnis in den Evangelien*; no page cited.

67 Ibid., 59.

scriptures. Wilhelm Bousset, professor of New Testament at the University of Göttingen, argued that the title "son of man" was not a formal title within Judaism and rather came from a syncretistic Hellenistic context, which was influenced by Indian, Persian and Greek cultures.[68] Heschel refers to this form of Hellenism as a "witch's brew" that only acknowledged the peripheral contribution of Judaism, through eschatology.[69]

According to Heschel, a third example is that Jesus's identity as a non-Jewish Galilean was put forth by Walter Bauer, also a professor of New Testament at Göttingen, who argued that Judea and Galilee possessed very distinct political, cultural and religious identities, and that Jesus understood himself to be a "heavenly son of man," a concept taken from the Hellenistic world, and not a Jewish messiah.[70] The opposition between Jerusalem and Galilee was further developed by proponents of two kinds of eschatology, a "Jewish eschatology" seeking a Messiah, and a "Gentile eschatology" seeking a son of man. This was supported by Rudolf Otto and Ernst Lohmeyer.[71] The analysis of Tillich's history of religion and history of revelation, occurring in Chapter Five of this book, shows that some of these ideas need not lead necessarily to an eradication of the historically Jewish roots of Christianity.

Chapter 5 of *Aryan Jesus* focuses on the faculty of theology at the University of Jena, including the "Nazification of the curriculum," which was based on the "principle of dejudaization," the imperative to purge the Christian church, and ultimately the surrounding culture, of all Jewish influence.[72] This included an attempt, not entirely successful, to revise the theology curriculum in all of Germany's universities so that it would never be taught that Christianity had Jewish roots. Relevant to this discussion was an April 1938 memo prepared by Heinz Eisenhuth, Institute member and dean of the theological faculty at Jena.[73] The memo was addressed to a national conference in Halle, recommending a thor-

68 Ibid., 59. This syncretistic Hellenstic context provides the raw material for much of Schelling's history of religion, as appropriated by Tillich, which will be discussed in Chapter Two. It will be seen that, even at this relatively early stage of Tillich's intellectual formation, he does not draw Aryan Christian conclusions.

69 Ibid., 59.

70 Ibid., 60. Heschel refers to Walter Bauer's article '*Jesus der Galiläer*', 16 – 34.

71 Ibid., 61 – 62. Heschel refers to Rudolf Otto's *Reich Gottes und Menschensohn* (Munich, 1934), 14 – 15, and also to Rudolf Bultmann's analysis of Otto's book in *Theologische Rundschau* n.s. 9 (1937): 1 – 35; for Lohmeyer, see his *Galiläa und Jerusalem* (Göttingen: Vandenhoeck & Ruprecht, 1936).

72 Ibid., 225 – 232.

73 Ibid., 217 – 219.

ough reform of theological education using a racialized understanding of the various subfields of theology: (i) the professorship in Old Testament would be replaced by a chair in the "History of Religions of the Near East," in which religions of the Orient would be examined, seeking Semitic influence; (ii) New Testament would be replaced by the "Study of the Gospels and the Origins of Christianity," and Jesus would be studied in the context of his religious and "volkish" environment; (iii) Church History would be the history of Germanic piety, and the religions of the East would be examined to identify their "Aryan religious element;" and (iv) Systematic Theology would reflect on how the gospel would influence a pious German life; Heschel correctly observes that *present-day experience* would be the hermeneutical key to truth.[74] While this proposal for curriculum reform was not fully implemented in all German universities, it is illustrates the fundamental way in which a racialized history of religions could influence the academic establishment.

Heschel's book is rich in detail and its indictment of numerous mainstream Christian theologians and Biblical scholars influenced by the History of Religions school deserves further examination, as none of the reviews to date explore this topic.[75] However, for the purposes of this argument, her contribution convincingly demonstrates the pervasive problem of anti-Jewish Christian theology within Germany, and especially at the highest levels of the theological community. Aryan Christianity attempted to solve two of the most powerful threats to the legitimacy of Christianity. The first is the ancient problem of the status of Judaism, and the second problem is the historical relativity of Jesus with respect to Christian origins.

1.3 The Use and Abuse of Judaism within the Western Tradition

The reader will notice the frequency with which the phrase "role" or "function" is appended to Judaism, Jewish prophetism or any of the equivalent terms, in the following chapters. For example, in Chapter Six I will discuss Tillich's religion of

74 Ibid., 226 – 227; the original memorandum cited is Heinz Eisenhuth's 'Denkschrift zu den Fragen der Studienreform und Fakultätsreform der theologischen Fakultäten' (UAB Akten der Ev. theol. Fakultät, vol. 35) – ibid., 227 note 94. Also see 202 – 203 for additional elaboration.

75 The three reviews of Heschel's *Aryan Jesus* that I have read scarcely touch upon her extraordinary claims about the History of Religions school. Kyle T. Jantzen, *Church History* 79/4 (December 2010): 968 – 971; Kevin Madigan, *Journal of the American Academy of Religion* 77/3 (2009): 742 – 748; Michael A. Madigan, *Modern Judaism* 30/1 (February 2010): 120 – 122.

the concrete spirit, which reflects the dialectical unity of the sacramental/mystical and prophetic/ethical elements. The prophetic/ethical elements possess a specific function within Tillich's dialectical history of religions, which may not be related to specific Jews in a particular time or place. Such a theoretical use of Jewish prophetism might strike us as peculiar. However, according to David Nirenberg's magisterial *Anti-Judaism: The Western Tradition*, this has been a pervasive practice. Nirenberg shows, in many and various ways, that using "Judaism" to express or describe something else, pre-dated the emergence of Christianity, and has occurred repeatedly into the modern period. After summarizing Nirenberg's argument, I will use his analysis of German Idealism to illustrate the complex ways that negative associations attached to Judaism, and became part of the context inherited by Tillich. It should become evident that Tillich's spirit of Judaism, also originating within the context of German Idealism, was positive by contrast.

For Nirenberg, "Judaism," and its correlate "anti-Judaism," have been busy playing supporting roles in the unfolding drama of western civilization, first appearing in antiquity, and have made appearances at decisive points into the modern period. Nirenberg uses the metaphors of "work" and "working" repeatedly to characterize the many ways in which "Judaism" and "anti-Judaism"[76] function within the western tradition, quite often apart from reference to specific communities of Jews. In this respect, the constructs Nirenberg refers to are similar to Tillich's spirit of Judaism and its synonyms, such as Jewish prophetism.

Nirenberg's argument has three relevant aspects. First, his "Judaism" does not primarily refer to the specific religion of a specific people, but is rather "a category, a set of ideas and attributes with which non-Jews can criticize and make sense of their world."[77] The correlate of Nirenberg's "Judaism," is "anti-Judaism," which for him is not simply a negative attitude toward Judaism, but is also a way of critically engaging the world.[78] The terms are not strictly opposites, depending upon how the function of "Judaism" operates within the particular context. For example, if "Judaism" or "being Jewish" has a negative association by being associated with irrationality, then the historic religion of Judaism and its practitioners are impugned. Most of the examples Nirenberg uses work like this.

76 Since Nirenberg uses both "Judaism" and "anti-Judaism" in a specific sense, when his terms are referred to, each will be presented in quotation marks to distinguish them from more customary senses.
77 Nirenberg, *Anti-Judaism*, 3.
78 Ibid.

Second, for Nirenberg, both "Judaism" and "anti-Judaism" reflect "habits of thought" that developed to help us understand our world.[79] For Nirenberg, academic disciplines were influenced, and sometimes transformed by changing senses of "Judaism" – epistemology, which is concerned with the relation between the "knowing subject" and the "known object;" metaphysics, which is concerned with the relation between spirit and matter; hermeneutics, which is concerned with the relation between "letter" and "spirit;" and political theory, which is concerned with power relations between rulers and ruled. For Nirenberg, echoing Marx, each of these questions became, in one way or another, "Jewish questions."[80]

Third, Nirenberg deliberately refrains from an analysis of anti-Semitism in order to isolate the ideas that helped to make the Holocaust possible.[81] Methodologically, Nirenberg strongly supports the use of intellectual history, while acknowledging its limitations, including the problem of historical causality. This means that he is aware of the potential to incorrectly infer that *since* a person or group maintains negative perceptions of Jews, they will act in antagonistic ways towards Jews. Nevertheless, at the end of the final chapter, Nirenberg correctly concludes that "the Holocaust *was inconceivable* and *is unexplainable*" without the "deep history of thought" that he provides, underscoring the importance of the history of ideas to explain these phenomena:[82]

> There are undoubtedly many reasons why the extermination of millions of Jews became not only imaginable but implementable in mid-twentieth-century Germany and not in some other place and time. But none of those factors functioned independently of the history sketched in this book. The "Jewish" terrors that assailed Germany and many of its neighbors in the first half of the twentieth century were not reflections of reality, or eccentric fantasies imposed on a populace by a powerful propaganda machine ... They were rather the product of a history that had encoded the threat of Judaism into some of the basic concepts of Western thought, regenerating that threat in new forms fitting for new periods, and helping far too many citizens of the twentieth century make sense of their world. We will fail to understand these terrors or their effects if we sunder them from what came before.[83]

It is revealing, for example, that the vast majority of associations with Nirenberg's "Judaism" are negative, and this coheres with the general understanding that there have been periodically virulent strains of theological anti-Judaism and

79 Ibid., 2.
80 See introduction, 2–5, and chapter 13 of Nirenberg, *Anti-Judaism*.
81 Ibid., 3.
82 Ibid., 459.
83 Ibid.

anti-Semitism within western Christianity and society. However, Nirenberg's primary goal is to isolate the many ways in which "Judaism" functions within the western tradition, allowing him to explore the habits of thought that have made possible antagonism and hostility towards real, living Jews.

One of the first examples Nirenberg uses is from the Apostle Paul's first letter to the Corinthians, where Paul contrasts God's wisdom with human wisdom. According to Nirenberg, Paul's view of human wisdom has two expressions, Jewish and Greek: "Since in the wisdom of God the world was unable to recognize God through wisdom, it was God's own pleasure to save believers through the folly of the gospel. While the Jews require signs (*semeia*) and the Greeks look for wisdom (*sophia*), we are preaching a crucified Christ: a scandal to the Jews, to the gentiles foolishness."[84] Nirenberg makes two observations about this. First, Paul's proclamation about Christ totally transforms what humans can know and how they can know it.[85] Second, this fundamental aspect of human knowledge is understood, in part, with reference to "Jews," although the meaning of the term "Jews" is already becoming extended to something other than "real Jews." In this context, Nirenberg observes that both "Jewish signs" and "Greek learning" represent human arrogance and foolishness, in contrast to God's wisdom.[86] This is the first of many oppositions between something "Jewish" and something desirable in the western tradition. Due to the limits of space, Nirenberg's entire book cannot be summarized here, although it is revealing that he analyzes the phenomena of "Judaism" and "anti-Judaism" in thirteen chapters across the vast territory of the following periods: (1) ancient Egypt and the Roman Empire; (2) early Christianity and the formation of the Christian Gospels; (3) the Christian Patristic period through Augustine, including Augustine's "witness doctrine;"[87] (4) the emergence of Islam; (5) medieval Europe; (6) the Roman Catholic Inquisition and the expulsion of Jews from Spain; (7) the Protestant

84 1 Corinthians 1:21–23; translation not specified. Nirenberg, *Anti-Judaism*, 53.
85 Ibid., 53–54.
86 Ibid., 54.
87 Augustine's "witness doctrine" holds that the Jews must be permitted to exist within Christian society, albeit as outcasts, so that their ongoing physical presence and use of their scriptures – the Old Testament for Christians – can "testify" to the fact that Christians did not fabricate the Old Testament prophecies concerning Christ to fit the facts of Jesus' life and crucifixion. Augustine cites Psalm 59:11 to support this view: "Slay them not, but scatter them in your might, lest your people forget your Law." Nirenberg argues that this is an example of Augustine's "historical realism," which sought to retain elements of historical truth in the Old Testament, as opposed to "spiritualizing" it away, like the Manichaeans, Marcionites and docetists; cf. Ibid., 130–131. For a detailed analysis of the hermeneutical issues surrounding the witness doctrine, see Paula Fredriksen's *Augustine and the Jews: A Christian Defense of Jews and Judaism* (New York: Doubleday, 2008).

Reformation and Martin Luther; (8) Shakespearean England; (9) the importance of "Israel" in sixteenth- and seventeenth-century Christian political theory; (10) the Enlightenment revolt against "Judaism;" (11) the revolutionary impulse starting with the French Revolution; (12) the role of "Judaism" in German Philosophy, including Fichte, Kant, and Hegel; and (13) the modern period, discussing Marx, the social sciences and the scientific study of religion. The pervasiveness of discourse involving "Jews" and "Judaism," while not always negative, is undeniable in scope.

1.3.1 German Idealism's "New Science of Hating Judaism"

Nirenberg argues that the potential for anti-Jewish sentiment was "endemic to the whole project of German Idealism,"[88] based upon the habits of thought emanating from it. His analysis begins with Johann Gottlieb Fichte's (1762–1814) *Addresses to the German Nation*, delivered in Berlin in 1807/1808. Nirenberg observes that the *Addresses* are similar to numerous earlier ideologies, since they interpret the history of the world as a war between two forces; in Fichte's case, love and self-interest.[89] According to Nirenberg, Fichte contrasts Romantic German virtues to Enlightenment French vices. For Fichte, the French are just like the Jews, in that both are incapable of apprehending the depths of reality, and are deceived by appearances. By contrast, Fichte's Germans love their soil, tribe and nation, which together have a divine quality.[90] For Nirenberg, not only do Fichte's lectures foster negative perceptions of Judaism, they also exemplify a new "critical science," based upon the Enlightenment view of human reason freed from dogma and tradition. According to Nirenberg, this new critical science, the tool of German Idealism, led to an "entirely new species" of Jew hatred, as initially noticed by Jewish bookseller Saul Ascher in Berlin in 1794.[91]

According to Nirenberg, Immanuel Kant (1724–1804) deepened this anti-Jewish narrative. Kant made possible new understandings of freedom, thereby adding epistemological, metaphysical and ethical dimensions to the construct "Judaism," through his revolutionary views of human knowledge (epistemology) and human freedom (ethics). For example, in the material world of "things," Kant moved beyond British empiricism, whose view of human reason was subject to natural laws, making human beings "slaves of necessity," like Jews.[92]

88 Nirenberg, *Anti-Judaism*, 405.
89 Ibid., 388.
90 Ibid., 389–390.
91 Ibid., 390.
92 Ibid., 391–392.

For Nirenberg, Kant's view of reason actively shaped our understanding of the material world, through the categories of space, time, causality and substance, instead of passively receiving sense impressions.[93] Nirenberg points out that this radically limited what can be thought of as "knowledge," and posited a sharp dichotomy between what can be truly known, "things-in-themselves," and mere "appearances."[94] For Kant, it was erroneous to confuse reality with mere appearances, which was something the Pharisees (i.e. read "Jews") were guilty of.[95] However, the corresponding benefit, in relation to the British empiricists, is to free the knowing subject so that it may be free to constitute the laws of nature and not simply respond to them.

Nirenberg argues that Kant also sought to free morality from the fear of punishment, by translating the Apostle Paul's distinctions between "inner" and "outer" circumcision, and "hearers and doers of the law," into the secular language of rational philosophy.[96] Kant's "categorical imperative" describes how it is rational to act "as if" we are subject to a universal moral law, in accordance with reason.[97] Nirenberg argues that Kant's "dualism" between the material world of necessity, and the spiritual world of human freedom, was central to his thought and caused him to associate "Judaism" with the material, sensible realm of un-freedom.[98] For Nirenberg, both Fichte and Kant, as representatives of German Idealism, were latter-day "Manichaeans" and Marcionite dualists who "amplified the language of anti-Judaism" to create the new science of hating Judaism.[99]

1.3.2 Hegel's Incarnational Dialectic

Nirenberg's account of German Idealism peaks with his exposition of the thought of Georg Wilhelm Friedrich Hegel (1770–1831), who attempted to transcend the aforementioned dualisms through an "Incarnational dialectic." Whereas for Kant and Fichte, "Judaism" was associated with the material dimension of the matter/spirit dualism, for Hegel, it was the dualisms themselves that were "Jewish:"

---

93 Ibid., 392.
94 Ibid., 392.
95 Ibid., 392–393.
96 Ibid., 393.
97 Ibid.
98 Ibid., 394–395. This may have been what led the Nazis much later to portray Jews as purveyors of "sensuality."
99 Ibid., 395.

> Hegel was like St Augustine, a convert from "dualism" to synthesis. In youth an ardent Kantian, by his early thirties he was convinced that Kant's "ideal does not come to terms with reality ... the real remains absolutely opposed." This opposition, he claimed, was simply a new version of "the Jewish principle of opposing thought to reality, reason to sense; this principle involves the rending of life and lifeless connection between God and the world." This "Jewish" opposition of thought to reality could lead neither to religion nor to philosophy, for the one task of every living religion and true philosophy was to "[strip] off the forms of dualism from its extremes, rendering the opposition in the element of Universality fluid, and bringing it to reconciliation." Christ had once shown humanity how to achieve this reconciliation through his crucifixion. Now it was Hegel's calling to do so through his philosophy.[100]

According to Nirenberg, it was Hegel's understanding of the history of religion and his Christology that sought to reconcile and transcend the dualisms inherited from Kant. In exploring these themes, Nirenberg draws mainly upon Hegel's *The Spirit of Christianity and its Fate* (1799).[101] In *Spirit*, Hegel makes several arguments that criticize Kant's ethics, although the starting point is the history of religion. First, Hegel interprets the history of revelation as the unfolding of a contest between two peoples, forces or principles (like Fichte and others), in this case Noah and Nimrod. According to Nirenberg's view of Hegel, Noah represents the Kantians, who rely upon thought and reason, and Nimrod represents the British empiricists, who sought to master nature through physical strength.[102] Second, for Nirenberg, Hegel interprets Abraham's sojourn out of Ur of Chaldees in Genesis 12 as a rupture with, and alienation from creation, making the Jews slaves to the material world: "all the miseries of Israel are rooted in Abraham's rejection of the world in favour of a 'sublime' God."[103] Third, according to Nirenberg, Hegel's Jesus differed greatly from Kant's moralistic Jesus, by calling for "fulfillment" of the law, which could be attained through a synthesis of love and law, subject and object, and universal and particular.[104] Nirenberg summa-

---

100 Ibid., 397 – 398. The quotes from Hegel are from *The Spirit of Christianity and its Fate*, trans. T. J. Knox, in *Early Theological Writings* (Chicago: University of Chicago Press, 1948; reprint Philadelphia: University of Pennsylvania Press, 1971). Hereafter cited as *Spirit*.

101 *The Difference Between Fichte's and Schelling's System of Philosophy. An English translation of G. W. F. Hegel's Differenz des Fichte'schen und Schelling'schen Systems der Philosophie*, prepared and edited by H. S. Harris and Walter Cerf (Albany, NY: SUNY Press, 1977). *Lectures on the Philosophy of Religion*, trans. E. B. Speirs and J. B. Sanderson, 3 vols. (New York: Humanities Press, 1962). Elsewhere in the chapter, Nirenberg also quotes from the Peter Hodgson edition of Hegel's *Lectures on the Philosophy of Religion* (Berkeley: University of California Press, 1984 – 1987).

102 Nirenberg, *Anti-Judaism*, 398, citing Hegel, *Spirit* (no page given).

103 Ibid., 399 – 400.

104 Ibid., 401.

rizes Hegel's Christological dialectic in this way: "(his) philosophy posits as its goal the dialectical overcoming of all oppositions, a process explicitly patterned on the overcoming of the difference between God and man, in the Incarnation and Passion of Jesus Christ. By writing the man-God union across all the fundamental oppositions of religion and philosophy – infinite and finite, love and law, spirit and letter, reason and nature – Hegel seeks to synthesize (technically *sublate*) all of them in the dialectical movement of the spirit across the ages."[105]

According to Nirenberg, Hegel's negative view of "Judaism" lessened to some degree in his 1827 *Lectures*, by assigning to Judaism a necessary role in the dialectical unfolding of Spirit throughout history, rather than alienation from that which is fundamentally human, as in *Spirit*.[106] Nevertheless, for Nirenberg, Hegel still wrestled with the issue of why the Jews as a people refused to renounce their faith and "exit the stage of history once their assigned moment was over."[107] Despite Hegel's Christological dialectic, which sought to reconcile all opposites into a higher unity, this did not elevate the status of Judaism within Hegel's history of religion.

Nirenberg concludes his analysis of German Idealism by observing that this process of attaching this complex set of features to "Judaism" occurred during periods of great social, political and economic upheaval. He is referring to the period from the start of the French Revolution in 1789 to the beginning of World War One in 1914, across "the long nineteenth century."[108] According to Nirenberg, during this period of immense change and dislocation, observers typically worried that European culture was becoming "more Jewish," and envisioned a future that involved the overcoming or elimination of whatever form of "Judaism" they feared.[109] Nirenberg observes that this confluence of ideas was germinating and taking hold at the same time that the Jewish population of western Europe swelled.[110] For Nirenberg, the great irony is that as the numbers of real Jews increased, the various kinds of philosophical roles played by "Judaism" also increased in number, and were typically negative in tone and/or content.[111]

---

105 Ibid., 402.
106 Ibid., 403–404.
107 Nirenberg adds: "But Judaism after Christ will remain for him a type of necrophilia: a dead man walking, an undigestible remnant expelled from the guts of history." He appears to be quoting Hegel here, but the note does not cite which of Hegel's works. Ibid., 404.
108 Ibid., 421.
109 Ibid.
110 Ibid., 422.
111 "just when it became most necessary to perceive the differences between real Jews and figures of Judaism, critical thought blurred them once again into one." Ibid.

The way in which Tillich uses the German Idealist framework results in a more favorable view of Judaism, when contrasted with the brief sketches of Fichte, Kant and Hegel provided above. Fichte, as portrayed by Nirenberg, understood European history as embodying a dualistic conflict between the godless French Enlightenment and divinely inspired German Romanticism, with the Jews being located on the godless side of this divide. Tillich, by contrast, did not interpret history dualistically, but dialectically, with a religious or historical movement enduring to the extent that it possessed critical and creative capacities, with Jewish prophetism being the model of critical capacities. This will be borne out in the primary source analysis culminating with Tillich's final public lecture in 1965.

Kant, as portrayed by Nirenberg, maintained a dualistic epistemological framework, resulting in the distinction between the "mere appearances" and the "things-in-themselves," with (Jewish) Pharisees unable to correctly discern one from the other. Tillich responded to Kant's epistemology, with his concept of the "depth of reason" in which the subject–object dichotomy is not the starting point of the analysis, but is preceded by a wider view of rationality that has an existential component, and that also raises the question of revelation.[112] In the following chapters it will be shown how Tillich assigns ethical values to the metaphysical concepts of time and space, with Jewish prophetism being associated with time, and idolatry with space. In addition, as portrayed by Nirenberg, Kant's ethics assumed a dualism between the material world of necessity, which the Jews were not able to transcend, and the spiritual world of freedom. In contrast, Tillich's view of freedom is fundamentally different from Kant's dualism, of freedom and necessity. For Tillich, freedom is not "indeterministic contingency," and it is not opposed to necessity, which thought of as "mechanistic determinacy." Rather, "Freedom in polarity with destiny is the structural element which makes existence possible because it transcends the essential necessity of being without destroying it."[113] For Tillich, this has nothing to do with Jews or Judaism.

112 *ST* I, 79–83.

113 The full passage reads: "Man is man because he has freedom, but he has freedom only in polar interdependence with destiny. The term 'destiny' is unusual in this context. Ordinarily one speaks of freedom and necessity. However, necessity is a category and not an element. Its contrast is possibility, not freedom. Whenever freedom and necessity are set over against each other, necessity is understood in terms of mechanistic determinacy and freedom is thought of in terms of indeterministic contingency. Neither of these interpretations grasps the structure of being as it is experienced immediately in the one being who has the possibility of experiencing it because he is free, that is, in man. Man experiences the structure of the individual as the bearer of free-

As portrayed by Nirenberg, for Hegel it was the dualisms themselves, like thought versus reality, that were Jewish. As described above, Hegel's Christology sought to "sublate" all of the fundamental oppositions of religion and philosophy – finite and infinite, love and law, spirit and letter, reason and nature. This bears some similarity to Tillich's doctrine of the Christian logos, which is the dialectical relationship between absolute concreteness and absolute universality. In these ways, both Hegel's and Tillich's Christologies seek to be dialectically "unitive," and not divisive. However, as seen above in Nirenberg's account of Hegel's history of religion, Judaism is deemed to inferior to Christianity. Subsequent chapters will demonstrate that Tillich's view of the role of Judaism within the history of religion is more favorable than Hegel's, on the face of it.

1.4 Tillich's Method: The Dialectical History of Religion

In Chapters Two through Six, relevant primary sources will be analyzed that span Tillich's entire career, from 1910 through 1965. In these primary sources, Tillich's idea of Judaism develops over time, and informs his understanding of Christianity in profound ways. However, prior to engaging in the analysis of the primary sources, it is essential to demonstrate the fundamentally dialectical structure of Tillich's thought, making note of the various polarities, contradictions, tensions and syntheses that employs throughout. These features are prominent in his dialectical history of religion, which is the venue in which continuity between Judaism and Christianity occurs. In Chapter Six, the "inclusive" nature of Tillich's history of religion will be discussed.

Tillich employs two forms of dialectic that influence his understanding of the relationship between Judaism and Christianity, and I have created two grammatically parallel terms to highlight the distinctive role of each. The first kind is a "historical dialectic of progression," in which religions emerge, conflict with one another, and become transformed by this conflict. Tillich always employs this kind of dialectic when he discusses the history of religion, and he consistently argues that historic Judaism contributes essential elements to the emergence of Christianity. Taken by itself, this understanding of the history of religion is not unique, and is compatible with the historic Christian faith, meaning that Judaism was the unique foundation of Christianity. This structure also opens up

dom within the larger structures to which the individual structure belongs. Destiny points to this situation in which man finds himself, facing the world to which, at the same time, he belongs." *ST* I, 182–183.

the question of "supersessionism" which will be touched upon in Chapter Seven.[114] The second kind of dialectic is an "ontological dialectic of balance," in which there is a reciprocal, mutual relation between two phenomena, with neither one being annihilated in the conflict, and with each possessing a fundamental integrity which may contribute to the creation of a new unity. In some instances, a permanent balance of two principles held in tension is viewed by Tillich as the optimal relation; in others, this balance itself is thought of as a new unity. My tentative thesis is that the historical dialectic of progression is ultimately subordinated to the ontological dialectic of balance, based upon the cumulative findings of the primary source analyses in Chapters Two through Six.

When the first volume of Tillich's *Systematic Theology* appeared in 1951, much commentary was generated concerning Tillich's distinctive theological method, the "method of correlation." Tillich's method of correlation proceeds by raising questions about the human condition, which is the domain of philosophy, and answering those questions, which is the domain of theology.[115] In addition to this question and answer format, there are numerous other dynamic features to Tillich's thought, which occur in the form of polarities, contradictions, antinomies, and creative unities and syntheses. These provide Tillich tremendous flexibility, but can also be confusing. This section will illustrate the pervasive presence of dialectical relationships within Tillich's thought, according to several essays by notable Tillich scholars, demonstrating the scholarly interest in the topic.

In 1952, an important collection of essays appeared in response to *ST* I,[116] with notable contributors such as the process theologian Charles Hartshorne,[117] Columbia's intellectual historian John Herman Randall, Jr.,[118] philosopher of religion Nels Ferré, economist, *kairos* circle member and long term friend of Tillich, Eduard Heimann,[119] Reinhold Niebuhr,[120] in addition to major Tillich schol-

---

114 For an important historical treatment, see Rosemary Radford Ruether, *Faith and Fratricide: The Theological Roots of Anti-Semitism* (Minneapolis, MN, Seabury, 1974); and, "The *Adversus Judaeos* Tradition in the Church Fathers: The Exegesis of Christian Anti-Judaism;" *Essential Papers on Judaism and Christianity in Conflict: From Late Antiquity to the Reformation*; ed. Jeremy Cohen (New York: NYU Press, 1991); 174–189.

115 Tillich, ST I, 18–28; and, specifically, "The method of correlation explains the contents of the Christian faith through existential questions and theological answers, in mutual relation."; ST I, 60.

116 Kegley and Bretall's *Theology of Paul Tillich* cited in the previous note.

117 Kegley and Bretall, *Tillich*, ch. 8, "Tillich's Doctrine of God," 198–229.

118 Kegley and Bretall, *Tillich*, ch. 7, "The Ontology of Paul Tillich," 166–195.

119 Kegley and Bretall, *Tillich*, ch. 15, "Tillich's Doctrine of Religious Socialism," 358–371.

ars Langdon Gilkey[121] and James Luther Adams.[122] In many of the essays, attention was drawn to the dialectical structure of Tillich's thought. One essay by James Luther Adams[123] on the types of dialectic present in Tillich's theology will receive special treatment. The Adams essay will permit me to introduce the two types of dialectic, referred to above, that will be used to interpret the Tillich primary sources discussed in later chapters.

John Herman Randall, Jr., observes that for Tillich, reason is finite, self-contradictory and ambiguous, "under the conditions of existence," and that Tillich employs three "polarities" that give rise to "conflicts," which generate "quests" for resolution.[124] For example, there is a polarity between static and dynamic elements in reason, which gives rise to a conflict between absolutism and relativism, which leads to a search for "the concrete-absolute."[125] In explicating Tillich's view of "knowledge," Randall also observes that a "balance" between two polarities is the optimal situation. Randall notes that knowledge for Tillich, especially knowledge as "understanding," is a *balance* of union and detachment.[126]

The most comprehensive essay that discusses the dialectical structure of Tillich's thought is James Luther Adams' "Tillich's Interpretation of History." According to Adams, Tillich exhibits the importance of dialectic in two ways: (i) by underscoring the importance of the philosophy of history as the most pressing problem of our period; and (ii) by arguing that the dialectical method can be the only basis for a prophetic and Protestant philosophy of history.[127] Adams observes that many of these ideas took shape for Tillich during his religious socialist period, in the 1920s and 1930s, and that it was Tillich's critique of the demonic powers in history, both secular and ecclesiastical, that drove him to develop his philosophy of history.[128]

Adams identifies four levels of dialectic in Tillich's thought: logical, ontological, historical and religious. Each level involves the other three, and each level main-

---

120 Kegley and Bretall, *Tillich*, ch. 10, "Biblical Thought and Ontological Speculation in Tillich's Theology," 252–263.

121 Kegley and Bretall, *Tillich*, ch. 1, "Tillich: The Master of Mediation," 26–58.

122 Kegley and Bretall, *Tillich*, ch. 14, "Tillich's Interpretation of History," 330–355.

123 "Tillich's Interpretation of History," in *The Theology of Paul Tillich: A Revised and Updated Classic*, ed. Charles W. Kegley and Robert Bretall, 2nd edn (New York: Pilgrim Press, 1982), 330–355 (1st edn; New York: Macmillan, 1952).

124 Randall, "Ontology," in Kegley and Bretall, *Tillich*, 177.

125 Ibid.

126 Ibid., 179–180.

127 Adams, "History," 330–331.

128 Ibid., 350.

tains features of identity and contrast.[129] While it is not clear how each level always involves the other three, it will be evident below in my analysis that the religious and ontological levels of dialectic have a historical dimension. For Adams, Tillich's *logical dialectic* has two aspects. First, it is expressed in the process of inquiry, of testing, affirmation and negation, designed to discover empirical truth.[130] The second aspect is that this inquiry and testing can also uncover a deeper level, penetrating to something's essence, or being.[131] This level applies to all areas of inquiry, including the natural sciences, and is fundamental to all life: "In a dialectical description one element of a concept drives another. Taken in this sense, dialectics determine all life-processes and must be applied in biology, psychology, and sociology. The description of tensions in living organisms, neurotic conflicts, and class struggles is dialectical. Life itself is dialectical."[132] This dynamic and comprehensive understanding of reality will be seen in Chapter Two, which explores the influence of F. W. J. Schelling on Tillich.

According to Adams, Tillich's *historical dialectic* refers to the process whereby "the configurations of social existence" drive beyond themselves to a new relationship of identity and contrast, in perpetually recurring syntheses and disruptions.[133] Adams compares Tillich to Clement of Alexandria in promoting "the great synthesis between the Old Testament of Yahweh and the Parmenidean idea of being."[134] Similarly he claims that, like Augustine, Tillich sought the "communion of Jerusalem and Athens."[135] This level of dialectic applies most directly to Tillich's understanding of the history of religion, which is not a merely historical description, but a deeply theological enterprise.[136]

---

129 Ibid., 332–333.

130 Ibid., 333.

131 "To see the limits of existence is to see beyond existence to its essential ground. Dialectic should penetrate to the depth, "the ousia", the "essence" of things, that which gives them the power of being ... This is their truth, the "really real" " (Ibid., 336–337). Tillich citation is from *ST* I, 101. In addition, "Dialectical thinking is rational, not paradoxical. Dialectic is not reflective, in so far as it does not reflect like a mirror the realities with which it deals. It does not look at them merely from the outside. It enters them, so to speak, and participates in their inner tensions. The tensions may appear first in contrasting concepts, but they must be followed down to their roots in the deeper levels of reality" (*ST* II, 90).

132 *ST* II, 90.

133 Adams, "History," 333.

134 Ibid., 349. Adams does not give a citation for Clement.

135 Ibid. Adams does not give a citation for Augustine.

136 Unlike Karl Barth, who provides extensive footnotes in his theological writings, Tillich seldom provides direct citations to specific works of theologians and philosophers. He is extremely eclectic, and borrows freely from the entire western philosophical and theological traditions, using them for his own distinctive views. This makes his unacknowledged usage less egregious.

For Adams, Tillich's *religious dialectic* refers to the identities and contrasts within humanity itself, and between humanity and the infinite.[137] More specifically, this encompasses Tillich's understandings of finite and infinite, the divine and the demonic, *kairos* and *logos*, and relationship between autonomy, heteronomy and theonomy.[138] For Adams, Tillich's *ontological dialectic* embodies a "metaphysics of history that rests upon a metaphysics of being," that is deeply influenced by Schelling's existential, anti-Hegelian dialectic, and is expressed in polarities and contrasts that pervade the *Systematic Theology*.[139] Adams identifies views of God from the history of theology that inform Tillich's ontology: Luther's distinction between God's wrath and God's love; Jakob Böhme's triad of "ground," "abyss" and the "God beyond God;" and Schelling's triadic formula of "being," "non-being" and "supra-being."[140] For Adams, these all inform Tillich's understanding of creation, estrangement and reconciliation, and come together especially in Tillich's Christology and his concept of the New Being.[141] Tillich's derivation of a philosophy of history from ontology bears strong similarities to Schelling's dialectic of the potencies, which deeply informed Schelling's own theological understanding of history. This relation of history to ontology informs Tillich's view of the relationship between Judaism and Christianity.

1.4.1 The Dialectical Structure of Tillich's *Systematic Theology*

This section on the dialectical structure of the *Systematic Theology* is intended to demonstrate the importance of dialectical method in Tillich's *magnum opus*, which is Tillich's most comprehensive work. It will be left to Chapter Five to demonstrate how the two types of dialectic, the historical dialectic of progression, and the ontological dialectic of balance, manifest themselves in that work. Tillich begins the Introduction to his *Systematic Theology* (*ST*) with the assertion

---

137 Adams, "History," 333.

138 Ibid., 349.

139 Ibid., 350. In the discussion of Tillich's 1961 Bampton lectures later in this book, it will be shown that Tillich had a negative view of Hegel's dialectic as applied to the history of religion. For an excellent recent discussion on the relative contributions of Hegel and Schelling on Tillich's thought, see Andrew O'Neill, *Tillich: Guide for the Perplexed*; New York: Continuum / T&T Clark, 2008, especially Part III, Chapter 6, "Philosophical Concepts and Structures," 103 – 123.

140 Ibid.

141 Ibid. "If applied symbolically to the divine life, God as a living God must be described in dialectical statements. He has the character of all life, namely, to go beyond himself and to return to himself. This is expressed in the Trinitarian symbols ... Trinitarian thinking is dialectical and rational, not paradoxical" (*ST* II, 90 – 91).

that Christian theology must satisfy two needs of the church, the statement of the truth of the Christian message, and the interpretation of this truth for every generation.[142] From the very beginning of the *Systematic Theology*, Tillich creates a polar relationship between "timeless" Christian truth, and time-bound expressions of that truth to address a particular situation.

> Theology moves back and forth between two poles, the eternal truth of its foundation and the temporal situation in which the eternal truth must be received. Not many theological systems have been able to balance these two demands perfectly. Most of them either sacrifice elements of the truth or are not able to speak to the situation. Some of them combine both shortcomings. Afraid of missing the eternal truth, they identify it with some previous theological work, with traditional concepts and solutions, and try to impose these on a new, different situation. They confuse eternal truth with a temporal expression of this truth. This is evident in European theological orthodoxy, which in America is known as fundamentalism.[143]

Right from the start, Tillich's theology addresses a permanent polarity, which ideally is addressed by "balance." The entire three-volume *Systematic Theology* is an extended exercise of seeking an appropriate balance between numerous polarities, the most comprehensive being that of "essence" and "existence." For Tillich, to the extent that an appropriate balance is maintained between essence and existence, then a new creative unity is established, in the drive towards essentialization. The drive toward essentialization is the focus of parts IV and V, comprising Volume Three of the *Systematic Theology*. For Tillich, this is where existential questions raised by the ambiguities of existence and history are answered in discussions of, respectively, the Spirit and the Kingdom of God.

For Tillich, his systematic theology proceeds by the "method of correlation:" (i) the human situation is analyzed and "existential" questions are drawn out of an analysis of culture; and (ii) Christian theology attempts to answer those questions through its symbols.[144] Tillich's *Systematic Theology* has five parts,[145] with each of the five parts asking a unique existential question, or set of related ques-

142 *ST* I, 3.
143 Ibid., 3.
144 Ibid., 62.
145 In Tillich's introduction to the first volume of the *Systematic Theology*, pages 66–67, he introduces the following order of the five parts. Part I: "Being and God;" part II: "Existence and Christ;" part III: "Life and the Spirit;" part IV: "Reason and Revelation;" and part V, "History and the Kingdom of God." In the main text of the work, "Reason and Revelation" is actually part I, and "Being and God" is part II, "Existence and Christ" is part III, "Life and the Spirit" is Part IV, and part V is "History and the Kingdom of God." Volume I contains parts I and II; volume II contains part III; and volume III contains parts IV and V.

tions. Within each part, an answer is also provided, using a Christian symbol, which is derived from the sources, medium and norm of Christian theology.[146] The questions are generated by the experience of "self-contradiction" or "estrangement,"[147] with Tillich frequently using the phrase "under the conditions of existenc"' in his detailed phenomenological descriptions. For Tillich, the presence of contradiction and/or estrangement clearly implies an *ideal* state, meaning a normative posture toward the world. This exemplifies Tillich's fundamental distinction between "essence," what *ought* to be, the realm of salvation and "existence," what *is*, the realm of creation.

> In each of the five parts of the system which are derived from the structure of existence in correlation with the structure of the Christian message, the two sections are correlated in the following ways. In so far as man's existence has the character of self-contradiction or estrangement, a double consideration is demanded, one side dealing with man as he essentially is (and ought to be) and the other dealing with what he is in his self-estranged existence (and should not be). These correspond to the Christian distinction between the realm of creation and the realm of salvation.[148]

As seen in the *Judenfrage* lectures and elsewhere in the primary sources to be analyzed, the "Is/Ought" polarity is fundamentally important to Tillich's theological idea of Judaism.

Part I of the system, titled "Reason and Revelation," analyzes human rationality, its relation to the rational structure of reality, and elicits questions implied in human finitude, self-estrangement and the ambiguities of reason. According to Tillich, these questions find their answers in "revelation."[149] Part II, titled "Being and God," analyzes the relation of human finitude, and finitude in general, to the essential nature of reality. According to Tillich, this analysis gives rise to questions that can only be answered by the Christian symbol "God."[150] Part III, titled "Existence and the Christ," analyzes human "existential self-estrangement," which implies questions that can only be answered by the Christian symbol of "the Christ."[151] Part IV, titled "Life and the Spirit," analyzes humanity as living, as expressing the power of actual being within the ambiguities and distortions of existence. For Tillich, this phenomenon of humanity as living generates existential questions that can only be answered by the Christian symbol of

146 *ST* I, 34–52.
147 Ibid., 66.
148 Ibid.
149 Ibid., covered in *ST* I, 71–159.
150 *ST* I, 66, covered in *ST* I, 163–289.
151 *ST* I, 66, covered in *ST* II, 19–180.

"the Spirit."[152] Part V, titled "History and the Kingdom of God," analyzes the historical existence of humanity, in conjunction with history in general, giving rise to questions implied in the ambiguities of history. According to Tillich, these questions can only be answered by the Christian symbol "Kingdom of God."[153]

1.4.2 Two Types of Dialectic

In Chapter Two, which will analyze Tillich's 1910 and 1912 Dissertations on Schelling, the historical dialectic of progression will predominate. Tillich employs Schelling's "dialectic of the potencies" as a fundamental framework to interpret reality. There is an organic quality that causes the participants in the dialectic to make enduring contributions to the next stage in the dialectic. For example, in the 1910 Dissertation, only Judaism provides the key concepts that enabled the shift from the particular to the universal. Tillich consistently comes to this conclusion in any discussion of the history of religion. Therefore, he would not have subscribed to Aryan Christianity, as described above.

In Chapter Three, especially in the discussion of *The Socialist Decision*, both the historical dialectic of progression and the ontological dialectic of balance are present. Similar to the 1910 Dissertation, Tillich understands the history of religion as the realm of contradictions and transformations, in which Jewish prophetism emerges to resolve the contradictions inherent in pagan polytheism. Tillich identifies Jewish prophetism as the first historical manifestation of justice, giving rise to the maxim "justice is the true power of being." In addition, in *The Socialist Decision,* Tillich introduces the polarity between space and time, which is one instance of the ontological dialectic of balance. "Time" is granted ethical and theological significance, and becomes associated with prophetism, while "space" becomes associated with idolatry. This polarity will assume other aspects in Tillich's *Judenfrage* lectures.

In Chapter Four, which analyzes Tillich's *Judenfrage* lectures, three sets of polarities are employed, Is/Ought, priestly/prophetic, and space/time. These are the most notable examples of the ontological dialectic of balance in all of Tillich's works. Unlike the historical dialectic of the 1910 and 1912 Dissertations and *The Socialist Decision,* in which human history expresses the forward movement of contradictions and transformations, the aforementioned three polarities must be kept "in balance," otherwise a distortion will occur regarding any relat-

152 *ST* I, 67, covered in *ST* III, 11 – 294.
153 *ST* I, 67, covered in *ST* III 297 – 423.

edness to the divine. When these poles are kept in the appropriate tension, "in balance" so to speak, then the divine is manifest more transparently. This is Tillich's "dialectic of the Holy." This is in addition to Tillich's observation in the first lecture that historic Christian theology exhibited anti-Jewish aspects that later served as part of the ideological structure of modern anti-Semitism.

Chapter Five will discuss Tillich's *Systematic Theology.* In Tillich's *Systematic Theology*, especially in volume I (*ST* I), the most detailed presentation of the history of religion is found, in which both the historical dialectical of progression, and the ontological dialectic of balance are present. As in the prior sources analyzed, historic Judaism served as a foundation for Christianity, despite periodic "life or death struggles" to save the Old Testament. In addition, it will be shown that the unfolding of Tillich's history of religion is *rational*, in the sense that the history of religion is driving toward an optimal balance between the particular and the universal. For Tillich, this optimal relation is paradigmatically expressed in the Christian Logos, in the event of Jesus as the Christ, which would have been impossible without the contribution of the Jewish prophets.

In the final round of primary source analysis, Chapter Six will discuss Tillich's 1961 Bampton Lectures,[154] and Tillich's final public lecture, "The Significance of the history of religion for the systematic theologian."[155] In the Bampton Lectures, Tillich reflects more directly on his dialectical method than in any of his previous works, and he observes that his dialectical history of religion is "inclusive" insofar as it preserves elements of prior religions, as they are transformed into new religions. This observation about inclusivity is occasioned by Tillich's attempt to integrate Buddhism into his historical, revelatory scheme. However, I think it can also be applied retrospectively to his ongoing attempts to maintain continuity between Judaism and Christianity. In Tillich's 1961 Bampton Lectures, which will be discussed in Chapter Six, the enduring influence of the dialectic of the Holy is evident.

---

154 *Christianity and the Encounter of World Religions*, Fortress Texts in Modern Theology, Foreword by Krister Stendahl (Minneapolis: Fortress Press, 1994). This will be noted as "Tillich, *Bampton Lectures.*"

155 The Fortress Press edition of Tillich's Bampton Lectures has an appendix with Tillich's final public lecture, "The Significance of the History of religion for the Systematic Theologian." Editor Stendahl notes that this lecture was recorded on tape, was delivered from ten pages of carefully outlined notes, and was transcribed and edited by Jerald C. Brauer in its final form. The Brauer edition, which was reprinted in the Fortress volume, first appeared in Brauer's *The Future of Religions* (New York: Harper & Row, 1966.). This will be noted as "Tillich, *Significance.*"

Chapter Two: Schelling's Cosmic Dialectic, the Jewish Critique of Idolatry, and Descent into Legalism

2.1 The Importance of Schelling for Tillich

It is difficult to fully appreciate Tillich's thought without understanding the influence of Friedrich Wilhelm Joseph Schelling (1775–1854). Throughout his career, Tillich remarked on the significance of Schelling for his own thought. For example, in Tillich's 1936 autobiography, *On the Boundary*,[1] in the chapter titled "Between Theology and Philosophy," he recalls how he had voraciously read classical German philosophy, especially Kant and Fichte, and later Schelling. His interest in Schelling was stirred by both a predisposition ("inner affinity") towards the relationship between nature, mysticism and history, and unexpectedly finding the complete works of Schelling in a used bookstore, what he came to refer to as the "the accident of a bargain purchase."[2] In addition, in a 1954 lecture in Stuttgart on the hundredth anniversary of Schelling's death, Tillich stated: "Never have I forgotten my dependence upon Schelling in the development of my own thought. At all times, even in a land of half-foreign culture, his basic ideas have been a help to me in the most varied fields. My work on the problems of systematic theology would have been unthinkable without him."[3] In the foreword to volume 1 of Tillich's 1959 collected works, he writes: "The influence of my Schelling studies on the whole of my further development

---

1 Tillich, *On the Boundary*, 46–47.

2 Ibid., 47. Tillich's biographers, Wilhelm and Marion Pauck, report that Tillich purchased the set of Schelling's works impulsively, wanting to know more about the history of philosophy, and that his romance with Schelling determined his entire philosophical point of view. *Tillich*, 16. Also, in Tillich's lectures on the history of Christian thought, at the beginning of a discussion of Schelling's critique of Hegel, he relates how originally obtained Schelling's works: "I recall the unforgettable moment when by chance I came into possession of the very rare first edition of the collected works of Schelling in a bookstore on my way to the University of Berlin. I had no money, but I bought it anyway, and this spending of nonexistent money was probably more important than all the other nonexistent or sometimes existing money that I have spent. For what I learned from Schelling became determinative of my own philosophical development." Tillich, *History of Christian Thought*, 438.

3 'Schelling und die Anfänge der existentialistischen Protestes', Gedächtnisfeier zum 100. Todestag von Friedrich Wilhelm Joseph von Schelling am 26. September 1954, *Zeitschrift für philosophische Forschung* 9/2 (1955): 197–208; cited by Daniel J. O'Hanlon, S.J., *The Influence of Schelling on the Philosophy of Paul Tillich* (Rome: Pontifica Universitas Gregoriana, 1958), 17–18.

is very strong."[4] And finally, when he had completed the third volume of his *Systematic Theology* in 1963, Tillich remarked that Schelling was the teacher and he was merely the student.[5] Therefore, the importance of Schelling remained with Tillich throughout his entire life.[6]

Tillich quotes Schelling liberally and at length, displaying in intimate knowledge of Schelling's work, underscoring the difficulty of separating Schelling's

---

4 Tillich adds: "Decisive confirmation of my own evaluation of Schelling came to me, for the first time, when I encountered Nietzsche and the philosophy of life, and, next, when I became involved in the philosophy of art and existentialism. Both movements are, to a great extent, dependent upon Schelling. The specific topic of the present work on Schelling has also proved its continuing significance. Even today, the problems of mysticism and guilt-consciousness play a decisive role within the traditional theological task and in the encounter of Christianity with Asiatic religions."; *GW* I, foreword, cited by Victor Nuovo, translator of Tillich's 1912 Dissertation on Schelling, Introduction, 9.

5 Pauck and Pauck, *Tillich*, 236.

6 This is not to ignore other significant influences from the German idealist tradition, especially Hegel and Fichte, and a tendency to over-emphasize the influence of Schelling. For example, Marc Boss has persuasively critiqued a "well established historiographical tradition" that Tillich experienced an "existential turn" in light of his experiences in World War One. This view holds that Tillich underwent a shift from a "negative," "philosophy of identity," or philosophy of essentialism, being primarily influenced by Hegel and Fichte, to a "positive," existential philosophy, initially influenced by Schelling. This shift followed a similar shift in Schelling, from "Schelling I," the essentialist Schelling, to "Schelling II," the existentialist Schelling. Based upon recent archival analysis, Boss concludes that "Tillich refuses to subordinate the negative philosophy to the positive, or the positive to the negative," observing that Tillich discovered Schelling I *after* Schelling II and that Schelling II provides the interpretive key to Schelling I, with respect to autonomy and human freedom. Cited from "Paul Tillich and the Twentieth Century Fichte Renaissance: Neo-Idealistic Features in his Early Accounts of Freedom and Existence;" *Bulletin of the North American Paul Tillich Society;* Vol. XXXVI, Number 3, Summer 2010, 14–15. If I understand Boss correctly, there is a Schelling I and Schelling II, but not a "Tillich I" and "Tillich II," with the former being the "essentialist" and the latter being the "existentialist." In addition, also recently, Christian Danz demonstrates that "Tillich's way to Schelling goes through Fichte," cited from "Freedom as Autonomy: Observations on Paul Tillich's Reception of Fichte;" *Bulletin of the North American Paul Tillich Society;* Vol. XLI, Number 1, Winter 2015, 14. In the same article, Danz also observes that in Tillich's reading of Fichte, there are two fundamental types of religion or notions of God, a voluntaristic type associated with Judaism, and an intellectualist type associated with the ancient Greeks, and that Christianity was a synthesis of voluntarism and intellectualism (Ibid., 16). In my argument, however, the role that Judaism plays in both Schelling dissertations undoubtedly provides an illuminating starting point for the development of Tillich's spirit of Judaism, which will be analyzed in primary sources in later chapters. Whether or not the idea of Judaism in each was normative for Tillich at the time is less important than the supposition that these ideas undoubtedly influenced his later views.

views from Tillich's. I have adopted the view of Russell Re Manning, who argues that while it is difficult to separate the views of Schelling and Tillich in the two Schelling dissertations, it is the fact of their interpenetration that is important.[7] As Re Manning notes, "to a large extent Tillich simply incorporates Schelling's later metaphysics and ontology into his own, such that it is often difficult, especially in the Schelling dissertations, to know for sure where Schelling finishes and Tillich begins ... The point here is that Tillich makes Schelling's thought his own – he absorbs it as the subterranean foundations of his own thought."[8] Therefore, where Schelling refers to Judaism, as quoted by Tillich in his two Schelling dissertations, it can be reasonably inferred that Tillich has the same understanding of Judaism. This understanding is fragmentary, and there is no indication that before World War I Tillich sought to develop a "theology of Judaism." However, there are aspects that will emerge in the Schelling dissertations and recur in his later works, and are therefore important. Due to the absorption of Schelling by Tillich, following Re Manning, I will refer to Tillich's use of Schelling as "Tillich's adaptation of Schelling," or "Tillich's Schelling."

Tillich's analyses of Schelling in his two dissertations draw heavily upon three of Schelling's works,[9] all of which are considered part of the later Schelling ("Schelling II"), and instances of his "positive philosophy;"[10] volume 7, *Philosophical Inves-*

---

7 Russell Re Manning, *Theology at the End of Culture: Paul Tillich's Theology of Culture and Art*, Studies in Philosophical Theology (Dudley, MA: Peeters, 2005), 78–79 note 63.

8 Re Manning, *Theology at the End of Culture*, 59 note 4.

9 The first complete edition of Schelling's collected works was published by his son, F. K. A. Schelling, between 1856 and 1858, in two parts of ten and four volumes, respectively. This edition is called the *Sämmtliche Werke*, and is here identified as Schelling, *SW* I and II followed by the volume number. Since there was no further edition of Schelling's collected works until 1927, it appears that Tillich used this edition in the 1910 and 1912 dissertations. However, in the English translations by Victor David Nuovo, the extensive parenthetical references to Schelling by Tillich use volume numbers 1 through 14. It appears that Nuovo used the 14 volume collection edited by Manfred Schröter, cited as *Werke*, 14 vols. (Munich: C. H. Beck, 1927). References to this edition are typically cited as *GW* 1–14. For example, Schelling's major essay translated as *On Human Freedom*, which is included as the seventh volume to both the F. K. A. Schelling and Schröter editions, would be cited as *SW* I/7 and *GW* 7, respectively. As a second example, the Berlin lectures translated as *Philosophy of Mythology*, vols. 11 and 12 of 14, are referred to as *SW* II/1 and *SW* II/2 in the F. K. A. Schelling edition, and *GW* 11 and *GW* 12 under the Schröter edition.

10 Positive philosophy is attributed to the later Schelling ("Schelling II"), which emerged in 1809 with *On Human Freedom*, and is contrasted with "negative," rational philosophy. With respect to God: "Whereas God as infinite potency is the starting point of rational philosophy, God as absolutely transcendent being is the principle of positive philosophy. Whereas rational philosophy is aprioristic and deductive, positive philosophy is aposterioristic and empirical. Experience is the only means of proof in positive philosophy." Tillich, 1910 Dissertation, 66. With respect to theology: "Historical philosophy is the domain of freedom, will, and act, which, in

tigations into the Essence of Human Freedom (*'On Human Freedom'*);[11] volumes 11 and 12, *Historical-Critical Introduction to the Philosophy of Mythology* (*'Philosophy of Mythology'*);[12] and volumes 13 and 14, *Philosophy of Revelation.*[13] Schelling's expansive treatment of the history of religion was contained in his *Philosophy of Mythology* and *Philosophy of Revelation.* The latter two works are compilations of student notes and Schelling's papers from lectures he delivered at the University of Berlin, beginning in 1841. Schelling's lectures were published after his death in 1854, by his son, F.K.A. Schelling, in 1856, 1857 and 1858. Anxious to fill the prominent position with someone to combat Hegelianism, King Wilhelm IV invited Schelling, at age sixty-five, to fill the spot.[14] The lectures were attended by numerous major nine-

---

the final analysis, is religion. The subject of historical philosophy is divine history whose nucleus is the history of religion. Its task is to interpret actual religion. It is concerned with the great acts of freedom that found the divine-human relationship, namely, creation, fall and redemption. It treats the latter in a three-fold sense: extrinsic redemption in paganism, mediated redemption in Judaism, intrinsic, unmediated redemption in Christianity." Tillich, 1910 Dissertation, 148. According to Karl Jaspers: "A schematic comparison of negative and positive philosophy shows: negative philosophy is the science of essence (*Wesenwissenschaft*) while positive philosophy is the science of existence; negative philosophy is regards to the Ideal while positive philosophy is in regards to the Real....Negative philosophy concerns itself with necessity while positive philosophy concerns itself with freedom;....The former is rational *a priori* science while the latter is an *a posteriori* science of actuality....In negative philosophy God is treated as the end while in positive philosophy he is treated as the beginning. In the former God is treated as a mere concept, an immutable God, while in the latter God is treated as an existing God, an acting God." *Schelling: Größe und Verhängnis* (Munich and Zurich: Piper, 1986), 98, cf. Schelling, *Philosophy of Mythology*, Foreword, x.

11 Parenthetically cited as Schelling, *GW*, vol. 7, under the title, *Philosophische Untersuchungen über das Wesen der menschlichen Freiheit und die damit zusammenhängenden Gegenstände*. This has been published in English as *Philosophical Investigations into the Essence of Human Freedom*, trans. with an introduction and notes by Jeff Love and Johannes Schmidt, Contemporary Continental Philosophy series (Albany, NY: SUNY Press, 2006); hereafter cited as Schelling, *On Human Freedom.*

12 Parenthetically cited as Schelling, *GW*, vols. 11 and 12, under the title, *Einleitung in die Philosophie der Mythologie.* Excerpts of Lectures 1 through 10 have been published in English as *Historical-Critical Introduction to the Philosophy of Mythology*, trans. Mason Richey and Markus Zisselberger, foreword by Jason Wirth, Contemporary Continental Philosophy series (Albany, NY: SUNY Press, 2007); hereafter, Schelling, *Philosophy of Mythology.*

13 Parenthetically cited as Schelling, *GW*, vols. 13 and 14, under the title *Philosophie der Offenbarung.* Excerpts have been published in English as *The Grounding of Positive Philosophy: The Berlin Lectures*, trans. with an introduction and notes by Bruce Matthews, Contemporary Continental Philosophy series (Albany, NY: SUNY Press, 2007), hereafter, Schelling, *Philosophy of Revelation.*

14 Schelling, *Philosophy of Revelation*, Translator's Introduction, 6. Also, according to Howard V. Hong and Edna H. Hong, Schelling had initially lectured on positive philosophy at Erlangen in the 1820s. At Berlin, Schelling intended "to consummate his philosophical program by devel-

teenth-century intellectuals, including Søren Kierkegaard, Friedrich Engels, Mikhail Bakunin, Arnold Ruge and Jacob Burckhardt, who at times provided stinging negative commentary.[15] It is possible that Tillich was unaware of these criticisms, because he does not mention them, nor does he offer a defense of Schelling against them. However, Tillich wholeheartedly appropriated Schelling's doctrine of the potencies as a means to respond to Kant's antinomies, regarding epistemology, ethics and aesthetics, all in a defense of a theological interpretation of culture. For my purposes, the dialectic of the potencies informs the theological history of religion, as articulated by Tillich's Schelling, in both the 1910 and 1912 Dissertations.[16]

Tillich wrote two dissertations on Schelling. The first is titled "The Construction of the History of Religion in Schelling's Positive Philosophy: Its Presuppositions and Principles," which was submitted in 1910 for his doctorate in philosophy at the University of Breslau. The second is titled "Mysticism and Guilt-

oping positive philosophy, the philosophy of 'that' a philosophy of nature, history, art, mythology and religion, a philosophy of freedom, of existents, under the title *Philosophie der Offenbarung* [manifestation, revelation]." Historical introduction, *The Concept of Irony, with Continual Reference to Socrates*, and *Notes on Schelling's Berlin Lectures*, ed. and trans. Howard V. Hong and Edna H. Hong (Princeton, NJ: Princeton University Press, 1989), xix – xx; hereafter, "Hong, Hong, Historical Introduction, *Concept of Irony*."

15 According to Kierkegaard, "Schelling talks the most insufferable nonsense ... His whole doctrine of the potencies betrays the highest degree of impotence" (letter to his brother, Peter Christian, February 1842); Hong, Hong, Historical Introduction, *Concept of Irony*, xxii – xxiii. According to Burckhardt, "I attended his lectures a couple of times as an outsider during the most turgid of dogmatic discussions, and explained it all to myself as follows: Schelling is a Gnostic in the proper sense of the word, like Basilides. Hence all that is sinister, monstrous, formless in this part of his doctrine [*sic*]. I thought that at any moment some monstrous Asiatic God on twelve legs would come waddling in and with twelve arms take six hats off six heads. Little by little even the Berlin students will not be able to put up with his frightening half-nonsensical, intuitional, contemplational form of expression. It is awful to have to listen to long historical explanations and discussions of the destiny of Messias, epically drawn out, complicated and entirely formless. Anyone who can love Schelling's Christ must have a large heart." See Thomas Albert Howard, *Religion and the Rise of Historicism: W. M. L. de Wette, Jacob Burckhardt, and the Theological Origins of Nineteenth-Century Historical Consciousness* (Cambridge: Cambridge University Press, 2000), 145.

16 I have reviewed the following works on Tillich's reception of Schelling, in alphabetical order: Bernet-Strahm, 1982; Crary, Yale Dissertation, 1955; Mokrosch, 1976; Neugebauer, 2007, O'Hanlon, Rome Dissertation, 1958; Re Manning, 2005; Scharf, 1999; Sommer, Duke Dissertation, 1960; Steinacker, 1989; and Zeitlow, Chicago Dissertation, 1961. Complete citations appear in the Bibliography below. Only four, Neugebauer, O'Hanlon, Zeitlow and Re Manning, discuss in any detail the function of the history of religion in Tillich's theology, and those contributions will be cited below, where applicable.

Consciousness in Schelling's Philosophical Development,"[17] which was submitted for the licentiate in theology at the University of Halle. In the introduction to the 1910 Dissertation, Tillich argues that while Schelling was in a sense the teacher of Hegel and Schleiermacher, the latter two became the objects of extensive scholarly commentary, while Schelling regrettably fell into neglect.[18] In the simplest terms, in the 1910 Dissertation, Tillich appropriates Schelling for philosophical purposes, and then in the 1912 Dissertation, Tillich appropriates Schelling for theological purposes, with philosophy providing a necessary foundation for theology. However, there is considerable overlap between philosophy and theology in Schelling, as Tillich observes that idealism possesses an essentially religious dimension ("self-consciousness"), expressed in Schelling's concept of "philosophical religion."[19]

2.2 The Doctrine of the Potencies

The metaphysical foundations for Schelling's dialectical view of reality employs three "potencies," which are principles that characterize possibility, drive, contradiction, transformation and reconciliation, within God, nature, humanity and history.[20] The term "potencies" appears to have come from Schelling's speculative physics; they are not only concepts, but "vital fields," "transcendental horizons of all being," "a striving ready to leap to fulfillment," and they function as mediators between the Absolute and the universe, between the divine will and history.[21] In addition, they are "the deeper meaning of the Christian Trinity,"

---

17 I will refer to two dissertations as the "1910 Dissertation" and the "1912 Dissertation," respectively. Pauck, Pauck, *Tillich*, 33–35.

18 1910 Dissertation, 39–41.

19 "Idealism is not only a scientific movement, it is above all a religious movement. Theologians or philosophers may reject joining philosophy and theology in a unified and systematic world view. Nevertheless, they cannot avoid considering the Idealist Movement from the standpoint of the history of religion as an expression of Christian religious life. Idealism itself makes this claim, and therefore must be appreciated as such, at least in a purely historical sense. The religious self-consciousness of Idealism is characteristically expressed in Schelling's concept of 'philosophical religion.' " 1910 Dissertation, 40–41.

20 O'Meara, "Schelling's Philosophy," 50–54. Thomas F. O'Meara, O.P., " 'Christianity is the Future of Paganism:' Schelling's Philosophy of Religion;" in Leroy S. Rouner, ed., *Meaning, Truth and God* (Notre Dame: University of Notre Dame Press, 1982).

21 O'Meara, "Schelling's Philosophy," 221.

through whom the God of monotheism becomes worldwide, historical and therefore trinitarian.[22]

According to Tillich, Schelling's three potencies are subject, object and spirit. In the most simple terms, subject is "what *can* be," or pure potency;[23] object is "what *must* be," or pure act; and spirit is "what *ought to* be," or the goal. With respect to God, they also have a Trinitarian association. "Subject" corresponds to the Father, the God of desire and wrath; "object" corresponds to Christ, the God of love; and "spirit" corresponds to the Holy Spirit, the God of hope.[24] In the conflict between subject and object, neither is completely annihilated, and each potency makes an enduring contribution to spirit, in teleological fashion, according to its success or failure in the struggle. Tillich's Schelling believes that the optimal relationship between the first two potencies is one of "equilibrium,"[25] but this is seldom, if ever, achieved, and it is the enduring presence of tension, conflict, contradiction, and attempted resolution that drives history forward and that exhibits the dynamic nature of reality. The notions of "enduring contribution" and "optimal relation" will re-appear later in this analysis to characterize the

---

22 Ibid. In addition, the translator of Tillich's 1912 Dissertation, Victor Nuovo, at page 177 note xxvi cites a passage from Schelling's *Philosophy of Revelation*, *SW* XIV, 66, observing that *Homoousia*, the communion of the Father and the Son in the Holy Spirit, is the goal of history: "The idea of the trinity passes through three moments: it must proceed from *tautousia*, where only the Father is the dominating *ousia*–where the Father comprehends all; it must proceed from *tautousia* through *heteroousia*, which lasts as long as there is tension [between the potencies] until the final reconciliation, to *homoousia*, which, therefore, is the only final moment, which is totally incomprehensible apart from the two that precede it."

23 Tillich points out that in *On Human Freedom*, Schelling introduces the theme of "the irrational moment within the absolute," a " 'potency' for self-contradiction." According to Tillich, this sense of *possibility* is the origin of the term "potency' as used by Schelling. This irrational event is the cause of the creation of the physical world and humanity, and ultimately results in the creation of human history. 1910 Dissertation, 48.

24 Nuovo, translator's introduction, 1910 Dissertation, 16–17. O'Hanlon adds the aspect of time to this: "The Can-be, Must-be and Should-be correspond to past, present and future. These are distinct and yet simultaneous 'times;' and it is only in this way that God's eternity can be reconciled with his entrance into time" (*Influences*, 99). There are also Christological and heresiological analogies: (1) Being in its primordial, subjective unity ("Tautousie") is compared to Sabellianism; (2) Being in its objective, determined existence ("Heterousie") is compared to Arianism; and (3) the eventual, reconciled union of subjective identity and objective diversity can be expressed as "Homousie," which appears to be analogous to the Nicene, or perhaps even Chalcedonian, understanding of God. Harold Zeitlow, *The Living God: The Existential Systems of F.W.J. Schelling and Paul Tillich* (Chicago: University of Chicago Press, 1961), 15. Also, see note 22 above for Nuovo's citation from Schelling's *Philosophy of Revelation*, regarding the analogy between the potencies and the Trinity, as quoted in 1912 Dissertation, 177 note xxvi.

25 See 1910 Dissertation, 45, 46 (twice) and 49 for uses of "equilibrium."

role of Judaism within the history of religion, and its relation to Christianity. Before "the Fall," the polarities within God were in harmony, with "one-sidedness" creating a distortion that seeks resolution by a harmonious relationship between the two poles. The terms "one-sided" and "one sidedness" are used more frequently in the 1912 Dissertation, but they do appear notably, if infrequently, in the 1910 Dissertation.[26]

It is beyond the scope of this book to discuss the doctrine of the potencies in great detail. The most important theme is that *contradiction* emerges within God, with additional contradictions replicated in the realm of nature and human history. It is the presence of contradiction within human history, especially between the first and second potencies, that seeks resolution in the history of religion: "Schelling portrays the struggle of both potencies in the world process and the gradual conquest and transfiguration of the first by the second by means of the categories of the philosophy of nature ..."[27] While somewhat cryptic, this suggests the cosmic importance of the conflict between the first and second potency, and also the analogy with the natural process. Freedom within God became the ground for differentiation within God, and therefore the positing of something that was "not God," specifically, the world of ideas, nature and humanity: "But this ground is the irrational will, the principle of subjectivity, whose contradiction of the principle of objectivity, of the will to love, is the condition of particularity, of selfhood and creaturehood. For by means of contradiction, the world process, whose task is to reconcile that which contradicts, gets underway."[28] Whereas the first differentiation within God occurred, effectively, in a pre-temporal realm, sometimes expressed as God having two wills,[29] history

26 For example, in Tillich's summary of Schelling's second potency, Schelling is cited as saying that deism is vacuous, moralistic and one-sided, because it lacks the potency of subjectivity, the "power of procreation," meaning the power of "going forth from itself and becoming unlike itself." Ibid., 53; cf. Schelling *GW* 12:41.

27 Ibid., 48 – 49.

28 Ibid., 55.

29 "When Schelling found himself forced to the conclusion that there was an irrational element within the Absolute itself, the second main period of his development was opened, the period beginning in 1809 with his Doctrine of Freedom. The acceptance of an irrational 'moment' in the Absolute turned the stress, which had been diverted, at the start of Plato's influence, toward the universal, strongly back to the *will* as a principle. An examination of the dual nature of the will itself indicated a solution to the problem. The will itself had a 'power' to contradict itself. The freedom which the Absolute gave to the Ideas was this power to be not-at-one with itself ... There can be no genuine freedom without the 'power' of setting self against itself. The conclusion (notes Tillich) is that there must be an irrational self-contradiction in the Absolute" (O'Hanlon, *Influence*; 35 – 36).

became the arena for the reconciliation of estranged reality back to God. Tillich's Schelling argues that "a new process is necessary to restore to the potencies their 'lordship over being;' that process is history."[30] This dialectical process will inform the analysis of each of Tillich's dissertations on Schelling.

2.3 The Emergence of the Religious Consciousness

Part II of the 1910 Dissertation, called "The History of Religion," employs the dialectic of the potencies in a development of the history of religion. It has two sections, A, titled, "Mythology," and B, titled "Revelation." The discussion of section A on mythology begins by recapitulating the account of the Fall, discussed above, which occurs in "absolute prehistoric time."[31] Tillich's Schelling develops six key features of the phenomenon of history. First, history is the realm of estrangement away from God and reconciliation back to God.[32] *Immediacy* with God was lost through the Fall, and through the *mediation* of history, humanity will return to a consciousness of the divine.[33] Second, human history is the history of religion, so all cultures and religions, to one degree or another, manifest aspects of a consciousness of the divine. All mythology has some revelatory content. Third, every history manifests a duality of principles, generating a conflict that seeks resolution.[34] Fourth, human history after "the Fall" was con-

---

30 1910 Dissertation, 76.

31 This is a critical concept in Schelling's philosophy of history. In part I, on the doctrine of the potencies, Tillich underscores this: "The qualitative notion of time that emerges in the concept of 'eternal becoming' is a foundation stone for Schelling's system, especially of his philosophy of history." (Ibid., 58).

32 Re Manning says this is reminiscent of the neo-Platonic process of *exitus et reditus. End of Culture*, 89.

33 Tillich begins part A with this summary statement: "History is essentially the history of religion. This assumption follows directly from Schelling's anthropology. Human consciousness is substantially God-realizing consciousness. Immediacy is lost on account of the Fall. Through the mediation of history, a conscious realization of God will take place. History is the process in which consciousness becomes indirectly what it was directly, namely, religious in the absolute sense. Everywhere, the cultural process has its roots in the religious, and in its completion returns to it. Even the cultural process can be viewed from the standpoint of the history of religion." This underscores the importance of religion as the basis of a theology of culture. 1910 Dissertation, 77.

34 Regarding the duality of principles, Tillich says: "It is necessary to assume a prehistorical condition because every history, at the very least, presupposes a duality of principles that contend with each other. However, on account of the Fall, consciousness has come under control of the first potency, which seized it and, what is more, keeps it for the present in a condition anal-

trolled by the first potency (God the Father), with humanity mired in a state of "total unconsciousness." Fifth, in a confusing but very important move for this historical dialectic of progression, the religious culture manifest in this state of unconsciousness is characterized simultaneously as "polytheism," "original monotheism," and "relative monotheism." This period can be thought of as the time when the first potency ruled, a period of " 'utter unconsciousness' (of God) ... not a monotheism which consciously excluded other gods, but a simple unawareness of the possibility of other gods."[35] Christianity is referred to as "absolute monotheism." Without debating the merits of this terminology,[36] it is clear that original/relative monotheism is "one-sided," demanding resolution with greater equilibrium. Tillich quotes from Schelling's *Philosophy of Mythology* (11:139): "Polytheism was ordained for mankind, not in order to destroy the true One, but the one-sided One, that is, in order to destroy a merely relative monotheism."[37] Sixth, the second potency (God the Son, or Logos) is engaged in a perpetual struggle to bring God-consciousness to humanity.[38] In the beginning of the section on revelation, which contains an analysis of two religions of revelation, Judaism and Islam, Tillich's Schelling underscores the cosmic role of the second potency, the original harmony present "before the Fall," the emergence of the natural world as something external to God, and the goal of reuniting estranged being to God.[39]

ogous to that total unconsciousness which prevailed before the beginning of the natural process" (Ibid., 78).

35 O'Hanlon, *Influence*, 60. See Section 2.4.2 below for a description of the mythological process and revelation.

36 Tillich explains: "An original, but relative monotheism can be ascribed to mankind, for the possibility of another God had not yet appeared to consciousness, although in fact it was already there. This monotheism lacked comprehensiveness; it was a monotheism mythologically conceived. It was 'in fact a genuine polytheism, because it had not abolished the possibility of other gods' (11:127)"; 1910 Dissertation, 78.

37 Ibid.

38 With respect to the perpetual struggle of the second potency against the first, Tillch writes: "there is an incessant struggle of the second, forward driving potency against the first that resists it, a struggle that will not end until the third potency is fully realized" (Ibid.).

39 "Throughout the world-historical process the second potency is active: the elevation of the first potency is the starting point of the process, the realization of the third potency is the goal, but activity belongs only to the second. Just as it is necessary to distinguish in the concept of God between nature in God and the divine Self, so it is also necessary to distinguish between logos as cosmic potency and logos as personality within God. To be sure, at the conclusion of the original natural process both aspects of the logos were in perfect harmony, for God was realized in the unity of the potencies. But on account of the Fall and the separation of the potencies, nature has come to exist outside God, and in this externality the second potency has also

Unlike most analyses of Schelling's influence on Tillich, I will discuss each dissertation separately, since each has a distinct argument, and each makes a distinct contribution to this topic. The 1910 Dissertation presents Judaism within the vast sweep of the history of religion, and it serves as a transitional phase from historically and culturally particular mythological, pagan religions, to the universal and revelatory religion of Christianity. In the 1910 Dissertation, there is a historical dialectic of progression, in which there is a progression from Judaism to Christianity. The 1912 Dissertation assumes a similar transitional place of Judaism within the history of religion, but employs a deeply Kantian framework that seeks to resolve "antinomies," with Judaism being put in dialectical opposition to paganism. In the 1912 Dissertation, Christianity not only comes after Judaism with a more adequate expression of divine revelation, it also resolves the contradiction posed by Judaism within the dialectical history of religion. As Tillich's history of religion develops over time, he will become more tentative about the ability of Christianity to maintain its definitive position as the "resolver of contradictions," and Judaism will increase in stature, to where it has permanent and not only transitional role, in a permanent reciprocal relation to Christianity. In both dissertations, Judaism receives a different emphasis, but plays an essential preparatory role for Christianity.

2.4 The 1910 Dissertation: Judaism and Islam ("Mohammedanism")

The only discussion of Judaism in the 1910 Dissertation appears at the beginning of the discussion of revelation, at the end of Part II, "The History of Religion," and it follows a lengthy analysis of the mythological process, which is punctuated by a description of how "rational religions" failed to fully stimulate the emergence of consciousness of the divine.[40] In the prior section on rational religion, Tillich's Schelling clearly stated that human reason was insufficiently voluntary, spiritual and personal to convey the fullness of the divine,[41] which established

come to dwell. At the same time, the second potency pursues God-estranged being in order to unite with it and to lead it back to God. In this process, the logos, according to its nature, operates as cosmic potency."; 1910 Dissertation, 102–103.

40 The analysis of Judaism appears in Part II, B,I, "*Revelation:* Judaism and Mohammedanism," 102–107.

41 "The ego finds its salvation only when it possesses God in actuality, and when it is united (reconciled) to him, that is, by means of a voluntary, spiritual, personal religion that brings the

the need for revelation. In the discussion of revelation, the portrayal of Judaism by Tillich's Schelling is not entirely clear, although he provides enough guidance to enable a reasonable estimate. It is clear that both Judaism and Islam, religions of revelation, are superior to rational religions, and unaided human reason. Yet, it also becomes clear that both Judaism and Islam are inadequate, compared to Christianity. Despite its final inadequacy, Judaism manifested some features that have enduring theological value, and these will be discussed below. In addition, despite the overwhelming "world historical" significance of Islam, it is deemed to be theologically inferior to Judaism.

The argument proceeds in five sections, which will be discussed in sequence. Despite some difficulties, the guiding principle can be expressed in a paradox identified in the fourth section of the analysis. The unfolding of revelation possessed an inner logic that sought final expression in an absolute, exclusive form of monotheism, specifically Islam. Tillich's Schelling portrays Judaism as being transformed over time by adapting to culturally specific practices and forms, seeking to universalize them, but ultimately lapsing into narrow, legalistic, beliefs and practices. However, the universal aspects of the Jewish prophetic tradition made an enduring contribution to Christianity. Islam, however, skips over the interaction with any cultural context and manifests a primordial, absolute, violent and destructive form of monotheism.

2.4.1 The Logos as the Agent of Revelation

Revelation is the process of how the awareness of God becomes manifest within human history. This awareness of God is stimulated by the second potency, which is the "logos," or cosmic potency."[42] The cosmic potency is the instrument of reconciling creation with God, as it "pursues God-estranged being in order to unite with it and lead it back to God."[43] The cosmic potency has a personal character, meaning that it acts with intention, and its presence emerges over time, within non-Israelite culture and history, and within the history of Israel.[44]

---

old world in its entirety to an end (11:567). The catastrophe of the rational process is the true end of paganism." 1910 Dissertation, 102.

42 "Throughout the world-historical process the second potency is active: the elevation of the first potency is the starting point of the process, the realization of the third potency is the goal, but activity belongs only to the second." Ibid., 102–103.

43 Ibid., 102.

44 "Revelation is the term for the action of God as personality, or, since it is the logos who acts, it is the term of the action of the logos as personality within God." Ibid., 103.

> "There is a twofold history of the mediating potency; there is, as it were, a *historia sacra* and a *historia profana* of its action" (14:119). The Old Testament contains the *historia sacra*. Whereas it is the task of the *historia profana* to set forth the universality of the potencies, it is the task of the *historia sacra* to reveal their unity. The former is secular for it is based on a natural process that is external to God. The latter is sacred for it is based on a supernatural process within God. The former presupposes the separation of the potencies outside God, the latter, the unity of personality within God.[45]

This progressive revelation of a personal God is what Schelling refers to as the "mythological process."[46]

2.4.2 Revelation, the Mythological Process and Idolatry

For Schelling, the mythological process begins with a universal, "primordial," nameless God of pre-history, known as Elohim, or "the first God."[47] Over time, "the true God," who possesses the personal name "Jehovah," becomes revealed."[48] Yet, the first God does not pass away, but remains the "ground," or ontological substratum, of the revealed personal God. The two are inseparable, as the first God *constantly mediates* the true God.[49] Tillich's Schelling draws directly upon this mediated relationship, as revelation must initially occur in "natural" or specific historical and cultural contexts. This is also referred to with the noun "substance," or the adjective "substantial."[50] Throughout

---

45 Ibid., 103.

46 In one instance, Tillich's Schelling also refers to the mythological process as "the pagan principle." Ibid., 104.

47 Schelling, *Philosophy of Mythology*, 104–105.

48 Ibid., 104–105.

49 The "two Gods" are eternal and inseparable, as the ground of revelation must always be from the ontological substratum of reality itself: "In order for the true God to appear to him (i.e. Abraham), the ground of the appearance must remain the first God, in which alone that second God can become enduring to him. The true God is not merely temporarily mediated to him through the natural God, but is rather constantly mediated; he is to him never that which *has being*, but rather constantly only the one who *is becoming*, through which alone the name Jehovah would be explained, in which precisely the concept of becoming is particularly expressed. Thus Abraham's religion does not consist in him giving up that God of pre-historical time, becoming untrue to him; on the contrary, that is what the heathens do. The true God has become revealed to him only in that God, and for this reason is inseparable from it, inseparable from the God *who was from time immemorial*, from the *El Olam*, as he is called;" Schelling, *Philosophy of Mythology*, 116.

50 "Revelation occurs in this way: through the mediation of the second potency, the true God reveals himself to consciousness, which posits God in substance. God reveals himself within this

the history of Israel, God's presence was consistently mediated through a combination of non-Jewish, universal, "substance," and Jewish "forms." Jewish forms were seen previously in the name of "the true God," Jehovah. This non-Jewish substance sometimes provided the *basis* for worshipping "the true God," and sometimes it served as idolatrous temptation. Tillich's Schelling observes that Israel's leaders, when faced with idolatrous cultural practices, or non-Jewish substance, that conflicted with revelation, periodically resisted having to obey commandments from an inferior past.[51]

Tillich's Schelling pairs two Old Testament references to illustrate this ongoing problem with idolatry, the story of the Rechabites in Jeremiah 35 and the tradition that the Israelites needed the skill of the Phoenicians to build the Jerusalem temple.[52]

> They believed that they were held back by a past that was culturally inferior. And indeed, as the Rechabites and the Nazirites prove, they were correct. "It is an enduring characteristic that of the people of God that they were compelled to seek the builders of their temple among the Phoenicians" (11:239)." From this we can understand how strongly Israel was tempted toward polytheism....Not until the Babylonian captivity did the danger of polytheism disappear, for just at that time the mythological process had lost its power among mankind generally, because its goal had been reached (14:144).

First, the reference to the story of the Rechabites, found in Jeremiah 35, implies a critique of Israel's idolatrous combination of temple cult and the monarchy. The Rechabites were a nomadic tribe that had been instructed by their patriarch Jonadab the son of Rechab, to remain nomadic by not building houses, not planting vineyards, not owning lands, and not "drinking wine," which symbolized reaping the fruit of land-owning, agrarian society. In obedience to their patriarch, they camped in tents outside of Jerusalem during the reign of Jehoiakim, the last king of Judah. During the siege of Jerusalem by Nebuchadnezzar c. 605 BCE, the Rechabites were compelled to take refuge within the walls of Jerusalem. God commanded Jeremiah to invite the Rechabites into the Temple and offer

substance. Therefore, this substantial, natural content of original consciousness always remains the basis and medium of revelation." 1910 Dissertation, 104.

51 Ibid., 104.

52 A common interpretation is that since the Israelites had been wandering in the wilderness prior to the conquest of Canaan, they had not developed skills that would enable flourishing in agrarian (i.e. non-nomadic) society. For example, the Phoenician king, Hiram of Tyre, helped King Solomon build the First Jerusalem Temple: "And Hiram king of Tyre sent messengers to David, and cedar trees, also masons and carpenters to build a house for him." 1 Chronicles 14:1, Revised Standard Version.

them wine to drink, in violation of their vows. They refused, and survived the invasion,[53] unlike the Jews, whose earthly kingdom was destroyed, and only a portion of whom survived. The Exile was to become one of the defining moments of the history of the Jewish people, and a theological milestone for Tillich, as it became the unique foundation for the Cross, which was intended to be the ultimate critique of all absolutes and idolatry.

Second, the reference to the Phoenicians being the builders of the Jerusalem temple is also intended to be a critique of idolatry, because of the pairing with the story of the Rechabites. The reference to this in Schelling could be understood as an example of revelation emerging from non-Jewish substance, that is, architectural practices that succeeded in awakening consciousness of the divine.[54] However, Tillich's Schelling understands the Exile as a providential

53 "But to the house of the Rechabites Jeremiah said, 'Thus says the Lord of hosts, the God of Israel: Because you have obeyed the command of Jon'adab your father, and kept all his precepts, and done all that he commanded you, therefore thus says the Lord of hosts, the God of Israel: Jon'adab the son of Rechab shall never lack a man to stand before me.' " Jeremiah 35:18–19, Revised Standard Version. In addition, the Rechabites are associated with the primordial God referred to above, specifically with the human race *prior to* Noah's planting vineyards *after* the Flood. Schelling contrasts the Rechabites with the *descendants* of Noah, who were more vulnerable to polytheism and idolatry because of their participation in agrarian culture. Schelling, *Philosophy of Mythology*, 109.

54 Tillich may be taking some liberty with Schelling at this point. Tillich specifically refers to GW 11:239, which is found in Schelling's *Philosophy of Mythology*, which makes at least two points, the second of which is that revelation that occurred outside of the people of Israel is a good thing. First, Schelling critiques the widely held, "great...sacrosanct...principle" of his time about human progress, which assumes no revelation, and that progress occurred, by trial and error, in a blind and fumbling manner. Schelling agrees that history is unpredictable and contingent, but that it is replete with manifestations of revelation, and he ruminates at length on the divine dimension of sacred architecture that spans various cultures: "For the believers in revelation, who seek in the revelation that which guides, that *numen*, find themselves in part in a decisive minority, and in part they can prove that guidance only for a small part of the human species. And it always remains strange that the people of the true God had to seek the architect of their temples in the Phoenicians. But by what were these other peoples raised, through what were they prevented from losing themselves in the fully senseless, through what were they elevated to the greatness that we cannot deny to their conceptions? If it was not mere *chance* that let the Babylonians, Phoenicians, [and] Egyptians find the way to their elaborate and in part astounding structures [XI 240], then something else must have intervened, something *different* but yet analogous to revelation. Heathendom does not form a mere negation to the revealed religion but rather something positive of another type. This something other and yet something analogous was precisely the mythological process." Schelling, *Philosophy of Mythology*, 166–167.

way that permanently eliminated recurring temptations, which reached their high point in the Jerusalem monarchy and temple cult.[55]

2.4.3 The Jewish Prophetic Transformation of Pagan Substance

The Basis of Revelation: Pagan Substance and Revelational Form

Tillich's Schelling illustrates the mythological process by giving examples from the Old Testament that distinguish between "pagan substance" and "revelational form." His main example is the account of God's command for Abraham to sacrifice Isaac, found in Genesis 22. The pagan or mythological substance is the practice of human sacrifice, which Tillich specifically says has a parallel in ancient Phoenicia, but also occurred elsewhere in the ancient world; it was effectively a universal practice. The revelational form is the intervention of the angel of Jehovah, with the particular name being the distinguishing characteristic of divinity:

> A typical example of how the pagan principle, which is the basis of Judaism and which gives it reality, is governed by revelation and becomes potential through it, is the story of the sacrifice of Isaac. Elohim commands Abraham to sacrifice his son, as Kronos commanded the Phoenicians. To Abraham, this command has complete reality. But the angel of Jehovah prevents him from carrying it out. Jehovah, whom the angel manifests, is a definite and distinct God. In contrast to that nameless God of prehistory who is substance, he has a name, that is, a form (11:163). All the biblical narratives in which Elohim reveals his name Jehovah belong here: "The name is important, because there is no knowledge of the true God without difference. The worshippers of the true God are those who know his name" (11:165). In particular, pagan substance and revelational form are traceable in the statutes and ordinances of Mosaic religion [*Mosaismus*].[56]

Note the distinction between substance, the "nameless God of prehistory," Elohim, and form, the "true God," who has the name Jehovah.

Tillich's Schelling provides additional examples, including the significance of circumcision as a mitigation of the "cult of castration;" and the ark of the covenant and tabernacle corresponding to Egyptian prototypes.[57] Tillich's Schelling concludes that the pagan substance is fundamental to revelation: "Mosaic religion is inconceivable if one does not perceive within it the reality of paganism

---

55 "Not until the Babylonian captivity did the danger of polytheism disappear, for just at that time the mythological process had lost its power among mankind generally, because its goal had been reached (14:144)." 1910 Dissertation, 104.

56 Ibid., 104–105. Tillich quotes Schelling *SW* 11:163 and 11:165.

57 Ibid., 105. Tillich quotes Schelling *SW* 14:134 and 14:135, respectively, regarding these two phenomena.

on the one hand, and actual revelation on the other (14:145)"; and "The secret of the formation and the structure of the Old Testament is based, for the most part, upon the necessity to cherish and preserve this pagan substance (14:125)."[58]

The Prophetic Transformation of the Particular into the Universal

According to the dialectical history of religion presented thus far, the relationship between paganism and Judaism manifests the tension between the first and second potencies, with Judaism possessing sufficient revelational form to begin the transformation into the third potency, or Spirit. Second, in a manifestation of Spirit, Prophetism began to transcend the cultural limitations and superstitions of the Mosaic law, but some elements of it were permitted to remain. Therefore, the prophetic witness was a necessary bridge from an earlier, superstitious and ethnically particular form of Judaism, to a later, more sophisticated, universal form. The following is the core of Tillich's description of Prophetism:

> Spirit, the potency of the future, speaks already in the prophets of Israel and leads beyond the law, without, however, annulling it for the present. To be sure, 'that superstitious customs like those prescribed in the Mosaic ceremonial law' should somehow continue to develop during the age of the Kings of Israel was made impossible by the prophets (11:174n). But just as little was the importance of such customs for that present disputed. Prophetic universalism is supposed to be explained in the same way. For the present it let the boundaries of the chosen race remain.[59]

God's revelation through the law of Moses would be limited for a season, and would ultimately be expanded beyond ethnic and national boundaries, as Israel increased its "self consciousness." This process of the emerging self-consciousness of Israel, had its goal in "prophetic universalism."[60] However, according to Tillich's Schelling, it appears that historic Judaism failed to attain this level of awareness, and fell back into a legalistic, and/or ethnically insular expression.

58 Ibid., 105.

59 1910 Dissertation, 105–106.

60 "4) Just as paganism reached self-consciousness in the mysteries and also transcended itself, so did Israel in Prophetism. Spirit, the potency of the future, speaks already in the prophets of Israel and leads beyond the law, without, however, annulling it for the present." Ibid., 105.

2.4.4 The "Mantle of the Supernatural:" Jewish Legalism

The fourth part of the discussion of Judaism and Islam is critical to the entire analysis, but it unfortunately possesses some cryptic references. However, there are two observations that can be made, providing guidance for the overall argument. First, Tillich's Schelling says that the history of the religion of Israel underwent three periods, a Mosaic period, a prophetic period, and a "normative" period.[61] The first two periods reflect what has been discussed in detail above. The Mosaic period exhibited emerging revelation from culture, and the Prophetic period sought the transformation of particular cultural practices into universal religious experience, that transcended ethnic and national boundaries. There is a third period, "normative Judaism," which is not clearly characterized. On the one hand, it could refer to prophetic universalism, which appeared to be the goal of the transitional prophetic period discussed above. Terminologically, this would make sense insofar as this appeared to be the goal of Judaism, what Judaism "ought" to be.

However, Tillich's Schelling observes that, as a matter of historical record, this did not occur. The post-prophetic development of Judaism clung to the ritual aspects of Mosaic law, as if it were "the mantle of the supernatural," which made it difficult for Jews to free themselves from its ritual aspects.[62] If this is what Tillich's Schelling is saying, which is my argument, then his view would be another instance of the widely held understanding that the Jewish law was a legalistic burden.[63] Therefore, this suggests that the third period of Judaism manifested a failure to fully transcend the Mosaic law, and therefore relapsed back into a

---

61 "According to this construction, the history of the religion of Israel ran through three periods: a) the normalizing through revelation of the basic mythological religious functions (in brief, the development of Mosaic religion), b) the spiritual understanding of the Mosaic law and the prophecy of the spiritual religion of the future (Prophetism), c) complete rejection of mythology, together with legal fixation of the substantial, mythological, and the formal, antimythological elements of Mosaic religion (normative Judaism)." Ibid., 106.

62 "The mythological element was the foundation of the post-prophetic development of Judaism. For the Jews it became the mantle of the supernatural, and thereby holiness itself. Therefore, it was very difficult for the Jews "to free themselves from their ritual law, and from that purely cosmic element peculiar to it" (14:149)."; Ibid., 106.

63 As discussed elsewhere in this book, 19th and 20th century liberal Protestantism maintained a reductionist understanding of Jewish law as legalistic and contrary to the Christian gospel. Tillich, similar to nearly all of his contemporaries, maintained a negative view of Jewish law. For example, see Jon D. Levenson, *The Hebrew Bible, the Old Testament and Historical Criticism*, Jews and Christians in Biblical Studies (Louisville, KY: Westminster/John Knox Press, 1993).

legalistic reliance upon it.[64] While this seems to be a plausible reading overall, what follows is another difficult concept that is only partly clarified by the final section on Islam.

The second observation by Tillich's Schelling is that the transformation of Judaism over time manifested a paradox, which characterized the inner logic of how revelation unfolded through the mythological process. On the one hand, the mythological process, with its tension between revelation and culture, enabled great adaptability for Judaism over time and in changing contexts. On the other hand, it appears that there was something seductive in the context of post-prophetic Judaism that led the Jewish community back towards rigid cultural practices, instead of expanding outward with a more universalistic posture.[65]

Tillich's Schelling concludes that the mythological process ultimately led to a religion that exhibits a virtually *unmediated* and primal expression of divine power that makes no accommodation to culture, which fits the characterization of Islam, discussed in the fifth and final section: "the power of the mythological principle enjoyed its final triumph in the antimythological religion of revelation (11:150 *sic*)."[66] While Tillich's Schelling presents an unclear view of the third stage of Judaism, his portrayal of Islam is much more clear, and its theological failure is the opposite of the theological failure of Judaism. Judaism went through numerous changes as it was continuously engaged with the surrounding culture, at times

---

64 Elsewhere, Tillich observes that the law of Sinai was distorted by Judaism, and had to be reestablished by Christ. He also argues that the law of Moses is equivalent to natural law, which can be known by reason. See *A History of Christian Thought: From Its Judaic and Hellenistic Origins to Existentialism*, ed. Carl E. Braaten (New York: Simon & Schuster Touchstone, 1967, 1968), 44. Hereafter, "Tillich, *History of Christian Thought.*"

65 In Part III, Section II of the 1910 Dissertation, "The Concept of History," 149, Tillich's Schelling sheds additional light on how the history of religion unfolds, and that revelation has a "supra-historical basis: "The construction of the pre-Christian rational process begins with prehistorical time, which is characterized by a complete absence of culture. It demonstrates the progressive rise of culture until it reaches perfection and catastrophe in Hellenism. The philosophy of post-Christian history likewise begins with a condition of cultural bondage. It treats the growing autonomy of cultural life and points to its goal, that is, the development of the unity of religion and culture in philosophical religion. Whereas on the gound of paganism, religion and culture diverged until they reached their ultimate separation with the advent of revelation, in the history of Christianity they develop a tendency to converge."

66 The full passage reads, not without some difficulty: "In paganism, the purely cosmic powers became impotent in themselves through the metaphysical process. In Judaism, as the substrate of revelation, they held the power of the antitheological principle. The result was a paradox: the power of the mythological principle enjoyed its final triumph in the antimythological religion of revelation (11:150 *sic*)."1910 Dissertation, 106.

succumbing to idolatry. Islam, on the other hand, maintained its early, aggressive posture toward culture, and purportedly remained unchanged.[67]

2.4.5 Islam: The "World-Historical After Effect of Judaism"

For Tillich's Schelling, Islam ("Mohammedanism") is understood in a very negative light. The history of Israel manifests a complicated transformation from an ethnically insular sect with polytheistic tendencies in the time of Abraham and Moses, to a legalistic, absolute monotheism in post-prophetic (i.e. rabbinic) Judaism. Islam undergoes no such transformation, but explodes onto the scene from the primordial past, with an unambiguous monotheism, destroying everything in its path: "The awesome successes of Mohammed can only be explained as due to 'a prodigious force rising again from the past ... which burst forth destroying and laying waste the tradition and culture that by that time had evolved (11:167)."[68]

For Tillich's Schelling, Islam is simultaneously an overwhelming earthly geopolitical success but a destructive theological failure. Whereas the revelatory purpose of Judaism, how it provided enduring characteristics that were later appropriated by Christianity, is articulated in detail, the sole purpose of Islam is to

---

67 "Mohammed's teaching of unity could never bring forth this revolutionary effect if it was not from time immemorial in those children of Hagar, in whom the whole time from their ancestor up to Mohammed had passed by without trace. Yet with Christianity a religion had emerged that no longer simply excluded polytheism, like it was excluded by Judaism. Precisely there, at this point of the development where the rigid and one-sided unity was utterly overcome, the old primordial religion had to right itself again – blindly and fanatically, as it could appear no differently against the much more developed time. The reaction was not merely aimed at the idolatry that in Mohammed's time had partially spread even among the part of the Arabs that had not departed from nomadic life, but rather far more at the apparent [XI 168] successive polytheism of Christianity against which Mohammed opposed the rigid, immutable God of the primordial time. Here everything is connected: Mohammed's law also forbade wine to his adherents, just like the Recabites reject it." Schelling, *Philosophy of Mythology*, 117–118. The reference to Hagar recalls Genesis 17 and 25, in which Ishmael was also blessed by the Lord to be the "father of many," of "twelve rulers," of "a nation;" in Genesis 25, Ishmael has twelve sons, many with Arabic names. Translator's Notes, Schelling, *Philosophy of Mythology*, Lecture 8, Note 32, 215.

68 1910 Dissertation, 106. According to Schelling's history of religion, the forerunner of Islam in the "pre-historical" period is Melchizedek. Schelling engages in theological etymology, noting that the Hebrew *zedek* and *zaddik* mean "justice" and "just," but also observes that these derive from Arabic words for "steadfastness" and "rigidity." Therefore, Melchizidek is "the steadfast one" who "walks fully in unification with *Elohim*," the primal "first God" discussed above. In addition, Schelling notes linguistic parallels between "Salem," "Islam" and "Moslem," observing that Islam means "nothing other than the complete, that is, the whole, the undivided religion: a Moslem is he who is devoted entirely to the *One*." Schelling, *Philosophy of Mythology*, 117.

attack what it misunderstood to be the idolatry of polytheism, found especially in Christianity:

> Just at the moment when Christianity, which not only excluded polytheism as Judaism had done, but also assimilated it, had completely overcome 'the austere one-sided unity of original monotheism, the ancient, primordial religion arose once again – irrationally and fanatically – with the force of necessity' (11:167). Mohammed set the austere, impassive god of prehistory not only against the *polydaimonism* prevailing among his clansmen, but above all against the apparent polytheism of Christianity. 'Like the Rechabites, Mohammed even forbade his followers to take wine' (11:168).[69]

For Tillich's Schelling, Islam became a religious-political force of undeniable significance, but purportedly made no enduring contribution to the development of religious consciousness within the history of religion. In light of the association of Islam with the Rechabites, it appears that Islam's non-participation in surrounding culture is the source of its ability to survive. According to Tillich's own principles, this illustration from the history of religion could serve as a critique of idolatry, as opposed to seeing Islam as a purely destructive force. In later analyses of Tillich's history of religion, this view of Islam remains essentially unchanged.[70]

It is outside the scope of this book to fully analyze the relationship of Tillich's thought and Islam,[71] but the main weakness of his view, insofar as it is Tillich's view per se (not that of Tillich's Schelling!) from the standpoint of interfaith dialogue, is similar to the main weakness of Tillich's spirit of Judaism as a prophetic principle. Tillich intentionally does not provide a "phenomenological description" of either Judaism or Islam, but creates or adopts a construct of each to fit within his historical and theological scheme. He does not try to present either

---

69 1910 Dissertation, 106 – 107. See Note 66 above. Schelling, *Philosophy of Mythology*, 117 – 118.

70 For example, Tillich understands the Roman Inquisition of the Middle Ages to be a direct result of Islamic aggression in Europe and Iberia, which in turn led to religious anti-Judaism. See Chapter Six, and Tillich, *Bampton Lectures*, 23 – 25.

71 For comparisons of Bediuzzaman Said Nursi (1877 – 1960) and Paul Tillich, see Kelton Cobb, "Revelation, The Disciplines of Reason, and Truth in the Works of Said Nursi and Paul Tillich," in *Islam at the Crossroads: On the Life and Thought of Bediuzzaman Said Nursi*, ed. Ibrahim M. Abu-Rabi (Albany, NY: SUNY Press, 2003), 129 – 150. Also, see Umeyye Yazicioglu, *Reconciliation of Faith and Reason in the Modern Age: A Comparison Between Paul Tillich and Bediuzzaman Said Nursi*; M.A. Thesis, Hartford Seminary, April 2004. There are also numerous references to Islam in Tillich's early works, in the series *Ergänzungs und Nachlassbände zu den Gesammelten Werken von Paul Tillich* (Berlin: De Gruyter), abbreviated as "E," especially Volume XII, Berlin Lectures 1919 – 1920, 364, 448, 457, 474 – 478, 486, 489, 509f, 520, 530 and 548.

faith in terms of its own diverse self-understanding, going against his method of correlation. As a result, Tillich's view of Islam appears to be summed up as primitive, powerful, and destructive.

Did Tillich really believe in the history of religion as constructed by Schelling, as if it were empirically true in every detail? This is not likely, but Tillich viewed Schelling's analysis as a means to an end,[72] the end of articulating the process of how the third potency, spirit, emerges in consciousness. Tillich acknowledges that many, if not all, of the empirical details of Schelling's analysis of the mythological process have been overturned by modern research, although there is "an abundance of ingenious and profound observations upon which … many learned poor could feast."[73] It is perhaps for this reason, the questionable empirical validity, that Tillich believed that the 1912 Dissertation was more important. As will be shown below, the philosophical premises of his argument are what is pivotal, and the use of the history of religion involved very little empirical detail, certainly nothing questionable.

2.5.1 The 1912 Dissertation: The Failures of Paganism and Judaism

In the 1910 Dissertation, Tillich provided an extensive analysis of the history of religion, followed by a relatively brief religious and theological application. In the 1912 Dissertation, the emphasis is reversed, with most of the analysis devoted to problems posed by Kant, with a shorter concluding section devoted to their

---

72 At the beginning of a section titled "Gods and Idols," Tillich writes: "Obviously the construction of the history of religion given here comprehends only a fraction of the religions that actually exist. But for a systematic construction, this is of no consequence. What matters here is the process by which the spiritual potency becomes predominant in consciousness. In principle, it is enough if it has been realized at one point in history. Only the quality of the outcome is valid here. As in nature, so also in history, God's way goes from the broad to the narrow. Moreover, it should be noted that his construction confines itself to the Near East and the Mediterranean region (with the sole exception of India, whose special position within the history of mythology is most comparable to Christianity). The nations of these regions and their culture are entirely interlaced with the history of Israel, and together they flow into the Hellenistic culture of the Roman Empire. Therefore an external economy is attained here that puts the concept of the 'fullness of time' in a new light: when Christianity enters the world, its way is prepared in a positive sense not only by the religious history of Israel, but also by the history of paganism." Ibid., 93.

73 Tillich, 1910 Dissertation, part II, 165–166 note 1. The comment about "the learned poor" is attributed to Otto Pfleiderer (d. 1908), professor at the Universities of Jena and Berlin. Cf. Wikipedia, "Otto Pfleiderer" [accessed 03/25/2012]. I do not know what Tillich meant by this. O'Hanlon concurs that Tillich believed that the empirical features of religions as held by Schelling were problematic. O'Hanlon, *Influences*, 62.

resolution within the history of religion. The structure of Tillich's thought is deeply indebted to Kant, and Tillich throughout his career responds in one way or another to Kant. In the 1912 Dissertation, Tillich responds to Kant's three Critiques, with a particular "antinomy" characteristic of each,[74] and also situates his work within the context of the entirety of western philosophy. According to the translator Nuovo, "Tillich suggests in his introduction and in the early sections of the work that the true significance of the outcome of Schelling's philosophical development can be grasped only when it is viewed within an ever-widening circle that comprehends, first, classical German philosophy beginning with Kant, then modern philosophy since Descartes and Spinoza, and finally western philosophy since Parmenides."[75]

The opening sentence of the 1912 Dissertation summarizes the recurring problem of the contradiction between truth and morality as applied to religion.

> Mysticism and guilt-consciousness, the feeling of unity with the absolute and consciousness of opposition to God, the principle of the identity of absolute and individual spirit and the experience of contradiction between Holy Lord and sinful creature: this is the antinomy for whose solution religious thought in the Church in every age has struggled and must continually struggle.[76]

Tillich observes that there are two fundamental, common religious experiences. The first is the union between the individual and the divine, explained philosophically as "identity," and religiously as "mysticism." The second is fear of the holy, explained philosophically as the contradiction between self-interest and obligation, and religiously as "guilt-consciousness."[77] The paradigmatic expression of this second expression is the call of Isaiah in Isaiah 6: "The holy and exalted God of Israel, whose look is like a consuming fire, before whom no man can stand (cf. Isaiah 6)."[78]

Part I, called the "Historical-Dialectical Foundation of the Problem," provides a theoretical basis by demonstrating the recurring contradiction between the experience of oneness with God (mysticism) and the experience of alienation

---

74 In the first critique, *The Critique of Pure Reason*, there is an antinomy between "Consciousness in General" and the "Thing Itself." In the second critique, *The Critique of Practical Reason*, there is an antinomy between "Moral World Order" and "Radical Evil." In the third critique, *The Critique of Judgment*, there is an antinomy between "Organic" and "Inorganic." 1912 Dissertation, 33–44.

75 Nuovo, translator's introduction, 1912 Dissertation, 10.

76 Ibid., 27.

77 Ibid., 27–28. This is also noted by Neugebauer, *Tillichs frühe Christologie*, 243, note 413.

78 Ibid., 27–28.

from God (guilt consciousness). Part II discusses the variety of ways that mysticism and identity function within the earlier Schelling, in his speculative ("negative") philosophy, and the limitations of ethical concepts to comprehend and resolve the original contradiction between truth and morality. Tillich concludes part II by showing that one pole of the original contradiction, "guilt consciousness," cannot possibly resolve the contradiction, especially if it is expressed solely in intellectual terms. This sets the stage for a fuller development of theological concepts in part III.

In part III of the 1912 Dissertation, Tillich discusses Schelling's attempt to synthesize mysticism and guilt-consciousness in his later period, where he develops his "positive" philosophy, also known as his philosophy of freedom. There are two main sections, with the first discussing several overtly theological concepts, such as sin, guilt, wrath, and grace, called "The Solution in Principle." In the second section, called "The Religio-Historical Solution," Tillich revisits Schelling's views on history and religion, including the role of Judaism. Similar to the treatment of Judaism in the 1910 Dissertation, here Judaism plays a transitional role from paganism, characterized by its mythological elements, to Christianity, characterized by its revelatory elements. Like the 1910 Dissertation, there is a section devoted to the construction of the history of religion, beginning with a discussion of mythology, and ending with a discussion of revelation, and the discussion of mythology ends with a treatment of the "catastrophe" of mysticism and the rational process.

The penultimate section of the 1912 Dissertation, titled "The Struggle of the Law against the Contradiction: Judaism," contains the only explicit discussion of Judaism in the entire dissertation, and is less than two full pages.[79] Like the 1910 Dissertation, there is a comparison of paganism and Judaism, although here the differences between them are emphasized. Paganism failed by coming to its logical conclusion in mysticism, one pole of the dialectic, and Judaism failed by coming to its logical conclusion in guilt-consciousness, the other pole of the dialectic. This happens in two ways.

First, whereas paganism evolves in a purely naturalistic dialectic of the potencies, Judaism experiences a revelatory confrontation of the divine self against nature, through the call of Abraham and the giving of the law to Moses:

> In paganism, the potencies develop in a natural, necessary process; in Judaism the divine self enters into antithesis with the natural principle. Jewish consciousness is also substantially mythological, that is, it is subject to the principle of wrath. But this principle is not overcome in the inner life of consciousness, so that finally aesthetic and intellectual culture

79 1912 Dissertation, Part III, II.B(b), 122–124.

> might emerge; rather the divine will opposes it and tries to give it a divine form. Here will opposes will, and there is no identity to make the mystical relation possible. God is the lawgiver.[80]

Second, while paganism subsumes the individual in a mystical union with divinized nature, Judaism cultivates individual spirituality, in relation to a transcendent God and in response to the Mosaic law:

> Whereas in paganism God proved to be the absolute, that which comprehends all the potencies and is their spiritual bond, in Judaism he manifests himself as the culmination of abstract, individual spirituality. God is the All-one. Paganism demonstrates his totality and therefore his identity with every individual, that is, in mysticism. Judaism shows his unity, his separateness from every individual, namely, guilt-consciousness.[81]

In the 1910 Dissertation, there was more continuity between paganism and Judaism, with Judaism "emerging" as an expression of the second potency and contributing to Spirit because of its universal, revelatory elements. Recall the complex distinction between "pagan substance" and "revelational form" in the 1910 Dissertation, with historic Judaism possessing both, as discussed in Sections 2.4.2 and 2.4.3, above. In the 1912 Dissertation, paganism and Judaism are pushed to two contradictory poles, for both "go to ruin" on "one-sidedness,"[82] reflecting the spirit of the Kantian antinomy. According to Tillich's Schelling, pagan mysticism has inherent limitations, and it is the externality of the Law of Moses given by a personal God, that provides the basis for revelation.

Tillich concludes the penultimate section of the 1912 Dissertation, which explicitly discusses Judaism, by anticipating the distinct revelatory character of Christianity:

> In the fullness of time mysticism in its perfect form was crushed under the burden of the moral demand and of divine wrath in paganism, and guilt-consciousness was obscured by the highest, namely, religious elevation of the principle of selfhood in Judaism, but just then, in the pagan mysteries and in the messianic expectations of the Jews, the true God was prophesied.[83]

The contradiction posed by the one-sided, or imbalanced natures of paganism and Judaism is resolved, according to Tillich's Schelling, by a personal God who is distinct from nature and humanity. However, what is salvific about this

---

80 Ibid., 123.
81 Ibid., 123.
82 "Judaism goes to ruin on this one-sidedness, just as paganism does on the other side" (Ibid).
83 Ibid., 124.

God is identification with humanity, by subjecting God-self to bondage to nature and bondage to the Mosaic law:

> God assumes the form of selfhood and subjects himself to its curse so that he may have communion with those who are bound to selfhood. He redeems from the power of the pagan principle, he reconciles by conquering divine displeasure, he justifies by "acknowledging" the present condition of separation from God by dealing as a person with persons, and by encountering individuals as an individual. He is completely victorious over the contradiction, by subjecting himself to it.[84]

2.5.2 Additional Support for the Continuity Between Judaism and Christianity

Two footnotes appended to Tillich's analysis support the general thesis that Judaism plays an indispensable preparatory role in the emergence of Christianity. In footnote number 51 to Part III, Tillich says that paganism and Judaism have a common starting point, in that each is bound to God through God's wrath.[85] Paganism "loses itself" in this bond, the mystical union of the individual with divinized nature, although Judaism resists this bond, "creates a real solution" through a personal relationship to God in obedience to Mosaic law, but stalls at that stage as "guilt-consciousness remains the characteristic form of Jewish piety."[86] This is similar to the 1910 Dissertation, insofar as paganism and Judaism have a common starting point. However, the characterization of paganism as being in "bondage" to a wrathful god is a different emphasis, and it helps to heighten the distinction between paganism and Judaism.

At the same time, in footnote 50, it is this personal relationship with God through the law that anticipates Christianity, enabling Tillich to pair Judaism with Christianity:

> It might have been possible to treat Judaism together with paganism, inasmuch as in Judaism also the contradiction has not yet been overcome. On the other hand, it cannot be maintained that the contradiction prevails there. It was resisted, and in every act of obedience to the law it was overcome. But above all – and this is decisive for Schelling – in Judaism, God confronts the contradiction through revelation, i.e., personally, so that in this connection (which is the more important one) Judaism and Christianity belong together.[87]

---

84 Ibid., 124.
85 Ibid., 142 note 51.
86 Ibid.
87 Ibid., 142 note 50.

This understanding of revelation is very similar to the 1910 Dissertation, in that the giving of the law of Moses in Judaism by a personal god, a *particular* revelatory element was introduced. However, unlike the 1910 Dissertation, it appears that the giving of the law itself, by a personal God, serves to transcend the contradiction between mysticism and guilt-consciousness, without the additional steps of Prophetism and prophetic universalism. In the 1910 Dissertation Tillich made a distinction between historical forms of Judaism (Abrahamic/Mosaic and prophetic) that were unable to fully transcend their pagan roots, and "normative Judaism," which manifests the universality of revelation. In the 1912 Dissertation, such a distinction is assumed, and Judaism still provides an indispensable foundation for Christianity.

The foregoing primary source analysis yields numerous insights, with three to be restated here, in anticipation of the following Chapters, Three through Six in particular. First, the doctrine of the potencies, which expresses Schelling's cosmology and ontology, will inform Tillich's theological history of religions. In particular, the doctrine of the potencies provides a framework for an "inclusive" history of religion (Chapter Six), in which a religion may make an enduring contribution to the emergence and development of the religious consciousness. Second, for Tillich's Schelling, the cosmic potency or logos, is the instrument through which creation will be reconciled to God, through the stimulation of the religious consciousness. This view of the logos anticipates Tillich's later Christology, as seen in the *Systematic Theology*, to be discussed in Chapter Five. Third, the foregoing discussion of the paradox of the inner logic of the mythological process, raises up the issues of idolatry and the tension between religion and culture. These are two key themes that will remain central throughout Tillich's career. Judaism contributes to the history of revelation in profound and enduring ways, despite its theological subordination to Christianity. Chapter Three will discuss the decisive elevation of the prophetic dimension of Judaism within the history of religion, as a prophetic response to two world-historical froms of idolatry, international capitalism and religious nationalism, with the latter posing an imminent threat in German National Socialism.

Chapter Three: Jewish Prophetism as the Ontological Basis for Justice

Before World War I, it is not clear whether Tillich believed that Judaism retained any permanent theological value, or whether it could disappear off the world stage and remain just a historical relic, as the Aryan Christians would have preferred. Based upon Tillich's relatively brief presentation of Judaism in the two Schelling dissertations, it is possible that in this early stage of his theological development, that Tillich could have dispensed with Judaism, seeing it *only* as the historical precedent to Christianity. It may have been enough that the giving of the law to Moses, the call of Abraham, and the prophetic witness of the Old Testament *were recorded* in the Old Testament, and that the written record was adequate to provide the foundational ideas for Christianity. This chapter will primarily analyze Tillich's *The Socialist Decision,* which demonstrates that Judaism possesses a permanent theologiclal validity, derived from its prophetic dimension. This prophetic aspect, typically referred to by Tillich as Jewish prophetism, must persist as a critical principle against idolatry, especially for the benefit of Christianity.

The primary thesis of this chapter is that in *The Socialist Decision*, Tillich's dialectical history of religion enables him to attribute permanent validity to Judaism, in the form of Jewish prophetism. Tillich places the *prophetic dimension of Judaism* in primary opposition to nationalistic German religion, as found in Nazism. Jewish prophetism plays an essential role in Tillich's distinctive view of socialism, which has a critical and constructive program to transform society along humanistic and eschatological lines. References to Jewish prophetism are pervasive throughout *The Socialist Decision*; the notion is deeply embedded in its dialectical structure, and considerable effort will be made to explain the theoretical basis of his argument from its starting point. Tillich's dialectical history of religion enables him to derive the "ought" of justice from the "is" of being, and to posit the maxim, "justice is the true power of being." The unique and indispensible foundation of this maxim is Jewish prophetism, derived from historic Judaism.

The secondary thesis of this chapter is that Tillich's concept of Jewish prophetism responds uniquely to the dual problems of capitalism and German National Socialism. Whereas Tillich had begun to diagnose the problems with capitalism by the end of World War I, they endured into the 1930s. By that time, the problem of Nazism had emerged as a major threat to German society in the Weimar period. The concept of "belief-ful realism," as developed in *The Religious*

Situation,[1] possessed priestly and prophetic aspects, and was thought by Tillich to adequately criticize the spirit of capitalism, as he understood it in the 1920s. Due to the limitations of belief-ful realism, Tillich later developed the concept of Jewish prophetism to respond to religious nationalism, of which Nazism is one instance. For Tillich, Jewish prophetism posed an effective response to religious nationalism and Nazism because it provides a much 'deeper' critique than belief-ful realism. Jewish prophetism has ontological roots, enabling it to transform political romanticism "on the basis of its own presuppositions."[2] This will be most vividly demonstrated in *The Socialist Decision*, where Tillich derives the maxim "justice is the true power of being."

In order to establish a context to analyze *The Socialist Decision*, Tillich's identity as a socialist will be briefly summarized. In addition, his analysis of "the spirit of capitalism," or "bourgeois capitalism," as discussed in *The Religious Situation*, will be introduced, since it exhibits important themes that will reappear in *The Socialist Decision*.

3.1 World War I and Tillich's Adoption of Socialism

In a 1989 essay exploring Tillich's understanding of the relationship between Lutheran Protestantism and Marxism,[3] Ron Stone succinctly summarizes Tillich's service as an army chaplain in World War I:

> Tillich left his boyhood home of dreaming innocence, his pastoral work in Berlin, and his patriarchal home with everything in place to go to war. He had his Ph.D. in theology, he was married, his family represented the learned German clergy. His father had served as a chaplain to the Emperor on a trip to Jerusalem. It was a world of patriarchal capitalism, with empire and Lutheranism in a symbiotic relationship. He went to war in a siege of patriotism and without clear political convictions ... By the end of the war he had suffered nervous collapses repeatedly, he had helped bury the cream of the German officer corps,

1 *The Religious Situation* was originally published in 1925 in Germany, under the title, *Die religiöse Lage der Gegenwart* ("The Religious Situation of the Present"). It was translated into English and reprinted in America in 1956, under the title, *The Religious Situation*, accompanied by a preface from translator H. Richard Niebuhr. This exposition and analysis will use the 1956 translation. See 116, 217–219.

2 Tillich observes that the churches can respond in one of three ways to the spirit of capitalism: (i) rejection; (ii) surrender and accommodation; and (iii) transformation on the basis of its own presuppositions. *Religious Situation*, 182.

3 Ronald H. Stone, "Paul Tillich: On the Boundary Between Protestantism and Marxism," *Laval Theologique et Philosophie* 45 (October 1989): 393–417.

> his wife had become pregnant by his friend, and the empire had been defeated and thrown into revolution.[4]

By the summer of 1918, Tillich became deeply disillusioned, admitting in personal letters that on the battlefield there was deep economic class division between the officers and the enlisted men, and at home, the wealthy industrialists ("war profiteers") were relatively insulated from the effects of war, unlike the masses of impoverished workers in Berlin.[5] He attributed these gross injustices to nationalism and the curse "that its absolute pursuit had brought upon mankind."[6] Finally, in September of 1919, Tillich acknowledged in a circular to his friends that he had learned to see the World War as "an inevitable consequence of a special social order and special ideas linked with it."[7] Tillich had finally abandoned his war theology,[8] and adopted religious socialism. Simply put, Tillich "wanted a new order of society born of Christianity and socialism, in which the destructive powers of capitalism would be undone."[9]

This is a very important phase in Tillich's life, and it has rightly benefited from a significant amount of scholarly treatment.[10] It is outside the scope of this paper to comprehensively discuss the German political situation during the Weimar period, Tillich's extensive relationships with socialists, Marxists and social progressives, or his appropriation of Marxist theory. For our purposes, Tillich's identity as a socialist can be summarized by four well-known involvements.[11]

---

4 Ibid., 394.

5 *Ergänzungs- und Nachlaßbände zu den Gesammelten Werken von Paul Tillich* (Stuttgart: Ev. Verlagswerk, 1971– ; Berlin: De Gruyter, 1994); hereafter cited as *E* followed by volume and page numbers. Erdmann Sturm, "*Holy Love, Claims Life and Limb." Paul Tillich's War Theology (1914–1918)*, in *Zeitschrift für neue Theologeschichte* (Berlin: De Gruyter, 1995), vol. II, 60–84.

6 *E* V, 143. Cf. Sturm, *Holy Love*, 84.

7 Ibid.

8 See Sturm, *Holy Love*, for the numerous ways in which Tillich adapted his battlefield sermons to support the German imperial army.

9 Pauck and Pauck, *Tillich*, 69.

10 For example, see Stone, *Radical Social Thought*. See also Brian Donnelly, *The Socialist Émigré: Marxism and the Later Tillich* (Macon, GA: Mercer University Press, 2003); Guy Hammond, "Tillich, Adorno and the Debate About Existentialism," *Laval Theologique et Philosophie* 47/3 (1991): 343–355; Terrence O'Keefe, "Paul Tillich's Marxism," *Social Research* 48/3 (1981): 472–499; John R. Stumme, *Socialism in Theological Perspective: A Study of Paul Tillich, 1918–1933* (Missoula, MT: Scholars' Press, 1978).

11 Ron Stone argues that Tillich's lifelong "dialogue" with Marxism began as early as a December 1913 debate with Karl Liebknecht, who later organized the German Communist Party, citing Stumme, *Socialism in a Theological Perspective*, 55; cf. Stone, "Tillich–Boundary," 399.

First, in the spring of 1919, Tillich delivered a lecture with a translated title of "Christianity and Socialism" at a meeting of the Independent Socialist Party, which caused him to be reprimanded by the Protestant Consistory of Brandenburg.[12] Second, in 1920 in Berlin Tillich joined a discussion group that was known as the "*kairos* circle," which met to discuss potential opportunities for a new social order, along socialist lines. This group was comprised of no more than a dozen individuals, including Protestants like Tillich, secular and believing Jews, academics and professionals.[13] The group disbanded in 1925, as several members obtained positions in other German cities, although Tillich had left in 1924 for a theology position at the University of Marburg.[14] Third, Tillich became associated with the *Institut für Sozialforschung* (the "Institute"), an independently funded, interdisciplinary "think tank" located on the campus of the University of Frankfurt-am-Main. Tillich was never employed by the Institute, and he was already a full professor of philosophy at Frankfurt. Yet, Tillich's close proximity to the Institute, his interest in socialism, and his prior relationships with Adolf Löwe and Karl Mennicke, naturally led him to associate with the members of the Institute.[15] The Institute's main researchers, in Germany in the 1930s, were Max Horkheimer, Theodor Adorno, Herbert Marcuse, Erich Fromm, Leo Lowenthal, Walter Benjamin and Friedrich Pollock, all of whom were devoted to the teachings of Marx, and their applicability to the transformation of so-

12 Pauck and Pauck, *Tillich*, 68–69.

13 According to the Paucks (ibid., 70–71), the main members were as follows: (i) Günther Dehn, Protestant minister, a pacifist who later taught at the University of Halle and who was later dismissed from his university position in April 1933, along with Tillich, in the wake of the Reform of the Civil Service Act; (ii) Karl Mennicke, a Protestant minister; (iii) Adolf Löwe, a "believing, non-Orthodox Jew," professor of economics, and lifelong friend of Tillich; (iv) Eduard Heimann, an economist and also a lifelong friend of Tillich; (v) Alexander Rüstow, a Protestant economist and historian; (vi) Arnold Wolfers, a Protestant lawyer who later became director of the Berlin Institute of Politics.

14 Ibid., 74, 288.

15 Tillich, Adolf Löwe and Karl Mennicke are not typically mentioned in histories of the Frankfurt School, but there was some connection. "Tillich was a close friend of Horkheimer, Lowenthal and Pollock, belonging with them to a regular discussion group that included Karl Mannheim, Kurt Riezler, Adolf Löwe and Karl Mennicke. The *Kränzchen*, as it was called–an old-fashioned word meaning both a small garland and an intimate gathering–was to continue in New York for several years, after most of its members were forced to emigrate." Martin Jay, *The Dialectical Imagination: A History of the Frankfurt School and the Institute for Social Research, 1923–1950* (Berkeley: University of California Press, 1996), 24–25. I think some of the confusion can be cleared up by stating that neither Tillich nor Löwe nor Heimann were ever paid from the endowment by the Institute.

ciety. Tillich's relationship with the Institute has been treated elsewhere,[16] but one brief example of the connection is that he was advisor for Theodor Adorno's *Habilitationsschrift*, *Kierkegaard: Construction of the Aesthetic.*[17] In March of 1933, the Nazi government closed the Institute, its members emigrated, most of them ending up in New York City. Some comprised the faculty of the "University in Exile," which was established at New York City's New School for Social Research, to accommodate the large number of high profile intellectual émigrés from Europe.

The fourth example of Tillich's identity as a socialist was his involvement in the publication of two socialist journals. The first was *Blätter für den Religiösen Sozialismus* ("Pages for Religious Socialism"),[18] published from 1920 until 1927, with Karl Mennicke as head publisher.[19] This time period roughly corresponded to the gatherings of the "*kairos* circle." The second journal, titled *Neue Blätter für den Sozialismus* ("New Pages for Socialism"), was published from 1930 to 1933, roughly corresponding to the operation of the Institut in Frankfurt, and was edited by August Rathmann, Eduard Heimann, and Paul Tillich.[20]

3.1.1 Other Tillich Essays on Related Topics

Tillich wrote several articles in the 1920s and 1930s on related topics, and three of them have been translated into English and are widely available in the collection of essays, titled *Political Expectation.*[21] These essays provide additional background for the concept of "prophetism,"[22] a concept that will be explored in greater detail later in the analysis of *The Socialist Decision.* However, there is no discussion of Judaism, and therefore no discussion of Judaism as having

16 A recent treatment is a doctoral dissertation by Bryan Lee Wagoner, entitled "The Subject of Emancipation: Critique, Reason and Religion in the Thought of Theodor W. Adorno, Max Horkheimer and Paul Tillich" Harvard University, December 2011.
17 Jay, *Dialectical Imagination*, 66.
18 The title is translated in this manner, in Pauck, Pauck, *Tillich*, 74.
19 *Socialist Decision*, 163, foreword note 6.
20 Ibid.
21 Edited by James Luther Adams (Lanham, MD: University Press of America, 1971). The individual essays are, in chronological order: "Basic Principles of Religious Socialism" (1923), 58–88; "Protestantism as a Critical and Creative Principle" (1929), 10–39; "Religious Socialism" (1930), 40–57.
22 For example, prophetic criticism is "existential," and it "stands beyond life," favoring neither metaphysical pessimism or optimism. Tillich, "Protestantism as a Critical and Creative Principle," 11–12.

any temporary or enduring theological value. Therefore, these essays will not be systematically analyzed.

In addition, a very important work by Tillich, *The Interpretation of History*[23] ("*Interpretation*") will not be analyzed, also because it does not have a distinct discussion of Judaism. *Interpretation* is a compilation of seven individual essays, written as early as 1924, through the fateful year of emigration, 1933. It is one of Tillich's most expansive and incisive works, and can serve as an interpretive key to his later works, including his *Systematic Theology.* In *Interpretation,* Tillich introduces key concepts such as "*kairos*," "the demonic" and the Cross as the center of history. Also, *Interpretation* discusses numerous key terms and concepts that will be covered in the subsequent analysis of *The Socialist Decision.* These topics are, in order of appearance in *Interpretation:* Jewish prophecy (104), the two "demonics" of nationalism and capitalism (120), socialism, idealism and ideology (179), Marx (181–182), power and Nazism (199–200), consciousness and the emergence of the "demand" (206–208), tension and circularity in history (243–246), and the Jews as the "people of time," the importance of monotheism, and "time" versus "space" (263–264). Therefore, where necessary, reference will be made to *Interpretation,* to help clarify terms used in *The Religious Situation* and *The Socialist Decision.*

23 Tillich's *Interpretation of History* (1936) has several sources, all essays in German, dating from 1924 to 1933. They are, in chronological order: (i) *Kirche und Kultur,* aus: *Sammlung Gemeinverständlicher Vorträge* (Tübingen: Verlag S.C.B. Mohr, 1924); (ii) *Das Dämonische, ein Beitrag zur Sinndeutung der Geschichte,* Tübingen 1926, Verlag S.C.B. Mohr (Sammlung gemeinverständlicher Vorträge); (iii) *Kairos und Logos, eine Untersuchung zur Metaphysik des Erkennens,* aus: *Kairos, Zur Geisteslage und Geisteswendung,* herausgegeben von Paul Tillich, Darmstadt 1926, Otto Reichl Verlag; (iv) *Christologie und Geschichtsdeutung,* aus: *Religiöse Verwirklichung* (Berlin: Furche-Verlag, 1929); (v) *Eschatologie und Geschichte,* aus: *Religiöse Verwirklichung* (Berlin: Furche-Verlag, 1929); (vi) *Das Problem der Macht, Versuch einer philosophischen Grundlegung,* aus: *Neue Blätter für den Sozialismus, 2 jahr,* 4 parts (Potsdam: Alfred Protte Verlag, 1931); (vii) *Die beiden Wurzelen des politischer Denkens* (Potsdam: Alfred Protte Verlag, 1933). These works are listed on the acknowledgments page of *On The Boundary/The Interpretation of History,* trans. Rasetzki and Talmey.

3.2 The Spirit of Capitalism

3.2.1 Tillich's *The Religious Situation*

The Religious Situation identifies the "spirit of capitalism" as a critical problem plaguing German society in the mid 1920s.[24] He assesses whether the disciplines of science, philosophy and art have the ability to respond effectively to the spirit of capitalism. For Tillich, the capitalist spirit is the product of free market economics (for Tillich a "war of all against all") and the application of reductionist scientific methods to human society. These initially combined in the nineteenth century to create a European culture dominated by "bourgeois capitalism," which Tillich refers to as "the capitalist spirit." The capitalist spirit peaked in influence before the outbreak of World War I, and in Tillich's opinion – which was widely shared – its foundations were shaken by "war and revolution," in particular World War I, the Russian Revolution, the revolution in Germany after the November 1918 armistice, and the abdication of Kaiser Wilhelm II. According to Tillich, the capitalist spirit is truly "anti-religious," because of its reductionist view of human nature, its promotion of "self-sufficiency," and ability to diminish "self-transcendence."[25] This reductionist view of human nature was fostered by what I will call "economic atomism,"[26] in which individuals are primarily self-interested creatures whose interrelations are governed by the laws of supply and demand, and competition, in which the victor necessarily triumphs at the expense of others.

For Tillich, the capitalist spirit is dominated by three characteristics: i) *mathematical natural science* – pursues the goal of demonstrating that reality is governed wholly by its own laws and is rationally intelligible, and keeps skepticism at a distance; ii) *technique* – world-ruling technique with its will to conquer space, time and nature and to make "the earth a well-furnished dwelling for man;" (iii) *capitalist economy* – seeks to provide the greatest possible number of men with the greatest possible amount of economic goods, which seeks to arouse and to satisfy ever-increasing demands without raising the question as

24 Tillich uses the terms "capitalist spirit" and "spirit of capitalism" interchangeably. The concept of spirit will evolve over time and be discussed accordingly.

25 *Religious Situation*, 43–53.

26 For Tillich, "'Capitalist society, even according to the definition of the concept, is a human group analyzable after the fashion of natural science into pure individuals–the atoms of society–which are held together by economic purposes and needs–the natural laws of capitalist society" (ibid., 43; see also 111 in relation to "the mass").

to the meaning of the process.[27] According to Tillich, capitalism started out with an emancipatory program, but degenerated in the following manner: "It did not turn away from this which was its eternal meaning until emancipated personality engaging in the conflicts of capitalist economy had been filled with unlimited desire for economic power and until free competition had forced upon almost all social groups an unbounded striving after profits and so the war of all against all. Only after this had happened did liberal economy with the technique which supported it become the most powerful symbol of a self-seeking, time-fettered existence. Then it became for many, particularly for the masses, which were oppressed as a result of the conflict, not only a profane but also a demonic and anti-divine symbol."[28]

For Tillich, the original socialist political form, as expressed by Marx in the nineteenth century, possessed an eschatological dimension, a "transcendent element," an "eschatological tension'" and a "dynamic hopefulness."[29] These ideas are similar to those used later in the humanistic and eschatological socialism sought in *The Socialist Decision*, although there is no grounding in Jewish prophetism. Tillich believes that the German socialism of his time failed to manifest these characteristics. Instead, he argues that the more radical communists and Marxists succeeded in providing an alternative world view, by addressing all the theoretical problems of the capitalist spirit, such as the reductionist view of human nature, the class struggle, and the economic atomism referred to above.[30] In fact, the spirit of capitalism exploited the "inner contradiction" of German socialism:

> It was a great victory of the capitalist spirit, however, perhaps the greatest victory that it has won, when it took captive the strongest of the movements directed against it. The ultimately

---

27 Ibid., 47.
28 Ibid., 49–50.
29 Ibid., 112.
30 The "radicals" Tillich specifically names include Landauer, Georg Lukacs, French syndicalism, Russia's Bakunin, influences of the German youth movement, and Berlin's Karl Mennicke. He says: "All of these movements seek to interpret socialism as a part of a comprehensive spiritual movement, to make it an organic part of the whole anti-capitalist attitude and to eliminate all capitalistic elements from it. They reject the naïve absoluteness of the socialist party, as expressed by both leaders and the masses. They struggle for a new definition of the theoretical basis and the practical end of the movement. Hence they deal with the problems of community, of the attitude toward things, with the questions about human needs, about the formation of classes, with the problem of the masses in its economic and religious aspects, with the problem of property, the meaning of the liberal definition of the economic laws and with other similar questions. Their criticism of socialism is often radical, more radical and profound, indeed, than that which is exercised by capitalism; yet it is a criticism which is at the same time an affirmation of the socialist struggle" (ibid., 114–115).

> transcendent goal of socialism was made finite and temporal in its actual definition of ends. It looked to a point in time when that which is the negation of all time – the eternal – was to be realized. The necessary result of this inner contradiction was that socialism should become disillusioned, should begin to make compromises, to adopt the doctrine of progress and to become bourgeois in its temper.[31]

According to Tillich, German socialism adopted a *purely temporal* goal, and forfeited its eschatological orientation. However, Tillich's normative view of socialism is "religious," in the broad sense that any aspect of culture in which the eternal is made accessible.[32] However, he will conclude that, *in theory*, a form of Protestant theology that unites priestly and prophetic elements could provide *a basis* for the transformation of society.

3.2.2 Belief-ful Realism

Tillich argued that Germany needed to adopt a posture of "belief-ful realism," which takes seriously both the specific historical context, which is permeated by the spirit of capitalism, and yet maintains a hopeful orientation towards the eternal, to avoid the extremes of romanticism and utopianism.[33] These features will recur in *The Socialist Decision*, but will be enhanced by the influence of Jewish prophetism.

For Tillich, the spirit of capitalism could be effectively countered by a union of "priestly" and "prophetic" elements in Protestant theology. The priestly element is best expressed in Rudolf Otto's *The Idea of the Holy*, in which revelation transcends the Kantian subject–object dichotomy, recognizing the "ecstatic, form-destroying character of religion with its divine and demonic aspects."[34] For Tillich, the prophetic element is best expressed in Karl Barth's *Commentary on the Epistle to the Romans*, since "This theology lets the judgment of the unconditionally transcendent

---

31 Ibid., 112–113.

32 Ibid., 36–37.

33 "Religious socialism is shaken by the doubt which arises out of the question which is most fundamental and most difficult for it, How is it possible from the standpoint of religion or the eternal to reach any decisions which are applicable to the world of time? ... It above all others raises the demand for that which we have designated *belief-ful realism*, that is an unconditioned acceptance of the serious importance of our concrete situation in time and of the situation of time in general in the presence of eternity; such an attitude contains the negation of every kind of romanticism and utopianism but it includes the hope of a social and economic life in which the spirit of capitalism–the symbol of self-sufficient finitude–has been overcome" (ibid., 116).

34 Ibid., 215.

God fall upon every attempt of culture or religion to claim value before him."[35] The two must create a union of "belief-ful realism," which Tillich believes could lead a cultural transformation.[36] However, Tillich concludes that this could only happen if its proponents assume that knowledge has a participatory dimension, which anticipates the posture of *The Socialist Decision:*

> One thing however must be remembered in connection with all of these observations: they can have meaning only for those who are themselves engaged in the movement and for them they are not only meaningful but also full of responsibility. Such men are not permitted to stand aloof as non-participating observers, but it is demanded of them that they think and speak about the religious situation of the present with unconditioned, active responsibility.[37]

3.2.3 Judaism as Ally to Capitalism

Tillich's analysis of Judaism in *The Religious Situation* occurs as a brief (just under three pages) transitional section between a discussion of Catholicism and Protestantism. It is revealing for what it says, and what it does not say. Tillich makes three observations about Judaism: (i) it is a diverse religious phenomenon having liberal/humanistic, orthodox, and Zionist expressions; (ii) the prophetic aspect is mentioned briefly as a positive aspect of Jewish mystical Zionism, but it is not seen as a resource to counter the spirit of capitalism; and (iii) the liberal/humanistic Jewish communities have been so successful in helping to create capitalist society that they will not take place in a transformation of society, should it occur at all. At this point, in the mid 1920s, Tillich is not optimistic that any of the expressions of *institutional religion* could lead an anticapitalist transformation of society.

Tillich's analysis of Judaism is primarily concerned with the liberal/humanistic expression. He concludes that liberal Judaism has structural similarities with Protestantism and also with the capitalist spirit, generally rendering it ineffective to lead a cultural transformation:

> The close connection between religion and morality, the high evaluation of personality, the devaluation of the sacramental sphere, the secularization of nature, the exaltation of the law, re-

35 Ibid., 217–218.

36 "At all events abundant and strong life is moving in the Protestant theology of our time. There is apparent in it the will to break through futile antitheses within the bourgeois situation. The decisive turn if it is to take place anywhere in Protestantism may be expected in theology" (ibid., 218).

37 Ibid., 219.

> ligiously inspired intra-worldly activity – all this is present in Judaism as in Protestantism and in capitalist society. It is common to all three not only because they are related types but also as a result of the historical influence of Judaism on the rise of capitalist society.[38]

Here Tillich introduces the concept of "type," which he appears to have been adopted from Max Weber.[39] Tillich does not elaborate on what a "type" is, but the context indicates that it refers to structural similarities between phenomena that are being analyzed, e. g. the close connection between religion and morality. In this context, the two phenomena being compared are liberal/humanistic Judaism and Protestantism. A more sophisticated concept Tillich calls the "typology of the history of religion" appears in Tillich's *Systematic Theology*, which will be discussed in Chapter Five below. There is very little scholarly commentary on Tillich's concept of "type," but Ron Stone thinks it enabled Tillich to discuss traditionally religious concepts in harmony with Marxist thought, or at least prevent religion from being reducible to, or subordinate to, "the substructure of society."[40]

Tillich concludes that liberal, humanistic Judaism could not pose an effective intellectual critique, let alone provide the cultural resources to overcome the spirit of capitalism "on the basis of its own presuppositions," which is the only way to overcome something.[41] This ineffectiveness was due to the structural similarities noted above. Tillich concluded that too many Jews "readily and easily abandoned their religious heritage and transferred their loyalty to capitalist

---

38 Ibid., 189. In addition, "In many ways therefore there is evidence that in Judaism there is reaction–not without backslidings–against the spirit of capitalistic society. But the revolt encounters difficulties because of the close interrelation of large circles of Jews with the capitalist system and its exclusively commercial type of life" (191).

39 Stone makes this observation in "Tillich–Boundary," 395: "Max Weber haunts the socialist writing of Paul Tillich. Basic concepts are taken over, utilized, and usually not acknowledged. I want to suggest that the importance of this is that Tillich had integrated Max Weber into his socialism by an early date (1926) ... The central concept of *The Religious Situation* is "The Capitalist Spirit". It does not differ from Weber's "The Spirit of Capitalism". The explanation of the use of the term makes use of Weber's ideal type methodology. Tillich writes: "It is rather a symbol for an ultimate, fundamental attitude toward the world." Tillich, *Religious Situation*, Author's Preface, 27." Other than these comments by Stone, I have been unable to locate any scholarly commentary on Max Weber and the use of "types" in Tillich's thought. This includes the discussion of the influence of Weber on Tillich (and Adorno and Horkheimer) as recently presented by Wagoner, in his dissertation, *Emancipation*.

40 According to Stone, "The utilization of Weber's method to describe Marxist ideas began to transform Marxism. Religion could never be only a byproduct of the substructure of society" ("Tillich–Boundary," 397).

41 Tillich claims that there are three possible responses by the churches to the spirit of capitalism: (i) they can reject it; (ii) they can surrender to it; (iii) they can overcome it on the basis of its own presuppositions. *Religious Situation*, 181 – 182.

society."[42] Despite this negative appraisal, Tillich remarks, "Yet the spirit of ancient prophecy continues to be effective even in religiously liberal circles."[43] Tillich is referring to Jewish Marxists, whose attempts failed to triumph over the spirit of bourgeois society, since they neglected "the religious heritage,"[44] meaning the prophetic dimension of Judaism.

Tillich's assessment of orthodox Judaism recognizes "valuable religious resources," which he does not enumerate, and concludes that it does not have a significant effect on the present religious situation.[45] Tillich's recognizes that Zionism has a mystical and prophetic dimension, but does not elaborate on the importance of the prophetic dimension. He observes that Zionism embodies a "peculiar mixture" of national and religious motives, and draws upon a past ideal, that seeks "a return to the original unity of religious prophecy and national existence."[46] Tillich does not say when this ideal occurred, but it probably refers to the prophetic critique of the monarchy, before division and conquest destroyed Israel's national existence.[47] For Tillich, Zionism poses a threat because it might become a secular ideology, losing its universality, messianism and world-uniting mission.[48] For Tillich, the finest expression of Zionism is Martin Buber's "mystical Zionism," which is to "become a powerful symbol and emanative force for the rest of the world."[49] However, Tillich concludes that even this expression must maintain a prophetic dimension: "Buber's presentation of Jewish mysticism ... belong(s) to the whole mystical movement against the spirit of capitalism. But this Jewish mysticism is always connected with the prophetic element of hope of the consummation."[50] Tillich concludes that while Judaism has features that run counter to the capitalist spirit, the critical mass of Jews are too

42 Ibid., 189.
43 Ibid.
44 Ibid., 190.
45 Ibid.
46 Ibid.
47 This also differs from "normative Judaism" as discussed in the 1910 Dissertation; see Chapter Two above.
48 *Religious Situation*, 190–191.
49 Ibid., 191. The most succinct presentation of Tillich's view of Buber is the essay "An Evaluation of Martin Buber: Protestant and Jewish Thought," chapter 14 in Tillich's *Theology of Culture*, ed. Robert C. Kimball (Oxford: Oxford University Press, 1972), 188–199. (This chapter was revised by Tillich from an earlier essay, which appeared in *Commentary* 5/6 (June 1948).) In this essay, Tillich comments on the three ways in which Buber's thought is significant for Protestant theology: (i) his existential interpretation of prophetic religion; (ii) his rediscovery of mysticism as an element within prophetic religion; and (iii) his understanding of the relation between prophetic religion and culture, particularly in the social and political realms (188).
50 *Religious Situation*, 191.

beholden to the commercial enterprise to lead a cultural transformation, as noted above.

3.3 *The Socialist Decision:* Context, Method and Critical Principles

Banned, Burned and Bombed? A Contested History

The Socialist Decision is a highly theoretical work since it discusses concepts that are associated with Marxist political theory, such as the bourgeoisie, the proletariat, socialism, capitalism, and historical and dialectical materialism. Communism is denounced, Hitler is never named directly, and the term *Führer* appears five times, four times in a purely descriptive capacity. The most inflammatory comment is an oblique reference to Hitler within an analysis of the socialist view of human nature about halfway through the book. Tillich observes that the German socialism of the Weimar period is unduly influenced by a "bourgeois" view of human nature, which valorizes harmony, fails to account for the limits of rationality, the inevitability of conflict, and the recurring economic crises brought on by the competitiveness of capitalism and wars caused by nationalism and imperialism. For Tillich, in the context of Weimar Germany in the early 1930s, socialism had failed to raise up powerful and charismatic leaders, and at the same time had permitted "a personality with trivial power of being" to "become the symbol and *Führer* of revolutionary political romanticism,"[51] presumably referring to Hitler and German National Socialism.

As described in Chapter One, Tillich was suspended from his teaching position at the University of Frankfurt in April of 1933 because of his socialist political beliefs, which were forcefully articulated in *The Socialist Decision.* While Tillich asserted throughout his life that it was *The Socialist Decision* that caused the unbreakable rift with the Nazi government, there is some question as to whether

---

51 *The Socialist Decision*, 74. *The Socialist Decision* was completed in late 1932 and it was released for sale in early 1933, so the book's contents were finalized prior to Hitler being elected chancellor in January 1933. Nevertheless, the term *Führer* ("leader") had been used within German political circles since the 19th century, notably being applied to Austrian politician Georg Ritter von Schönerer (1842–1921), who sought the union of German speaking areas of the Habsburg Monarchy with the German Empire. It is clear that Hitler was influenced by von Schönerer. Richard J.E. Evans, "The Emergence of Nazi ideology," 26–47, in *Nazi Germany, The Short Oxford History of Germany*, ed. Jane Caplan (New York: Oxford University Press, 2008), 35. In addition, the "leadership principle," or *Führerprinzip*, was in use by the Nazi Party and its predecessors since the 1920s. Dietrich Orlow, *The History of the Nazi Party, 1919–1933* (Pittsburgh: University of Pittsburgh Press, 1969), 25, 74, 85–86, 259 and 305.

the book was banned by the Nazis and consigned to the flames in the Frankfurt book burnings of May 1933.[52] The condemnation of Tillich flowed from the fact that he had been determined to be "politically unreliable," and was suspended from his position at the University of Frankfurt.[53] However, Tillich's unwillingness to retract it caused an irreconcilable rift between him and the German government. Tillich was quite proud of this work, and his Jewish friend Adolf Löwe remarked that it was Tillich's "most Jewish book."[54] The publisher, Alfred Protte of Potsdam, was forbidden to circulate copies, and the book experienced very limited circulation.[55] In addition, during World War II, the warehouse of Alfred Protte, who had also published many works on socialist political theory, including the journal *Neue Blätter für Sozialismus*, was bombed by the Allies, destroying many copies of Tillich's book.[56]

The immediate context of *The Socialist Decision* is Tillich's critique of German socialism in the early 1930s. On the one hand, according to Tillich, German socialism tried to disassociate itself from revolutionary forms of communism, which were atheistic. As a result, German socialism lost its eschatological dimension. On the other hand, German socialism assumed fundamental characteristics of bourgeois capitalism, and was unable to liberate the proletariat. This meant that German socialism lost its humanistic dimension. Tillich's distinctive view of socialism, which has humanistic and eschatological aspects, draws upon the Jewish prophetic tradi-

---

52 Tillich's biographers claim that the book itself was banned and burned; see Pauck and Pauck, *Tillich,* 132. However, Friedrich Wilhelm Graf argues that *The Socialist Decision* was not banned, nor was it burned in the Frankfurt book burnings of May 1933. See " 'Politische Romantik' und 'Sozialistische Entscheidung.' Eine freundschaftliche Annonce für Heinrich Meier zum 8. April 2013;" Zeitschrift für Neuere Theologiegeschichte, 2012; 19(2): 247–268.
53 Weaver, through José Miguez, reports that Max Horkheimer said after World War II: "after reading some sections of his writings, it was I who told him that, in my opinion, if he did not leave the country, he would pay with his life." Cf. "Rereading Tillich in Latin America: From Religious Socialism to the Exile." In *Religion in the New Millennium: Theology in the Spirit of Paul Tillich*, ed. Raymond F. Bulman and Frederick J. Parrella, 19–33. Macon GA: Mercer University Press, 2001. Weaver, *Religious Internationalism*, 98.
54 24 May 1972 interview with Adolf Lowe; *Socialist Decision*, editor's introduction, xxv.
55 "As it turned out, *The Socialist Decision* was written and published too late. When Hitler came to dictatorial power it was promptly banned and the publisher forbidden to circulate it. During the ensuing years a few copies were secretly handed from one person to another. The book thus had no noticeable influence. It is a noble document of Tillich's political outlook in the period between the two great world wars." Pauck, Pauck, *Tillich,* 128. Also see, Graf "Politische Romantik."
56 Stone, "Tillich-Boundary," 397. Stone does not say whether the bombing of the German publisher Alfred Protte was intentional, or just collateral damage. Also, Graf "Politische Romantik," 253.

tion. The humanistic element contrasts favorably to the reductionist view of humanity embedded in unrestrained capitalism, and in the bourgeois worldview, which Tillich first discussed in *The Religious Situation*.

Tillich's view of socialism is also distinct from scientific Marxism, which is materialist in two senses. The first sense of materialism means that changes in material, economic conditions are the drivers of history, which is taken from Marx. The other sense of materialism is the atomistic, atheistic kind, in which the human person is reduced to a crude set of needs and drives, characteristic of the later, scientific Marx.[57] This reductionist view of human nature was also seen in the "spirit of capitalism," which was the object of Tillich's critique in *The Religious Situation*. For Tillich, the human person is a complex combination of needs and drives, with "vital, aesthetic and erotic elements."[58] For Tillich, the eschatological element has the twofold function of criticizing unjust existing power structures, and also providing the drive for change, in the form of expectation.

Plan of the argument

In *The Socialist Decision*, the prophetic dimension of Judaism plays two essential roles, one critical, and the other constructive. This analysis shows how Judaism confronted the myths attached to soil, blood and social group, "the powers of origin." This is the critical role of Jewish prophetism. Tillich uses the following terms interchangeably for Jewish prophetism: "the Jewish spirit," "the spirit of Judaism," "Jewish prophetism," "prophetism" and "the prophetic tradition." Tillich states clearly that Judaism as a historical reality is not to be equated to these.[59] For example, Judaism under the heirs of the Davidic monarchy began to exhibit features of religious nationalism, which then led to generations of pro-

---

57 For Tillich, both scientific Marxism and the bourgeois principle assume that human behavior is reducible to a pain/pleasure, stimulus response form of "drive psychology." For Marxism, "as the suffering of the increasingly proletarianized masses became even greater and greater, a pain-reaction would result that would touch off the revolution." For the bourgeoisie, "Also completely primitive and removed from reality was the notion, derived from the liberal belief in harmony, that after the victory of the revolution, a universal and uniform satisfaction of human needs would prevail" (*Socialist Decision*, 133).

58 "Even such basic needs as hunger and thirst are inwardly complex. Apart from extreme cases of direst need which press one beyond the limits of human consciousness, the need for food and clothing and the like is also infinitely differentiated and determined by vital, aesthetic, and erotic elements, whose reciprocal effect causes radical changes even in the spheres of the most primitive need-satisfaction" (ibid., 136).

59 "Of course, prophetism and Judaism cannot simply be equated" (ibid., 22).

phetic critique. However, the Old Testament prophets provide a necessary historical reference point for Jewish prophetism.

In this analysis of *The Socialist Decision*, Judaism and its related concepts are treated in three sections, following an introductory section on the dialectical structure, analytical framework, and key terms. The first section will focus on part I, chapter 2, "The Break with the Myth of Origin in Judaism," and will contrast how Judaism confronted each of the mythical powers of origin. This is the *critical* dimension of Jewish prophetism, and it underscores the continuing importance of the history of religion for Tillich. The second and third parts of this analysis will be from part III, where Tillich attempts to resolve the inner tension of the proletarian situation through the principle of socialism. This is the *constructive* role of Jewish prophetism. In part III, chapter 5, "The Socialist Principle and its Roots," Tillich lays out the themes of "demand," "promise," and "expectation," acknowledging that each has its roots in Jewish prophetism, and that each plays an essential constructive role in his particular view of socialism. In this section, Tillich explicitly draws an analogy between Jewish prophetism and socialism. Finally, in part III, chapter 7, "The Resolution of Socialism's Inner Conflict through the Unfolding of the Socialist Principle," Tillich completes his constructive project by outlining the specific elements of the socialist principle, which are directly and indirectly derived from Jewish prophetism. The discussion of this section will explore two elements that *explicitly* draw upon Jewish prophetism, the transformation of nationalism to a universal humanity, and economic globalization. In *The Socialist Decision*, Jewish prophetism is deeply embedded in the dialectical structure of Tillich's argument, and the critique of the bourgeois principle and political romanticism could not have been formulated without it. Also, Jewish prophetism has an ontological basis that is deeper than belief-ful realism. In *The Socialist Decision*, Tillich coins the maxim "justice is the true power of being," which has its unique foundation in Jewish prophetism. This maxim responds to the "unconditional demand" of justice. For Tillich, this unique ontological basis and derivation of justice is the only appropriate response to the "powers of the myth of origin" as posed by political romanticism, the proxy for Nazism.

Dialectical Structure

Tillich's *The Socialist Decision* is written in three parts,[60] with an introduction, and the structure of the work is dialectical. The introduction is where key terms are in-

---

60 Part I is "Political Romanticism, Its Principle, and its Contradiction;" part II is "The Principle

troduced, including "being," "consciousness," and "principle," which will each be discussed below. Part I introduces the principle of "political romanticism," which possesses an inherent contradiction, and will not represent a normative position for Tillich. Political romanticism will remain at one "pole" of the dialectic, so to speak, but it helps to frame the argument by introducing key terms such as the "powers of origin," which play an important role in Tillich's distinctive view of socialism. The powers of origin are not eliminated, but rather *transformed*, by prophetic expectation, which has its foundation in Jewish prophetism.

Part II develops two themes. The first is the principle of bourgeois society, the dominant social and economic phenomenon present in Weimar Germany, which is deeply informed by the spirit of capitalism, which preoccupied Tillich in *The Religious Situation.* Tillich regarded bourgeois society as dominated by a post-Enlightenment rationalism that broke the primitive bonds of origin, and permitted the subjection of human nature to scientific and economic materialism. He believed bourgeois society was based upon a reductionist anthropology, in which persons acted strictly in accordance with a simple pain/pleasure principle, and that the arena of work, trade and economics was a "war of all against all." He felt this placed the working class, the proletariat, at a structural disadvantage from which it could not be liberated, as long as the assumptions of bourgeois capitalism remained operative. The second theme Tillich describes is specifically how the bourgeois principle creates tensions within aspects of Weimar German socialism that beg resolution. Therefore, this second part of the dialectical structure expresses an "inner drive" that seeks a resolution. Part III discusses how the inner tensions manifest in Weimar German socialism could be resolved in the "principle of socialism," which derives its key concepts from Jewish prophetism.

Key Terms

The key concept for Tillich common to all three parts of *The Socialist Decision* is the concept of "principle," which he introduces in order to characterize the specificity, fullness, dynamism and inner drive of historical, social and cultural phenomena. This stands in sharp contrast to the "type," which was limited to a com-

---

of Bourgeois Society and the Inner Conflict of Socialism;" part III is "The Principle of Socialism and the Solution of its Inner Conflict." Many of the same terms appearing in *The Socialist Decision* also appeared in a 1932 essay titled, "Der Geist des Sozialismus und der Kampf gegen ihn," in Tillich, E, Volume XI, *Religion, Kultur, Gesellschaft, Unveröffentliche Texte aus der Deutschen Zeit (1908–1933)*; 399–448. The term "poltical romanticism" appears to be drawn from the political theorist Carl Schmitt (1888–1985), who wrote *Politische Romantik*, München und Leipzig, 1919; cf. Tillich, E, XI, 408, note 2.

parison of structural similarities, as discussed in *The Religious Situation.*[61] First, Tillich contrasts this with the limitations of the a-historical Platonic concept of "essence,"[62] which derives from the ancient natural sciences. In its place, Tillich proposes a concept that appropriately reflects the historical and teleological complexity of the phenomenon being analyzed, the "principle." He provides two definitions of principle, and one example. The first characterizes a principle as a dynamic concept that "*contains the possibility of making understandable new and unexpected realizations of a historical origin.*"[63] The second definition is: "*A principle is the power of a historical reality, grasped in concepts.*"[64] I will take the liberty of creating a single, functional definition that captures the spirit of both: A principle must achieve three things when being used to analyze any historical, social, cultural or political phenomenon: (i) it must reflect its diversity and particularity; (ii) it must capture its power, inner drive, potentiality, teleology, and the potential for transformation; and (iii) it is something that must be apprehended by participation. The participatory aspect of the principle of socialism is what occasions the title of the book, *The Socialist Decision.* For Tillich, one cannot at the same time be politically engaged, and remain "a spectator to the spirit."[65] The breadth and depth of the concept of principle grants Tillich considerable flexibility in his analysis. As a result, each principle, political romanticism, the bourgeois principle, and the socialist principle, is treated somewhat

61 Stone, who was cited earlier in the discussion of "types," appears to observe that for Tillich, types and principles are effectively the same thing, but notes that principles emphasize the "spirit" of a movement, and also the "existential" or "decision" character of a movement. He writes: "*Principal* [*sic*] was a way to avoid the endless empirical particularities and to refer to dynamics of a movement or to its spirit. It also emphasized the decision or existentialist character of identifying a group with its central powerful idea. So with the term principal he can carry forward the typological, descriptive-critical work of *The Socialist Decision*" ("Tillich–Boundary," 396). These features of "spirit," existentialist character and central powerful idea could be applied to Tillich's "typology of the history of religion," which will be discussed in Chapters Five and Six.
62 Tillich elaborates: "the logic of essence is inadequate in the face of historical realities. The 'essence of a historical phenomenon' is an empty abstraction from which the living power of history has been expelled. Nevertheless, we cannot dispense with summarizing characterizations when we are dealing with a coherent movement. It is not enough to refer to historical continuity, since some selection must be made out of the infinite abundance of continuously linked events. Therefore, we must seek another method of historical characterization" (*The Socialist Decision*, 9). Tillich's concept of "spirit" or inner drive is ultimately his answer to the problem of deriving meaning from historical particularity.
63 Ibid.
64 Ibid., 10.
65 Ibid., 7.

differently, according to the contribution of each to an understanding of the proper transformation of socialism.

Framework for Political Analysis

As with all of Tillich's works, he begins with a statement of principles and presuppositions. A thorough presentation is necessary to appreciate the nuances of the dialectical structure, and the derivation of Jewish prophetism from Tillich's anthropology and ontology, grounding the maxim, "justice is the true power of being." Tillich begins by stating that all political thought and action rests on the duality of human nature and the two roots of political thought. Human nature, in all times and places, is comprised of "being" and "consciousness." Being refers to the bodily aspect of human existence, which is subject to the cycle of birth, growth and development, and death, and is something humankind shares with all living beings. On the other hand, consciousness is distinctive to human beings, and refers to their individual and collective reflective capacity, and their ability to ascribe *meaning* to being, which is the cycle of birth, growth and development, and death.[66] This anthropological duality is not unique to Tillich, but is common within twentieth-century Continental philosophy and has its roots in ancient Greek philosophy.

In addition, for Tillich, there are two roots of political thought. The first is the "origin" and the second is the "demand." In *The Interpretation of History,* Tillich elaborates that the origin is perpetually generating, and therefore existence is always bound to it, to some degree.[67] At the same time, existence seeks to separate itself from the origin, through the process of individuation, and through the expression of freedom. Therefore, the relationship of existence to the origin is one of tension between bondage to the origin (sometimes referred to as "necessity") and freedom.[68]

---

66 "Man finds himself in existence; he finds himself as he finds his environment established for him. To find oneself in existence means that one does not originate from oneself, that one has an origin outside of oneself, or to use the expressive word of Martin Heidegger '*Geworfensein:*' 'being thrown' into the world. From this situation follows the human question, 'Whence?' It does not appear as a philosophical question until very late. It was always asked, however, and its first answer is given in mythology and sets a standard for the whole future" (Tillich, *Interpretation of History,* 206).

67 Ibid.

68 "The origin is creative. Creation produces something new, which did not exist and which, after being produced, represents something independent and singular. Our life has this tension between dependence upon the origin that has produced us and the independence of it through individuality and freedom. The origin does not leave us free from itself, since it is not past only

According to Tillich, all societies seek to understand their origin, as their beliefs, practices and institutions answer the question, "Whence?" or "Wherefrom?" (*Woher?*), which Tillich refers to as the "myth of origin."[69] There was a detailed discussion of mythology in the 1910 Dissertation, although there was not a discussion of freedom as transcending the myths of origin, providing no basis for political thought at this stage.[70] Tillich believes that the combined results of myth research, depth psychology, sociology and ontology, are instrumental to discover "primordial" human experiences:

> The myth of origin envisions the beginning of humankind in elemental, superhuman figures of various kinds. Common to them all is the fact that they are expressions of the human tie to father and mother, and that by the power of this tie they want to hold consciousness fast, not allowing it to escape from their dominion.[71]

These universal phenomena, also described by Tillich as the "consciousness" of a society, yield a wide variety of mythological expressions across human history and cultures, as discussed in Tillich's dissertations on Schelling. While the content of these mythological expressions varies, they all have in common the attempt to understand the natural cycle of birth, growth and development, and death.

According to Tillich, "powers of origin" are "envisioned in myth" and "represented in cult."[72] He claims that there are three powers of origin that are relevant to political activity, soil, blood and the social group. According to Tillich, soil is the most universally present, and the most powerful: "It generates life

---

but present every moment. It gives us existence again and again; it reproduces us and *holds us fast* through its omnipresence" (ibid., 206; emphasis mine).

69 Tillich elaborates: "Every myth is a myth of origin, that is, an answer to the question about the 'Whence' of existence and an expression of dependence on the origin and on its power" (*Socialist Decision*, 3–4). In a supplemental article to be discussed in Chapter Seven, Tillich refers to this as "wherefrom." He elaborates: "The origine (sic) creates the law of circular motion. Everything which comes from it must return to it. There is nothing entirely new. The predominance of the question 'wherefrom' makes it impossible to ask seriously 'whereto.' The circle of circular motion can be narrower and larger." Tillich, *Two Types of Historical Vision*, 5.

70 According to Stone, "Schelling's early enthusiasm for the French Revolution and his activity as a leader of the Tübingen radicals in the 1790s had no direct political influence on Tillich, who found in him a metaphysical not a political guide. The early hopes of Schelling, Hölderlin, and Hegel that a change in consciousness would produce political change seem not to be reflected in Tillich's work on the philosophy of the later, more apolitical Schelling. Tillich's political innocence at the time of his dissertations prevented him from analyzing the political consequences of Schelling's philosophy of freedom." Stone, *Radical Social Thought*, 25.

71 Ibid., 13.

72 Ibid.

from itself, supports and nourishes it, and then takes it back into itself again. It holds everything under the spell of the cycle of birth and death. The deities of the soil are the holiest; they are the last to let the consciousness go free."[73] The second power of origin, blood, develops out of the soil, but through the struggle of selection and breeding, results in the distinction of "noble" and "common" types of people. The noble type accretes to itself all kinds of heroic features, which justify its social dominance.[74]

The third power of origin, the social group, is the only one of the three powers of origin that that can permit moving forward beyond the origin, although it is the context for struggle between past and future. While Tillich is not entirely clear on this point, it appears that a social group can be governed by either a matriarchy, or a patriarchy. Matriarchal cultures derive their identity to a greater degree from the powers of soil and blood, meaning leadership is given to those who have noble traits, and a vitality which may be distinctive to each culture. On the other hand, patriarchal cultures derive their identity from the primal ancestor, a "father figure," and leadership is passed from father to son. For Tillich, there is a "primordial demand," *found only in patriarchal cultures*, that creates the possibility of progress over against tradition.[75] This appears to be the mythological source of the "unconditional demand," found in Jewish prophetism: "Liberation from the origin becomes real only when a break with the social group can also be demanded, i.e., in prophetism."[76] Just how the "demand"

---

73 Ibid.

74 "Concepts such as 'noble blood,' 'noble race' and 'noble lineage' appear. Noble origin is divine origin, in the sense of special election ... the unity of youth and form is the highest symbol of animal power ... [this] is expressed in heroic ecstasy in which life and death, courage and melancholy, are one. 'Noble' means being consecrated to death, the return to the origin; not, however, out of mere resignation or obedience to duty, but ecstatically. Social dominance, the ruling power of the noble race, follows directly from this power of being" (ibid., 14–15).

75 While this seems to favor patriarchal cultures, in *Two Types of Historical Vision*, to be discussed in Chapter Seven, Tillich seems to say that the father can be an impediment to asking the normative question, positing the "ought:" "The circle is largest in the social realm where the question whereto is first asked. But the question remains unanswered as long as the power of the father, the main symbol of social origine (sic), is untouched. In all these realms even the priestly mysteries and revelations deal with the wherefrom and their rites and institutions are supposed to effect the return to the father, that is to the origine (sic)." Tillich, *Two Types of Historical Vision*, 5.

76 "While the origin of soil and blood is more commonly expressed in the mother symbol, in the social sphere the father symbol predominates. The father combines supportive and *demanding* aspects, whereas in the mother, in soil and blood, the immediate law of origin is more visible. The tie to the father therefore takes the form of a tie to the primordial demand, to the primeval ordinance that passes as a heritage from the father to the son. The line of ancestors is an expres-

first presents itself is not entirely clear, but is explained by the awareness of an "other," creating an "I-Thou" relationship, which was also discussed in the 1910 Dissertation, and also in *Interpretation.*[77] The mysterious emergence of this "demand," that makes possible an "I-Thou" relationship, is fundamental to both kinds of dialectic in Tillich's history of religion, the historical dialectic of progression, and the ontological dialectic of balance.

According to Tillich, when a culture fails to transcend this natural cycle, beyond what "is," it remains in *bondage* to the powers of origin.[78] This is the attempt by that culture "to hold consciousness fast," referred to above. He concludes, with emphasis, "*The consciousness oriented to the myth of origin is the root of all conservative and romantic thought in politics.*'"[79] With its emphasis on "soil" (territory) and "blood" (racial purity), and the "social group" (the Nazi party), German National Socialism is the boldest and most ominous expression of political romanticism, which tries to *restore* the broken myth of origin, broken by Enlightenment rationalism and the spirit of capitalism.[80] Nazism cre-

---

sion both of blood origin and of the continuity of the social group and its ordinances ... This primeval law shapes the unconscious; it works through the line of ancestors, holding the individual in thrall within the circle of the group and its patriarchal rule. And yet it is *the demanding character of the father-origin that makes it at all possible to break the myth of origin.* It is still only a possibility, however; the origin still rules. Integration into the group still is demanded. Liberation from the origin becomes real only when a break with the social group also can be demanded, i.e., in prophetism" (*Socialist Decision*, 15; emphases mine).

77 "Yet it is not enough to point out the simple contrast of the two factors of human being [being and consciousness]. The demand which man receives is unconditioned, but it is not strange to him. If it were strange to his nature, it would not concern him; he could not perceive it as a demand on him. It strikes him only because it places before him, in the form of a demand, his own essence. Only thereon rests the absoluteness, the inevitability, with which the demand approaches man and must be affirmed by him" (Tillich, *Interpretation of History*, 208–209).

78 Tillich elaborates: "The origin embodies the law of *cyclical motion:* whatever proceeds from it must return to it. Wherever the origin is in control, nothing new can happen" (*Socialist Decision*, 16).

79 Ibid., 4.

80 According to Stone: "The return to the myths of origin, with its search for meaning in soil, blood and social group, was an attempt to eclipse the rational consciousness and to obliterate the distinction between "is" and "ought." It was an attempt to make existence itself sacred and to justify a group by reference to its origins. Return to the soil was not economically feasible, but it attracted some political supporters. Return to one blood was anthropological nonsense, but built on the anti-Semitism that had been developing in Germany. Also, the appeal to race set the population up for a return to a social group using the model of a patriarchal community dominated by a leader rather than a rational group. Conservative and revolutionary romantics could lust together to overthrow liberal democracy and its bureaucracy even as they dreamed respectively of a monarch or a Führer." *Radical Social Thought*, 76.

ates myths about the German people having a unified, ancient racial lineage that is being threatened by modernity. For Tillich, a culture that manifests political romanticism takes the first step towards political thought, but fails to look beyond itself, to a "Thou." If a society remains bound to the powers of origin, or "what is," and never asks the question of "what *ought* to be?," or experiences[81] the "demand" referred to above, then that society cannot fulfill the second aspect of true political thought. To be truly political, a society or culture must respond to the "unconditional demand." Therefore, a society cannot be both: (i) "romantic," or bound to the myth of origin, to *what is*; and (ii) "political," or transcending the origin by being oriented toward *what ought to be*. This is the inherent contradiction of political romanticism.

The second root of political thought arises if a society transcends the cycle of being and becoming, and attempts to answer not simply "what *is?*," but "what *ought* to be?" ("Whither?" or *Wozu?*).[82] This "ought" does not occur as a continuation or derivation from what "is," but is "experienced" as an "unconditional demand" that "confronts" humanity.[83] When this occurs, the myth of origin, which is equated with the realm of necessity, is "broken," and human freedom enters human history, initiating human history. When the demand is experienced, Tillich concludes, again with emphasis: "*The breaking of the myth of origin by the unconditional demand is the root of liberal, democratic and socialist thought in politics.*"[84] For Tillich, all cultures dominated by Enlightenment rationalism have experienced a "break" away from their ancient founding myths of origin, with two common responses. The first and most common response is that of bourgeois capitalism,[85] which gained momentum in the nineteenth century, but was dealt severe shocks

---

81 Tillich uses the word *erfahren* five times in this discussion (*erfährt, erfahren*), which was translated as "experience" by Franklin Sherman. The verb *erfahren* could also be rendered "to find out," or "to learn;" however, the adjective *erfahren* is rendered "experienced;" cf. *Concise Oxford–Duden German Dictionary*, 893. The "demand" also "confronts us" (*über ... steht*) unconditionally. When confronted, a culture may obey, or disobey, the unconditional demand.

82 *Socialist Decision*, 4.

83 Ibid. Tillich says that the demand arises from the "ambiguity of the origin." In the 1910 Dissertation, Tillich's discusses the emergence of the demand of the moral law in the section on the limits of rational religion and the emergence of revelation; 98–101.

84 Ibid., 5.

85 "The conflict of the proletarian situation is rooted in the fact that, on the one hand, the proletariat must draw the consequences of the bourgeois principle, while, on the other hand, it stands in opposition to the bourgeois principle. It must, therefore, overcome the bourgeois principle by means of the bourgeois principle! This is an inescapable conflict, because proletarian existence is the consistent expression of the bourgeois principle. Objectification, depersonalization, and separation from the origin find undisguised expression in the proletariat" (Ibid., 97).

by World War I and the ensuing worldwide economic crisis, as Tillich described in *The Religious Situation.* Bourgeois capitalism is threatened by the other response, that of revolutionary political romanticism, which seeks to rekindle the ancient powers of origin. For Tillich, the threat in his immediate context was German National Socialism. In the words of Ron Stone, the choice for Germany, if it did not embrace humanistic socialism, then it would suffer the chaos of capitalism, or the barbarism of National Socialism.[86]

Justice is the True Power of Being[87]

For Tillich, every culture's *true nature,* the "fulfillment of its origin," can only occur if it reflects and acts upon the question, "What *ought* to be?," which is the "unconditional demand." Only when a culture responds to the unconditional demand of answering "what ought to be?," it then becomes aware of its "true origin," and can begin the process of true political activity.[88] It is only in community that the demand can be posed and received, meaning that the demand can only come from outside of one community, posed by another community. This is similar to what Tillich argued in his analysis of rational religion in his

86 Ron Stone, "Scenes from Paul Tillich and Reinhold Niebuhr," *BNAPTS* 38/2 (Spring 2012): 15. A different view of Tillich's posture towards Nazism in *The Socialist Decision* is offered by Reimer in *Hirsch–Tillich Debate.* Reimer argues that Tillich was ambivalent about Nazism because it offered a critique of the Enlightenment, which would have agreed with Tillich's understanding of a humanistic form of socialism. In addition, Reimer observes that there was great uncertainty and fluidity during 1932 and 1933, and it was difficult to pin down where every political party stood. Finally, Reimer demonstrates that there were significant formal similarities between Tillich's political theology, and that of Emanuel Hirsch (*Hirsch–Tillich Debate,* 226–227).

87 By the 1950s, in *Love, Power and Justice: Ontological Analyses and Ethical Applications* (New York: Oxford University Press, 1954), Tillich argued that love, power and justice are universally significant within the humanities and social sciences because of their common ontological roots (1–2); "power is the form of justice and the substance of love" (8); "Justice is just because of the love which is implicit in it" (15); and "It was our task to show that essentially, in their created nature, love, power and justice are united....Love, power and justice are one in the divine ground, they shall become one in human existence. The holy in which they are united shall become holy reality in time and space" (108–109).

88 "The questions 'Whence?' and 'Whither?' do not belong to different worlds. And yet, the demand is something unconditionally new over against the origin. This indicates that *the origin is ambiguous.* There is a split in it between the true and actual origin. *The actual origin is not the origin in truth.* It is not the fulfillment of what is intended for humanity from the origin. The fulfillment of the origin lies rather in what confronts us as a demand, as an ought. The 'Whence' of humanity finds its fulfillment in the 'Whither.' " Tillich goes so far as to say that the origin is "ambiguous," and when a culture recognizes this ambiguity, it entertains normative questions. *Socialist Decision,* 5.

1910 Dissertation on Schelling.[89] When a demand is received by one individual from another individual, an "I" – "Thou" relationship is created.[90] When the "I" and the "Thou" are granted equal dignity, *justice* is manifested.[91]

Tillich employs a distinction between "mere being" and "true being," in order to establish a definition of justice. This distinction elaborates on the aforementioned discussion of being and consciousness, the duality of human nature. Mere being is "impotent"[92] since it is associated with the failure to transcend the limitations of the myth of origin and the bondage to the actual origin.[93] On the other hand, true being has "power," insofar is it is associated with the breaking of the myth of origin through human freedom, and the recognition of the true origin by embracing the equal dignity of the "Thou." Power is associated with the inner drive, or fulfillment of something's "true being."

In a culture which is governed by "the unbroken myth of origin," Tillich says there is perpetual struggle and destruction, "the rising and perishing of forces that 'pay one another the penalty and compensation for their injustice according to the ordinance of time,' " quoting Anaximander.[94] For Tillich, the emergence of the demand of justice makes it possible for culture to transcend the "tragic cycle of existence," and to realize its true fulfillment as a culture:

---

89 1910 Dissertation, 98 – 100.

90 Ibid.

91 "The content of the demand is therefore that the 'thou' be accorded the same dignity as the 'I'; this is the dignity of being free, of being the bearer of the fulfillment implied in the origin. This recognition of the equal dignity of the 'Thou' and the 'I' is justice. *The demand that separates from the ambiguous origin is the demand of justice*" (ibid., 6).

92 Ibid.

93 In other sections of *The Socialist Decision*, Tillich employs the concept of "ideology," which can be defined as something that conceals an oppressive power structure. For example, in part II, 171 note 6, he writes: "The bourgeoisie conceals the class struggle ... it wages from above by means of ideology." Also: "All these things have been interpreted, and opposed, as ideology– i.e., as the *false consciousness* the bourgeoisie has concerning itself" (56). More comprehensively: "Socialism faces a challenge at the level of fundamental theory ... it is most important to clarify the polemical significance that the *concept of ideology* had for Marx, a matter that must not be forgotten when one employs this concept to probe the relationship of being and consciousness ... a false consciousness can only appear in a society if a true consciousness is also present, namely a consciousness that is united with the new being ... A false consciousness is nothing other than the willful self-affirmation of old social structures that are being threatened and destroyed by new ones" (116 – 117). Tillich's use of ideology is discussed thoroughly in Donnelly, *Socialist Emigré*, 27 – 62.

94 *Socialist Decision*, 6. On page 4, Tillich quotes Anaximander: "It is necessary that things should pass away into that from which they are born." Cited from Werner Jaeger's *Paideia: The Ideals of Greek Culture*, trans. Gilbert Highet (Oxford: Oxford University Press, 1945), vol. I, 159.

> The unconditional demand transcends this tragic cycle of existence. It confronts the power and impotence of being with justice, arising from the demand. And yet, the contrast is not absolute, for the ought is the fulfillment of the is. *Justice is the true power of being.* In it, the intention of the origin is fulfilled ... *Only when the myth of origin is broken and its ambiguity disclosed may it enter into political thinking.*[95]

For Tillich, Jewish prophetism is the paradigmatic example of how a culture can transcend what "is," and seek what "ought to be," and definitively manifest justice. Therefore, Jewish prophetism plays an indispensable role in human history, politics and theology.

3.3.1 The Contradictions of Polytheism, or "Might Makes Right"

Tillich's view of the history of religion, myth research and depth psychology, initially developed in the 1910 Dissertation, continued to inform his worldview into the 1930s. This is evident by the importance he assigns to the powers of origin, which were discussed above. In the 1910 and 1912 Dissertations, Tillich acknowledges that before the emergence of Judaism there were rational elements in Greek religion, which endured and later influenced Christianity. *The Socialist Decision* has a simplified view of the history of religion, and Tillich's characterization of pre-Jewish and pre-Christian religion is less favourable. Jewish monotheism is contrasted with everything else that came before it, which were polytheistic religions. For Tillich, polytheism manifested two types of contradiction, which only Jewish monotheism could resolve. The first contradiction stemmed from the fact that numerous localized deities cannot coexist with one another, since every deity has a tendency to transcend its local origin, potentially creating a conflict with other deities.[96] Tillich underscores that each of these deities retains its localized identity, or attachment to "the soil," one of the powers of origin. This is critical for understanding how the second type of contradiction works, and causes polytheistic societies to experience persistent conflict. In a difficult logical maneuver, Tillich argues that these polytheistic cultures have an impulse towards unification into one nation, what he calls

---

95 *Socialist Decision*, 6.

96 "The myth of origin necessarily takes a polytheistic form ... The creative powers of origin press beyond the original point of emergence. They want to subject to themselves other powers of origin and to enlarge their space. They make a universal claim; their ultimate goal is to encompass all of space ... And one's particular god becomes the god of the whole world, without ceasing to be a particular god" (ibid., 18).

"mythical-political imperialism,"[97] but the attachment to the soil is too strong, and any temporary unity deteriorates into factionalism.[98] Despite the questionable empirical validity of this argument, it makes sense in light of Nazism's ideology of German racial unity, when Germany, historically, was anything but homogeneous.[99] Tillich concludes that if a culture remains oriented solely toward the soil, it remains bound to *what is:* "There can be no 'ought' on the basis of unbroken being and sacred space ... This means, practically, that might makes right."[100] In the following discussion of Tillich's understanding of the Exile, it will be shown how Jewish prophetism explicitly countered the myth of origin, and the attachment to space.[101]

3.3.2 The Exile and the Elevation of Time over Space

In the 1910 Dissertation, the two definitive contributions from the Old Testament to the process of revelation were the giving of the Mosaic Law and Prophetism. As discussed in Chapter Two, the Mosaic Law possessed pagan substance expressed in revelational form, and it was this dual nature that provided a basis for Prophetism to effect the transformation of particular revelation into universal revelation. However, no reference was made to the Exile, or, more generally, to the destruction of idolatrous aspects of Judaism, to preserve God's people.[102] In *The Socialist Decision*, there is no discussion of revelation per se, because the purpose of *The Socialist Decision* is to promote a political program that will have a humanistic and eschatological form of socialism. For Tillich, this means the creation of political institutions and culture that enable human flourishing, a true "humanism," as opposed to the reductionist anthropologies of

97 Ibid., 19.

98 "The original attachment to the soil ... is stronger than any all-embracing unity ... Polarization and demonic divisiveness have the last word on soil that is space-bound" (ibid.).

99 "The attempt to create a unity bound to origin by means of the old-Germanic heritage is completely hopeless, since as soon as the Germanic people appeared on the scene of history, they were grasped by the major streams of tradition already in existence and deprived of their original structure. To be sure, the Germanic substance was at work in the adoption and reformulation of these traditions; but there is no such thing as an original Germanic, and hence national, tradition, and such cannot be created" (ibid., 34).

100 Ibid., 19.

101 Ibid., 20.

102 Below in Chapter Five, in the analysis of the *Systematic Theology*, pages 141–143, reference will be made to the Suffering Servant in Second Isaiah as being an example of preparation for the paradoxical concept of the Cross.

bourgeois capitalism and scientific Marxism. In addition, in the 1910 and 1912 Dissertations, there is no discussion of "space" as being problematic from a theological, political or ethical standpoint, nor "time" being correspondingly elevated. In *The Socialist Decision*, Tillich presents for the first time, in any detail, the problematic nature of "space," in terms of bondage to the myth of origin, and the metaphysical importance of "time" as something that breaks the ancient, never ending cycle of birth, development and death.[103]

Tillich's understanding of the Exile, presented here for the first time, is fundamentally important for his distinctive view of a humanistic, prophetic understanding of socialism. According to Tillich, God saved his people by destroying their idolatrous relationship to the promised land, the priesthood and Temple cult, and the monarchy, which together constituted Israel's distinctive identity as the chosen people of God.

> On the basis of a powerful social myth of origin, Jewish prophetism radicalized the social imperative to the point of freeing itself from the bond of origin. God is free from the soil, the sacred land, not because he has conquered foreign lands, but precisely because he has led foreign conquerors into his own land in order to punish the "people of his inheritance" and to subject them to an unconditional demand.[104] The bond of origin between God and his people is broken if the bond of the law is broken by the people. Thus the myth of origin is shattered – and this is the world-historical mission of Jewish prophetism.[105]

This destruction was punishment for the failure to maintain justice, as described earlier, as the equality of "I" and "Thou." For Tillich, the nation of Israel failed to maintain equality toward strangers in their midst: "The claim of belonging to the people avails nothing in the face of the unconditional demand, on account of which the alien can be held in equal, indeed, in higher esteem."[106]

The simultaneous destruction of the monarchy and the preservation of the descendants of Israel in exile signified for Tillich, in theological terms, two things concerning time. First, it signified the theological independence of

103 In *Interpretation of History*, Tillich acknowledges that the Jews became "the people of time," but the point is not developed in any significant way: "For polytheism corresponds with the category 'beside' of spaces, just as monotheism with the category 'toward' of time and its one direction. So prophecy simultaneously struggled for time against space and for monotheism against polytheism; and so the Jewish people became the people of time, necessarily provoking the attacks of all people who are bound to space and consciously or unconsciously defy the meaning of history" (263 – 264).

104 This is similar to the "threat of extinction" referred to by Tillich in *ST* I, 141 – 143. This is also referred to in Chapter 2 above.

105 *Socialist Decision*, 20.

106 Ibid.

time, in which something "new" can emerge: "the independent character of time is recognized; it means *the elevation of time over space.* Time acquires a direction; it moves toward something that did not exist but will exist and, once it is attained, will not be lost again."[107] This also means that the pagan mythological cycle of birth and death can be definitively transcended. Second, the notion of "expectation" is introduced, which will be discussed in more detail below, which introduces a teleological, eschatological and dynamic aspect to time: "The expectation of a 'new heaven and a new earth' signifies the expectation of a reality that is not subject to the structure of being ... The new being is intrinsically unontological. It cannot be derived from the original state. It goes beyond the origin into a second phase, so to speak, the phase of *the new in history.* Thereby the origin itself appears in altered guise."[108] This idea is difficult insofar as it suggests that "the new" has no basis in the structure of being, in that "it cannot be derived from the original state." Yet, there must be some continuity between the "structure of being" and "the new," if "the origin itself appears in an altered guise." Despite any difficulties, Tillich is trying to describe the process of transforming "what is" into "what ought to be."

3.3.3 Prophetic Transformation of the Powers of Origin

For Tillich, an additional implication of the Exile is that the "new" *transforms* the origin, in order that the origin can transcend its orientation to space and become temporally oriented, toward "the new." Memory of the origin is not eliminated, but this is the risk with Enlightenment rationalism, and even the heirs of the Jewish Enlightenment.[109] Tillich uses the doctrine of creation as an example of what he means by transformation:

> the origin ... receives the character of a beginning. In the myth of origin there is no temporal beginning; existent things forever emanate from the origin and return to it. Being is not the beginning of existing things, but rather their constant root. Prophetism transforms the ori-

---

107 Ibid.
108 Ibid.
109 Tillich acknowledges that some forms of Judaism, such as rationalist forms in western Europe, had a secularizing effect: "Now it is the tragedy of Judaism that its historical fate not only broke the hegemony of the powers of origin, but also frequently dissolved them altogether, insofar as no new ties to the soil were created in their place (though this did come to pass in east-European Judaism). This negative element, the critical dissolution of the myth of origin instead of its prophetic transformation, gives to anti-Semitism and political romanticism an apparent justification for resisting this tendency" (ibid., 22).

> gin into the beginning of the historical process: the creation, which itself is pictured symbolically as an historical act.[110]

For Tillich, the concept of creation has been transformed from a process of eternal generation, similar to Neo-Platonism or some forms of Gnosticism, to a single event, which is depicted as historical, through the use of symbols. Therefore, history as a linear, teleological process, is created, and the cycle of birth and death is transcended. Something truly "new" becomes possible.

3.3.4 Jewish Prophetism and the "Jewish Problem" of Nationalism

Tillich concludes his analysis of how his distinctive view of Judaism,[111] or Jewish prophetism, can solve two problems, the problem of rationalism, and the problem of lapsing back into bondage to the origin. According to Tillich, both Christianity and Judaism are vulnerable to each extreme. Historically, in the second century CE, Christianity was confronted with the related heresies of gnosticism and Marcionism, which, among other things, rejected the use of the Old Testament, allegedly because of its capricious, vengeful God. In Tillich's terms, these anti-Jewish forces were problematic because they were bound to the myth of origin.[112] For Tillich, the Christian church struggled to save itself by making "the spirit of Judaism its own," by affirming the fundamental importance of creation and the Old Testament.[113] While Christianity managed to solve that

---

110 Ibid., 20 – 21. The aspects of continuity and discontinuity in prophetism will be discussed again below, in the fifth section regarding the symbol of expectation. Specifically, this means the transcendence and immanence of prophetic eschatological expectation, and its analogue in socialism.

111 Tillich underscores that Judaism and prophetism cannot be equated: "Old Testament prophetism is the persistent struggle of the 'spirit of Judaism' with the *realities of Jewish national life*. For the actual life of the Jewish nation, like the actual life of every nation, is by nature pagan. Hence, we see the foolishness of certain nationalistic demands that the Old Testament be dismissed as an expression of alien identity" (ibid., 22).

112 Ibid., 21.

113 "Christianity, through severe struggles, made the spirit of Judaism its own foundation. It took over the Old Testament, the idea of creation, and other historical concepts, and defended them against attempts to reinterpret the Christian event according to the myth of origin. In these struggles Christianity came to the very edge of extinction as an independent religion. At last, however, it won out and affirmed the Old Testament as its indispensable basis" (ibid.). For Tillich, the Old Testament writings are "a continuous testimony to the struggle of prophetic Judaism against pagan, national Judaism. For this reason, and solely for this reason, the Old Testament is a book for humanity–because in it the particular, the bondage to space and blood and nation-

problem, in a historical sense, Tillich believes that there are two ongoing threats from the powers of origin. The first is from "the priesthood," with its rituals and ancient forms of worship, which could lead to idolatry.[114] The second potential threat is any Christian group that seeks to re-attach itself to the powers of origin, after it had originally transcended them. Tillich does not name his target here. However, this would characterize the German Evangelical Church ("GEC"), whose predecessors led the Protestant Reformation. In the mid 1930s, the GEC was not critical of Nazism, and at times supported it,[115] as discussed in Chapter One above.

For Tillich, Judaism is also vulnerable to the twin threats of rationalism and bondage to the origin. Above it was noted that the Jewish Enlightenment caused a complete break from the powers of origin, explaining anti-Semitism, in a highly qualified way.[116] For Tillich, the other problem is Jewish nationalism, which was seen at the height of the monarchy, as reported in the Old Testament, and is also seen in the Zionist movement of Tillich's day. For Tillich, Jewish nationalism is the distinctly "Jewish problem," because of the iconic historical and theological status of the promised land and monarchy for Jewish identity. The only solution for this is to consistently reject the "bondage to space," as paradigmatically expressed in Jewish prophetism:

> The "Jewish problem" can only be solved by a decisive affirmation of the prophetic attack on the dominion of the myth of origin and all thinking bound to space. Only in this way can the pagan element in the Christian peoples and the negatively critical element in Judaism

---

alism, are seen as things to be fought against" (ibid., 22). In Volume II of the *Systematic Theology*, Tillich refers to the "life and death struggle" against Gnosticism, to save the Old Testament. *ST* II, 89–90.

114 Tillich probably means the Roman Catholic priesthood, since he regularly uses the concepts of "Catholic substance," referring to sacramental and traditional aspects of religion, and "Protestant principle," referring to the critical and reformist aspects of religion.

115 *The Socialist Decision* was written before the GEC elections in the summer of 1933, in which the so-called "German Christians" won substantial victories and a Reich-bishop ("*Reichsbischof*") with Nazi sympathies, Ludwig Müller, was selected. See Klaus Scholder, *The Churches and the Third Reich*, vol. I, *Preliminary History and the Time of Illusions 1918–1934* (London: SCM Press, 1987), 219–549, "The Churches in the Year of the Seizure of Power." Also, technically speaking, the Confessing Church, which never formally broke away from the GEC, opposed Nazi ideology, although it did not exist when *The Socialist Decision* was written. For a discussion of the lack of explicit support of the Jews in the 1934 Barmen Declaration, see Gerlach's *And The Witnesses Were Silent: The Confessing Church and the Persecution of the Jews;* trans. Victoria Barnett (Lincoln, Nebraska, University of Nebraska Press, 2000), 73–76.

116 *The Socialist Decision*, 22.

> simultaneously be overcome. A *secessio Judaica*[117], on the other hand, would mean a relapse into the barbarism and demonry of an existence totally bound to space.[118]

For Tillich, both Judaism and Christianity must always embody "the Jewish spirit," to avoid persistently encroaching pagan tendencies:

> it remains the *function of the Jewish spirit* to raise the prophetic protest, both in Judaism and Christianity, against every new attempt to revive such bondage to the myth of origin, and to help time, the unconditional demand, and the "Whither" to be victorious over space, mere being, and the "Whence." The spirit of Judaism is the necessary and eternal enemy of political romanticism. Anti-Semitism is an essential element in political romanticism. Christianity, however, by virtue of its principle, belongs radically and unambiguously on the side of Judaism in this conflict.[119]

This underscores the permanent theological validity of Jewish prophetism. Therefore, this dialectical framework presents a *reciprocal* relationship between Judaism and Christianity, exhibiting an ontological dialectic of balance. This is in addition to a highly developed understanding of the emergence of Jewish prophetism within the history of religion, through a historical dialectic of progression.

3.4 *The Socialist Decision:* Expectation and the Socialist Principle

The preceding exposition of Jewish prophetism demonstrates its critique of political romanticism. This critique identified three aspects of Jewish prophetism that will be carried forward into Tillich's normative understanding of socialism: monotheism (versus polytheism), time (versus space) and the power of the origin (versus bondage to the origin). The preceding analysis illuminated the deficiencies of political romanticism, bondage to the origin, the critique of Jewish nationalism, and pagan Christian National Socialism. However, the positive application of Jewish prophetism must now be developed. In part III, chapter 5 of *The Socialist Decision,* Tillich initiates his constructive proposal, through a multi-dimen-

---

117 Meaning a Jewish secession or withdrawal. Translator: Franklin Sherman. This also appears to be a title of a book or essay by Hans Blüher, *Secessio judaica. Philosophische Grundlegung der historischen Situation des Judentums und der antisemitischen Bewegung.* Potsdam, 1922. Cf. Tillich, E, Volume XI, Religion, *Kultur, Gesellschaft, Unveröffentliche Texte aus der Deutschen Zeit (1908–1933)*; "Der Geist des Sozialismus und der Kampf gegen ihn," 416.

118 *Socialist Decision,* 22–23.

119 Ibid., 21–22.

sional "symbol," the symbol of expectation. Three things will be discussed. First, there are the three elements of the socialist principle, which Tillich uses as the basis to draw an analogy between socialism and the prophetic tradition. Second, prophetic expectation reflects the interpenetration of promise and demand, with the demand providing the basis for justice. This expression of equality and justice enables Tillich to call this a "true humanism." Third, the socialist principle incorporates a creative tension between prophetic and rational elements, which drives the transformation of symbols pointing to a future reality.

First, the socialist principle is grounded in the interaction of three elements: (i) an affirmation of the power of origin, a presupposition of political romanticism; (ii) an affirmation of the unconditional demand, also a presupposition of political romanticism; and (iii) a rejection of "the metaphysical core" of the bourgeois principle, the belief in harmony.[120] Tillich's distinctive view of socialism readily incorporates the first and second element, but the third element, the belief in harmony, is pivotal. According to Tillich, if harmony becomes the basis for society, then the relationship to the powers of origin is severed. Tillich says this is what happened with bourgeois capitalist society, drawing upon Enlightenment rationalism, causing capitalist society to utterly distance itself from the powers of origin. Alternatively, if harmony is rejected, then the relationship to the powers of origin can be retained, but they must be transformed, lest society become bound to them once again. Tillich summarizes the relationship this way: "*Socialism lifts up the symbol of expectation against the myth of origin and against the belief in harmony. It has elements of both, but it transcends both.*"[121]

By introducing the term "symbol" in this context, Tillich is enabling an analogy to be drawn between the prophetic tradition and socialism:

> By combining the three elements of the socialist principle in the symbol of expectation, the socialist movement is brought into explicit relationship with the prophetic tradition. For in the prophets, i.e. in the historical movement in which the second root of human existence was grasped in a radical manner, these three elements are likewise united: the bond of origin, expressed in the form of patriarchal religion;[122] the breaking of the bond of origin by the unconditional demand; and the fulfillment of the origin not in a present interpreted in terms of harmony, but in a promised future. This means that *the socialist principle, so far as substance is concerned, is prophetic.*[123]

---

120 Ibid., 100–101.
121 Ibid., 101.
122 In part III of *The Socialist Decision*, chapter 7, section 5, "Eros and Purpose in the Life of the Community," Tillich's view of socialism includes the "emancipation of women," which rejects "male patriarchalism" (ibid., 152).
123 Ibid., 101.

Second, Tillich's distinctive view of socialism reflects an "interpenetration of demand and promise."[124] This relationship is an outgrowth of the tension between "what *will* come to pass," which is not dependent upon human activity, and "what *ought to* come to pass," which is dependent upon human activity, and is rooted in the prophetic tradition.[125] The demand possesses features rooted in the Jewish prophetic tradition, and helps provide the basis for a humanistic socialism, as opposed to a reductionist, scientific socialism. For Tillich, "the demand" was also present in the mythological, that is, pre-Jewish stage, where it merely presented *the possibility* of transcending the origin (the "ambiguity of the origin").[126] In addition, he says that the prophetic and socialist "demand" subjects all aspects of culture, every power, "both high and low," to the standards of equality and justice.[127] In a more difficult move, Tillich argues that this demand for equality serves to elevate, uniquely in the history of religion, the status of "lowliness."[128]

Third, the socialist principle incorporates a creative tension between prophetic expectation and rational expectation, which results in a "fundamental openness" and a "living expectation." This tension trades on a juxtaposition of immanence and transcendence, and what is knowable and what is incalculable. For Tillich, rational expectation is "immanent," meaning that it looks for something "other," meaning that which *ought to be*, but at the same time within the realm of experience (no concrete example given). Also, prophetic expectation is something "transcendent," meaning that it points to a "new creation," something "wholly other."[129] Using the example of prophetic eschatological expectation, Tillich observes that the "coming order of things" presupposes a total transformation of the present, even a "suspension of the laws of nature," although the language used necessarily derives from everyday experience.[130] However, the

124 Ibid., 104.

125 "This tension corresponds precisely to the prophetic character of socialism, since the prophet is simultaneously one who demands and one who promises" (ibid.).

126 See Note 83 above.

127 Ibid., 105.

128 "The inescapability of the demand, a demand that is addressed to everyone, makes all persons equal. That which one has, the fullness of one's being, with its luminous power, becomes insignificant in the presence of the unconditionality of the demand. Thereby the extraordinary possibility arises that human being may be fulfilled through the severest diminution of being. Hence the value that the prophetic and Christian viewpoint places on lowliness" (ibid.).

129 Ibid., 110.

130 Ibid., 110–111. In summary: "*Prophetic expectation acknowledges factors in human life that are in principle incomprehensible; rational expectation, only factors that have not been comprehended*" (110).

prophetic and rational are not opposed, in the sense that one must be eliminated in favour of the other, but that *both* must be maintained, in tension, not opposition. For Tillich, this gives socialism more than a humanistic character, in addition to an eschatological dimension. Tillich argues that true socialism presupposes a radical transformation of society, meaning a transformation of human nature and the laws of society.[131]

From a practical standpoint, this involves the hard work of planning and legislation, aimed towards the goal of a just society, coupled with the understanding that there will be contingencies that may, or may not, be favorable to socialism:

> in the background [there is] a sense of transcendent destiny, and in the foreground historicoanalytical research and history-shaping policy. Neither inhibits the other. Even the most rigorously rational analysis contains within itself (not outside itself) an element that is inaccessible to it, not because it is too complex but because it cannot become the subject of analysis. And even the strongest prophetic belief in providence never refrained from analyzing the historical situation in detail.[132]

3.5 *The Socialist Decision:* Transformation of the World Order

In part III, chapter 7, "The Resolution of Socialism's Inner Conflict through the Unfolding of the Socialist Principle," Tillich completes his constructive project by demonstrating how the elements of the socialist principle, taken from Jewish prophetism, are essential to his particular view of socialism. In chapter 7, Tillich presents the specific elements of his distinctive view of socialism, which include: the classless society (130–131); a new view of human nature which integrates humanistic Marxism and Freudian psychoanalysis, enabling a richer and more complex understanding of human drives and needs (133–136); a new view of power that seeks justice and requires consent (138–140); the creation of a universal socialist culture through the development of appropriate symbols (147–150); a new view of the nation that frees particular nations from bondage to the origin by subjecting them to the prophetic demand (151–152); a new view of economic planning which ranks the satisfaction of material needs according social value, to be administered by a central authority (153–155); a new view of work and labour that enables work to serve people, and for the meaning of work to coincide with the meaning of life (157–158); and, a new orientation of economics to promote international trade, to oppose imperialist nationalism (or "au-

131 Ibid., 111.
132 Ibid., 111–112.

tarky"), and to place the largest economic assets, such as agricultural land, heavy industry and banking, in the hands of central planners (156–160).

Each of these new understandings could be tied back to Jewish prophetism, at least indirectly, in light of the latter's humanistic orientation, and overt attention to justice understood as equality. For our purposes, those aspects that Tillich *directly* attributes to Jewish prophetism will be discussed, completing the exposition and analysis of *The Socialist Decision.* In chapter 7, section 5, "Eros and Purpose in the Life of the Community," Tillich's view of Jewish prophetism serves directly as the basis for the transformation of two aspects of his distinctive view of socialism: the movements from nationalism to universal humanity and imperialist economic independence to economic globalization.

3.5.1 The Transformation of Nationalism

Tillich's desire to transform nationalism is in direct response to 'reactionary forces, which have taken possession of the family and the national community'.[133] This most likely refers to German National Socialism, a form of political romanticism. At the same time, he acknowledges the legitimacy of nationhood, which is consistent with his understanding that the "powers of origin" are not in themselves destructive, but can become objects of idolatry and the basis for oppression. Tillich is arguing that nationhood can be co-opted for unjust purposes, but that it does have a "genuine use."[134] For Tillich, the prophetic critique is twofold. First, it acknowledges the importance of the origin, insofar as prophets are always identified with a particular people. Second, prophetism reminds its particular people of origin that they do not exist only for themselves, but for a larger purpose.

---

133 Ibid., 150. He further says that socialism must "decisively and courageously unveil the bourgeois perversion of the nationalist idea, revealing that the spirit of patriotism is being used to justify and defend class domination at home and economic imperialism abroad." This observation points to Tillich's assessment of the opportunistic nature of bourgeois capitalism, which defends the reactionary Nazi policies.

134 "Even at present a considerable portion, if not the greatest portion, of the self-destructive nationalism of the European peoples can be traced back to such sources. *But it is here, too, that only what once had a genuine use can be misused.* The idea of the nation cannot be destroyed by pointing to its perversion. The idea of the nation has energies deriving from the origin, and therefore has a claim to fulfillment–meaning not uncritical support, but also not destruction. Soil, blood, tradition, the social group–all the powers of origin are combined in the nation" (ibid., 151).

> Soil, blood, tradition, the social group – all the powers of origin are combined in the nation. The prophetic tradition thus relates to a people neither in such a way as to confirm it in its immediate self-awareness (as the "false prophets" do), nor to dissolve it for the sake of an immediate transition to a universal humanity (as bourgeois cosmopolitanism does). It seeks rather at once to judge and to support the nation. *The prophetic is always addressed to all humanity, but it always proceeds from amongst a people*, exhibiting thereby the unity of origin and goal that is typical of it.[135]

For Tillich, socialism affirms the true purpose of a nation more profoundly than nationalism can.[136] He states the prophetic critique another way, since it intends to free the nations from bondage to the powers of origin:

> Nationalism can provide the nation with an empire, but it cannot so relate it to the course of history as to free it from the cycle of birth and death. Socialism performs a service for Christian peoples which the churches have relinquished, if not formally, then actually, among many of its groups and leaders: *It frees nations from the law of death by subjecting them to the prophetic demand.* Therefore prophetism alone truly serves the nation. It is the legitimate representative of the idea of the nation. And what is true for prophetism is also true for socialism.[137]

3.5.2 The Transformation of "Autarky" and the Elevation of Time

For Tillich, the goal of socialist economics is twofold.[138] The first goal seeks "the unification of world economic space," in opposition to "autarky," which refers to an individual nation seeking to achieve economic independence. The second goal is to ensure "the rational utilization of the earth's virtually unlimited productive capacity in the service of humanity as a whole."[139] The problem facing socialist economics, the "inner tension" reflected in the bourgeois principle referred to above, is that German socialism had to align itself with economic liberalism against "the restraints on economic rationality." (It is not clear why Tillich says this, since "economic rationality" usually means the dictates of the free market, something Tillich and socialism would aver. It could mean some kind of restrictions on capitalism imposed by the German National Socialists.) In ad-

135 Ibid.
136 Ibid.
137 Ibid., 152.
138 Ibid., 159. Tillich acknowledges the assistance he received from his economist friend, Adolf Löwe, in writing section 6 of chapter 7, "Nature and Planning in the Economic Order." Tillich also refers to an essay of Löwe's, "Der Sinn der Weltwirtschaftskrise," *Neue Blätter für den Sozialismus* 2 (1931) (ibid., part III,177 note 33)
139 Ibid., 159.

dition, according to Tillich, German socialism also needed to affirm central planning against the instability and recurring crises brought on by capitalism.[140]

Tillich's transformation of economics draws upon Jewish prophetism in two ways, picking up on threads sown earlier. The first thread is the elevation of time over space, a theme first seen in Tillich's critique of political romanticism in part I, and his understanding of the Exile. In this critique, the cyclical view of time is expressed as bondage to the powers of origin, and as the inability to transcend *what is.* In Tillich's constructive response, this view of time is meant to reflect *what ought to be.* The specific problem occurs, according to Tillich, when a nation seeks economic independence and self-sufficiency, and "absolutizes" itself, effectively sacralizing its geographic territory.[141] The solution, according to Tillich, is to prohibit granting any *absolute* status to any geographic space: "*An autarky of the national economy implies, in keeping with the myth of origin, tying production to a limited space, for the sake of the absolute sovereignty of this space.* But no one space is sovereign."[142]

The second thread is the extension of equality to "the alien," a cornerstone principle of Mosaic law, and the foundation of justice. The ethical and theological imperative experienced simply by the presence of "the other," first expressed in the 1910 Dissertation, and discussed above in *The Socialist Decision*, reappears in the culmination of this work. Tillich extends this to justify the internationalization of trade.

> International trade and exchange, of its own force, prevails over the economic independence of places bound to the origin. It is a path-breaker for the trans-spatial unity of humankind, for a common orientation to the forward movement of time. Hence the prophetic position affirms the international horizon also with regard to economic exchange. Prophetism protects the "alien" in the name of the same unconditional demand that compatriots and foreigners, one's own and other peoples, all confront: the demand of justice.[143]

140 Ibid., 153.
141 In Tillich's discussion of the bourgeois principle in part II of *The Socialist Decision* (55–56), he equates autarky, imperialism and bourgeois nationalism: "The powers inherent in the idea of the nation, which are very closely related to the myth of origin, are utilized in the struggle for the interests of the national bourgeois economic groups. Domestically, opposition to the domination of these groups is condemned as unpatriotic. Internationally, the economic struggle against them is interpreted as a struggle against the nation. Thus the bourgeoisie, with the help of the idea of the nation, succeeds in overcoming its political opponents at home, in enlisting in its service the prebourgeois forces that are still bound to the origin, and in reducing competition in the world market, either by political suppression of the competing nations or by barring their products (imperialism or autarky)."
142 Ibid., 158.
143 Ibid., 159.

Tillich's distinctive view of socialism, which has humanistic and eschatological aspects, is firmly rooted in the Jewish prophetic tradition. What had changed from the 1920s to the 1930s was the emergence of a new and ominous threat, German National Socialism, the paradigmatic example of Tillich's political romanticism. My supposition is that Tillich marshaled the resources of Jewish prophetism because they more effectively responded to the problem of "bondage to the myths of origin," as expressed in political romanticism. This can be seen particularly in the derivation of the "ought" of justice, in the experience of the unconditional demand, and in the maxim of "justice is the true power of being." The appeals to ontology and power are "deep" criticisms, that belief-ful realism did not provide, at least as expressed in the 1920s. As for the problem of capitalism, Jewish prophetism exhibited several key characteristics – like the impetus for economic globalization based upon recognition of "the alien" – that could address the reductionism of capitalism more effectively than belief-ful realism.

Further, Tillich's derivation of the maxim "justice is the power of true being" was rooted in his distinctive view of the dialectical history of religion. This means that only a culture that is governed by a patriarchal principle could foster the conditions for a "primeval demand," which is the unique basis for the unconditional demand of justice. For Tillich, Jewish prophetism was the unique and original expression of this concept of justice. Also, for the first time in Tillich's various analyses of Judaism, he proposes that Judaism assume a permanent, critical/prophetic role in relation to Christianity. This became the basis for what would later be a fully reciprocal relation between Judaism and Christianity, which will be demonstrated in later chapters, an ontological dialectic of balance.

Chapter Four: The Dialectic of the Holy and the Permanent Theological Importance of Judaism

In March of 1952, less than ten years after the end of World War II and the full revelation of the horrors of the Holocaust, the directors of the Deutsche Hochschule für Politik (the *Hochschule*) invited Tillich to give a series of lectures with the suggested topic, "the Jewish question – a Christian and a German problem."[1] These will be referred to as the "*Judenfrage* lectures." The occasion for these lectures is remarkable. The directors were very concerned that their students, who were too young to participate in the genocide, did not fully appreciate the importance of the Holocaust, by trivializing it through ignorance and denial, as it was not *their* problem.[2] Two of the directors of the *Hochschule* wrote to Tillich stating why they thought he would be the best person to address this topic:

> We do not know many people who would be able to do this thoroughly enough; in any case, you would be able to, and you would surely do us in Berlin in general and our students in particular a very great favor. I [Fränkel] know from our common work in New York, how intensively you have dealt for years not only with the problem as an ethical-philosophical problem but as a current political problem ...[3]

The term "the Jewish question" is not really a question, but it is a phrase that gained currency in the mid eighteenth and early nineteenth centuries to describe the implications of Jewish emancipation in a period of rising nationalism. Karl Marx wrote an essay in 1843 titled, "On the Jewish Question,"[4] which quite likely caused the professors at the *Hochschule* and Tillich to frame the issue in this way. Jewish people for centuries in Europe were subject to different laws within European countries, unlike other citizens. The term was then co-opted by the Nazis to say that for centuries the status of the Jews had been a perpetual problem in Christian Europe.[5] Further, as Gavin Langmuir points out, there are few

---

1 Earley Dissertation, 84.

2 Ibid., 84–85.

3 10 March 1952 letter from Herr Fränkel and Otto Heinrich von der Gablentz to Paul Tillich. Letter archive, Renate Albrecht, Duren, Germany. Earley Dissertation, 121 note 171.

4 See *The Marx-Engels Reader*, 2nd edn, ed. Robert C. Tucker (New York: W. W. Norton, 1978), 26–52.

5 For one example among many, see Adolf Hitler's "German Economic Goals and the Jewish Question," in "Unsigned Memorandum on the Four Year Plan," August 1936, *Documents on German Foreign Policy, 1918–1945*, Series C (1935–1937) (Washington, D.C., n.d.), vol. 5, 853–

words in western history and culture, from the Middle Ages to the present, that have elicited such a strong emotional response as the word "Jew."[6] For a complex variety of reasons, Jews periodically rose to heights in Christian society, and also periodically suffered the most intense forms of persecution.

The *Judenfrage* lectures, given seven years after the end of World War II in the summer of 1952, represent an early attempt by a Christian theologian to address the traumatic events of the Holocaust, and their theological implications. More specifically for Tillich, they represent the culmination of years of reflection on the problem of anti-Semitism, in relation to Germany and Christianity. In these lectures, Tillich attempts to show the historical, theological, psychological and sociological causes of anti-Semitism in Christian Germany, and sketches a path to reconciliation. Tillich's biographers report that these lectures were the only lectures that Tillich gave in Berlin after World War II that were not well received, although they do not say why.[7] If Tillich was correct in his assessment that after the end of World War II Germans typically remained in denial about their complicity in the Holocaust, then this cool reception is easily understood.

After World War I, Tillich looked to a humanistic and eschatological form of socialism to overcome the problems of international capitalism and religious nationalism. After the additional trauma of World War II and the Holocaust, it seems that Tillich was again driven to look elsewhere for answers, beyond theologically informed political structures, deeper into the human person, into the "psyche." Tillich's affinity for psychoanalysis is well-documented, although he was never formally trained in that discipline.[8] In the *Judenfrage* lectures, he applies psychology and sociology to the problems of anti-Judaism and anti-Semitism, adding more methodological tools to address a complex problem.[9] For example, in the second lecture Tillich applies new ideas such as "anxiety," and "insecurity" to the prior concepts of "space" and "time," as first analyzed in

---

862, cf. *The Jew in the Modern World: A Documentary History*, 2nd edn; ed. Paul Mendes-Flohr and Jehuda Reinharz (New York: Oxford University Press, 1995), 649–650.

6 Cited from his essay, "Majority History and Postbiblical Jews," in *Toward a Definition of Antisemitism* (Berkeley and Los Angeles: University of California Press, 1996), 22–41.

7 Pauck and Pauck, *Tillich*, 217.

8 A recent discussion of the role of psychology in Tillich's soteriology is chapter 3 of Wilder's dissertation "Existentialism and Exegesis," which is titled "Salvation as Healing: Psychoanalysis, Existentialism, and Soteriology in Tillich."

9 Tillich describes the second lecture as being mainly a sociological and social-psychological analysis. *Judenfrage* lectures, 455. Langmuir concludes that historical research needs to be informed by the social sciences, and that the study of anti-Semitism must appropriate the insights of social psychology, and he wagers that the history of the Jews will be better served as the influence of the social sciences on history increases. *Definition of Antisemitism*, 22–41.

The Socialist Decision. For Tillich, these psychological and sociological categories are deeply illuminating, and provide the basis for what is ultimately his theological interpretation of the Jewish problem. In the third lecture, Tillich will combine in new ways, the concepts of space and time, Is and Ought, priestly and prophetic, culminating in a multi-disciplinary, dialectical and theological concept referred to as "the Holy."

The *Judenfrage* lectures are comprised of five parts, an introduction and four lectures. The introduction presents "the Jewish question," and distinguishes how it relates to Jews, Germans and Christians. The presenting problem is the ambiguity of these classifications, which causes Tillich to adopt a wide array of analytical tools. The first lecture introduces the concepts of "anti-Judaism" and "anti-Semitism," through a historical analysis of western Christianity and the witness of the New Testament. The second lecture introduces psychological and sociological categories, and concludes that Germans and Jews have similar structural "corporate personalities," which exhibit a unique relation of mutual attraction and repulsion. In this chapter Tillich introduces the metaphor of the "mirror" of Jewish prophetism, which is to be perpetually held up to Christianity. The argument climaxes in the third lecture, in which Tillich argues that the sociological and psychological categories fundamentally assume a theological dimension. In this lecture, Tillich draws upon his understandings of Judaism in the 1910 Schelling Dissertation and *The Socialist Decision*, and he introduces the concept of "the Holy," echoing Rudolf Otto,[10] but given a characteristically Tillich-ian emphasis. In the fourth lecture, Tillich applies the theological concepts presented in the third lecture, to Jews, Germans and Christians, in an attempt to provide a path to reconciliation.[11]

---

10 Rudolf Otto, *The Idea of the Holy: An Inquiry into the non-rational factor in the idea of the divine and its relation to the rational*, trans. John W. Harvey (Oxford: Oxford University Press, 1958). Tillich does not mention Otto in the *Judenfrage* lectures, but discusses the importance of Otto's concept of "the Holy" in *ST* I, 215–216. Tillich appears to have drawn upon Otto's idea that God was at the same time both terrifying and fascinating.

11 The only extended analysis of the *Judenfrage* lectures is by Glenn David Earley, in "Paul Tillich and Judaism: An Analysis of 'The Jewish Question – A Christian and a German Problem' " (Earley, *Judenfrage* lectures). Earley's analysis reflects his criticisms of Tillich's view of Judaism, advanced in the Earley Dissertation, discussed in Chapter 1 above.

4.1 Existential Participation[12]

Tillich believes that if any progress could be made within Germany and Christianity with respect to Jews and Judaism, it must be based upon something more than intellectual understanding. Similar to his reasoning in *The Socialist Decision*, there must be existential participation. Tillich applies the concept of existential participation to himself, as part of his statement of method, and gives three reasons why these lectures are fundamentally important to him. First, Tillich has participated in Jewish/Christian dialogue for decades, and he sees this as a vital aspect of his calling as a Christian theologian: "It has been my destiny to participate in the questions which will be considered in these lectures. As a Christian theologian, I have participated in Jewish/Christian discussions for decades and have experienced the entire burden of the problems which are moving theological thinking today, as in the beginning of the Christian era."[13] This has two implications. The first implication is that the problems surrounding the relationship between Judaism and Christianity in antiquity recur in the modern period. Tillich's chief example, which he first discussed in *The Socialist Decision*, is the threat to Christianity by pagan syncretism, in the form of religious nationalism, which must be subject to the critique of Jewish prophetism. The second implication is that these problems are not peripheral, but central to Christian theology, and that they represent universally human problems. The second reason is that Tillich is a German by birth, so he is inevitably related to whatever is concluded about the role of Germans, and Germany, in resolving these problems. The third reason why these lectures are important to Tillich is that some of his closest friends over the years have been Jews.[14] This we know from his participation in the '*kairos* circle', and his associations with the Frankfurt School. These reasons combine to lead Tillich to address the question of guilt, to be discussed below.

---

12 The problem with Harnack's view of Greek philosophy was that it was "intellectualistic," to the exclusion of a fundamental, existential dimension. Tillich, *History of Christian Thought*, 517.
13 *Judenfrage* lectures, 420–421. The full quote is illustrative: "It has been my destiny to participate in the questions which will be considered in these lectures. As a Christian theologian, I have participated in Jewish/Christian discussions for decades and have experienced the entire burden of the problems which are moving theological thinking today, as in the beginning of the Christian era. I am not speaking of the many follies which occur in these debates, but of the questions which concern human beings unconditionally as human beings, and with which I have wrestled along with my Jewish dialogue partners."
14 Ibid., 421.

4.2 Ambiguity, Guilt and Multi-Disciplinary Method

Tillich begins the first of five parts, the Introduction, by noting the ambiguity of the terms "Jew," "Judaism," "Christian" and "German."[15] He asserts the term "Jewish-question" is ambiguous, since Judaism could have a sociological function as a minority, a religious function as a sacramental society, and/or a sociological function as an ethnic group, or "race."[16] Tillich also claims that the relationship between the religious and sociological functions is significant, and unresolved.[17] In addition, Tillich describes the ambiguity of the term "Christian," which has historical, institutional, denominational, and sociological associations.[18] Finally, the term "German" is also ambiguous, although Tillich highlights two specific senses, one having to do with "the German character," and the other relating to German history. Tillich asks whether there is something about the German character that is inherently antagonistic to Judaism, or whether there was some historical event, or catastrophe, that created a unique relationship between Jews and Germans.[19] To maintain maximum flexibility, Tillich assures the listener that none of the senses referred to for each of the three concepts will be excluded.[20]

Tillich proceeds to describe five types of guilt for the Holocaust, which have religious, sociological, psychological and legal aspects. When taken together, *all* Germans are implicated, even Tillich, in one or more ways. This layered phenomenon of guilt underscores the complexity of the problem, and enables Tillich to use a wide array of arguments as he attempts to answer the question of the Jewish problem for Christians and Germans. The first type of guilt is identified by direct responsibility, to those who participated in the immediate cause of an event. Tillich does not give examples, but he probably means those Germans who directly engaged in the process of identifying, imprisoning and executing Jews – Nazi government officials, prison guards, members of the security agencies and military. This kind of guilt cannot be

15 For Tillich, ambiguity plays a major role in the third volume of his *Systematic Theology*, but in this instance it simply refers to the confusion that can result from one word carrying more than one sense, or meaning.

16 Tillich acknowledges the problematic concept of race: "Do we speak of Judaism as a religious reality or race? If there was such a thing as the Jewish race (which I do not believe, just as little as I believe there is an Aryan race), the question would be: Is our theme a problem of race or is the Jewish question a matter of something special, that is, a race that is something more than a race? Does 'Jew' mean a representative of one of the great eleven religions which have universal character or do we speak of the Jew as a preparer of Christianity?" (ibid., 418–419).

17 Ibid.

18 Ibid., 419–420.

19 Ibid., 420.

20 Ibid.

attributed to the German people as a whole, but only to limited groups and individuals.[21] The second type of guilt implicates all Germans, including émigrés such as Tillich, the guilt of "a lack of the practice of responsibility."[22] Tillich extends this guilt back into the 1920s, inferring that the German people should have suspected the Nazis genocidal plans even then. Tillich faults himself and all other Germans for not opposing Nazi barbarism early on, preventing them from gaining popularity and strength.[23] He even says that what happened was "inevitable," not in a deterministic sense of being unavoidable, but because Germans were not strong enough to resist.[24]

The third sense of guilt is the repression of knowledge, which is only attributable to those in Germany after 1933, the year that Hitler came to power. This sense of guilt assumes a strong psychological dimension; it is the guilt of "knowing and yet not knowing," a complex combination of intuitive understanding combined with denial.[25] This sense of guilt assumes a complex combination of conscious and unconscious motives, self-deception and denial, and "mirror

---

21 Ibid., 422.

22 Ibid.

23 "Every German is guilty in this sense ... Why? Because in the years in which the reign of those who perpetrated these crimes was prepared, we were not strong enough to hinder them, nor willing to sacrifice, even if we protested and thereby became émigrés or sacrifices. Since the middle of the twenties, we suspected what would come. I often told my friends what I saw, as in a vision, the German cities in ruins" (ibid.). The Paucks recount that this "vision" came to Tillich in 1931: "In 1931 he had a dream which was an uncanny premonition of the consequences of a National Socialist victory for Germany. In Kampen, that summer, he and his friends had spent the night drinking wine, talking, dreaming out loud, reciting poetry, all on the theme of imminent doom. As they emerged from the cottage where they had gathered, at four in the morning, to watch the sunrise over the dunes, they were startled to hear Tillich say, "You will all see sheep grazing on the Potsdamer Platz one day." He had had in fact a dream in which he saw grass growing and sheep grazing on that busiest square in the center of Berlin. Fifteen years later, after the Allied invasion and the bombing of Berlin, he was excited and shaken to see that his dream had come true. A photograph in a New York newspaper showed sheep cropping grass in the Potsdamer Platz" (interview with Paul Tillich. Pauck and Pauck, *Tillich*, 124–125).

24 *Judenfrage* lectures, 422–423.

25 "This is a deep psychological problem, for it is a matter neither of conscious acts, nor of completely unconscious acts, but of acts which hang somewhere between conscious and unconscious. One knew what happened and yet did not know. I believe all who tell me that they did not know, and yet I believe no one, for I know that one knew enough to repress knowledge which one did not want to know. This is guilt which poses difficult psychological and ethical problems ... Who is able, even if he or she is only a little sensitive, to look at himself or herself in the mirror? One looks away from one's own image in the mirror" (ibid., 423–424).

imagery."[26] These factors make it a particularly fertile concept, which Tillich will exploit later in the second lecture. The fourth sense of guilt is similar to the third, because it contains an element of self-deception. This is the guilt of forgetting, not in the sense of literally not remembering what happened to the Jews, but the sense of not permitting that historical reality to shape one's actions in the present or future.[27] Here Tillich appeals to Max Scheler's concept of "remorse," which is not a sentimental feeling of pain over something that happened in the past, but has a decisive ethical dimension: "remorse is the expulsion of something false from the household of the soul."[28] For Tillich, the third and fourth senses of guilt are related because they both have a partially unconscious cause, which confers a tragic dimension upon them.[29]

The fifth sense of guilt employs a moral calculus of weighing the suffering of Germans experienced during and after World War II, and uses that as an offset against the guilt of assuming full responsibility for the Holocaust. Tillich expresses the mind-set of some Germans this way: "We have acted badly, but we have suffered correspondingly. The others have suffered through us, but now we have suffered through them and are even."[30] For Tillich, this represents the justice of proportionality, which is important in any understanding of justice, but is inadequate to address the culpability of Germans for the Holocaust.[31] Instead, Tillich favors a form of justice that accomplishes two things: it (i) recognizes that an objective standard ("the right") has been violated; and (ii) fosters reconciliation of that which is separated, God from humanity, and persons and groups from one another.[32] For Tillich, the biblical idea of justice requires recognition of the wrong and eradication of its causes.[33] The addition of reconciliation

26 The metaphor of the mirror will recur at the end of the second lecture, in a fundamental way.

27 *Judenfrage* lectures, 424. Earley observes that the third and fourth types of guilt are directed to the past and to the future, respectively. Earley, *Judenfrage* essay, 217.

28 "To what extent is this expulsion taking place and to what extent has it taken place? Everything depends on whether those elements, which led to the anti-semitic madness, are expelled from the soul, not forgotten, repressed, or hidden, but recognized and banned under the pain of remorse" (*Judenfrage* lectures, 424).

29 Ibid.

30 Ibid., 425.

31 Ibid.

32 "But there is another definition of the concept of justice. It does not deny the proportional element but goes beyond it. I am thinking of the Old and New Testament concept of justice in which the violation of the right and the consciousness connected therewith are recognized. But that is not the last word" (ibid.).

33 Ibid., 426. This is a new sense of the biblical idea of justice. Prior to this, it had been based on the equality of persons, as in an authentic I–Thou relationship (477).

to the concept of justice is a significant addition from the concept of equality expressed in *The Socialist Decision.* Tillich closes his analysis of guilt with a fundamental question that will inform the remainder of the *Judenfrage* lectures: "The true question is: Is reconciliation possible and what is necessary so that reconciliation becomes real?"[34] Tillich develops the complexity of the problem in the first three lectures, and then makes recommendations to achieve reconciliation in the fourth lecture.

4.3 First Lecture: Anti-Judaism and Anti-Semitism

The first lecture draws upon two unpublished papers that were prepared at the request of the American government in the early 1940s, as Tillich was asked to write on the relationship of Catholicism and Protestantism to the Jewish question.[35] Due to the limitations of space, these two papers will not be systematically discussed, but they will be cited where applicable. This lecture can be divided into six sections: (i) the distinction between anti-Judaism and anti-Semitism; (ii) an assessment of the New Testament witness, as the "completion" of the Old Testament, not "anti-Judaism;" (iii) an historical overview of western Christianity, focusing on the emergence of anti-Judaism, as occasioned by the encounter of Christianity with "paganism;" (iv) a discussion of the "deicide" charge, and the pervasiveness of theological anti-Judaism in the western church; (v) the question of "mission" to the Jews;[36] and (vi) an assessment of the Christian churches under Hitler.

---

34 Ibid., 426.

35 Weaver, *War and Peace*, 198. Weaver simply refers to the American government, and I suggest that it was the Office of War Information because that was the agency that asked Tillich to create the texts for the Voice of America broadcasts referred to in Chapter One above, and analyzed in Stone and Weaver, *Against the Third Reich.* Both papers are found in the Paul Tillich Archive of the Harvard–Andover Library at Harvard Divinity School. In 2012 the Tillich Archive was reorganized and recatalogued, with new document numbers being assigned. Here the old document number and new document number will be cited, in that order. The old document number is often accompanied by the abbreviation PTAH, which was created by Erdmann Sturm. The first paper is titled "Catholicism and Anti-Judaism", PTAH 416:009 / bMS649/62 (6). The second paper is titled "Protestantism and Anti-Semitism", PTAH 416:010 / bMS649/62 (7).

36 In "Protestantism and Anti-Semitism," Tillich surveys a number of American Protestant statements on anti-Semitism, which deal variously with alleged Jewish guilt for Christ's death and related topics. He observes that "Sectarian Christianity," the heirs of the Anabaptist tradition in America, was unequivocally against Christian anti-Semitism, because it adhered to "the basic principle of the divine in the ground of the human soul." There was a large theolog-

To one degree or another, each of these topics relates to the central thesis of this book. However, due to limitations of space, the discussion will be limited to the thesis that for Tillich Jewish prophetism must endure at all times to serve as a critique of paganism, or "Gnosticism," which is prototypically present in religious nationalism. Tillich identifies two principles that support this ongoing importance of Jewish prophetism. First, anti-Semitism, which has roots in 18th and 19th century science,[37] has earlier, theological roots, which Tillich refers to as "anti-Judaism." Second, for Tillich, theological anti-Judaism is present in all periods of all periods of church history: "Anti-Judaism has occurred in all of church history and represents the tragic guilt of the church."[38] Anti-Judaism is a recurring phenomenon, and emerges in any situation in which Christianity engages non-Christian culture. According to Tillich, any time Christianity engages non-Christian culture, there is a risk of "syncretism," or a compromising of Christian belief in order to be acceptable to the surrounding culture: "Anti-Judaism originates in the instant in which Christianity comes into the pagan world and must make itself understandable to paganism."[39] How this occurs will be illustrated in the following section.

---

ical discussion group based in New York City, about which Tillich makes the following observation: "In a theological discussion group, representing the highest level of American theology, we discussed, a few years ago, the question of Jewish mission; and it was astonishable [*sic*] how great the percentage of theologians was who rejected any aggressive mission, partly on the basis of the fact that there is no special denomination to which to come the Jews should be asked [*sic*], partly on the basis of the belief that the prophetic spirit of Judaism should be preserved apart from the Church as long as the Church is in danger to relapse into paganism. Such an attitude, of course, would undercut not only anti-Semitism but also Christian traditional anti-judaism [*sic*]" (9, 11–12).

37 According to Cornel West, racism in the western European tradition entered its first phase in the Enlightenment, although it drew upon concepts from Greek antiquity and the Renaissance: "To put it crudely, my argument is that the authority of science, undergirded by modern philosophical discourse guided by Greek ocular metaphors and Cartesian notions, promotes and encourages the activities of observing, comparing, measuring and ordering the physical characteristics of human bodies." See "A Genealogy of Modern Racism," in *Prophesy Deliverance: An Afro-American Revolutionary Christianity* (Louisville, KY: Westminster John Knox Press, 1982), ch. 2, 48. Also, see George L. Mosse, *Toward the Final Solution: A History of European Racism* (Madison, Wisconsin: The University of Wisconsin Press, 1985).

38 *Judenfrage* lectures, 428.

39 *Judenfrage* lectures, 429. In "Protestantism and Anti-Semitism," Tillich begins the paper with the assertion, "The distinction between antisemitism and antijudaism [*sic*] is valid for Protestantism as well as for Catholicism" (1).

4.3.1 Christianity, Paganism and Anti-Judaism

Tillich's assessment of "paganism" becomes more negative over time. The most positive characterization is in the 1910 Dissertation, where Tillich argues that paganism, or pre-Christian and pre-Israelite religion, was on a parallel track with Israelite religion, but later paganism "exhausted itself" in a "catastrophe of the rational process."[40] This development shows the influence of the dialectic of the potencies. Paganism contributed rationality to Judaism, but it did not have adequate revelatory capacity, due to its cultural particularity. Judaism, having both particular and universal elements, became the necessary precursor to Christianity. Therefore, there is an important element of continuity between paganism and Judaism. In the 1912 Dissertation, paganism is in heightened opposition to Judaism, as its dialectical opponent. According to Tillich, paganism represented capricious deities that could not be appeased even by sacrifice, so humanity sought other expressions, lest "human consciousness ... be inevitably destroyed."[41] According to Tillich's dialectic, paganism failed to transcend one pole of the dialectic, that of "mysticism," and Judaism failed to transcend the other pole of the dialectic, "guilt-consciousness."

In *The Socialist Decision*, paganism is still understood within a dialectical history of religion. Tillich only refers to "paganism" four times, as his primary object of criticism is political romanticism, but they are deeply interrelated. In the discussion of how Judaism "breaks" the myth of origin, Jewish monotheism is contrasted with everything else that came before it, which were pagan, polytheistic religions. For Tillich, only Jewish monotheism could resolve the contradictions of polytheism. Tillich's argument hinges on an interpretation of the Babylonian Exile. In the Exile, all the symbols of Israel's election, the monarchy, the temple cult and the promised land, are taken away because they had become idols. However, a righteous remnant endured in exile. For Tillich, it is this destruction of the idolatrous Jewish kingdom and the merciful sparing of the remnant in exile that is the basis for something "new," that can provide a basis to transcend the naturalistic, pagan cycle of birth, development, and death.

In the *Judenfrage* lectures, Tillich identifies three key historical instances when the Christian church assumed an anti-Jewish posture, with each instance representing a response to encroaching paganism. The premise of Tillich's argument is the following: "Anti-Judaism originates in the instant in which Christian-

---

40 1910 Dissertation, 103 – 104, and 107.
41 1912 Dissertation, 118.

ity comes into the pagan world and must make itself understandable to paganism."[42]

The first historical example is the creation of the "Pilate legend" in Egypt, asserting Pilate's innocence in the Crucifixion.[43] This is important, presumably, because the historical record clearly shows that Pilate was ultimately responsible for the crucifixion of Jesus, and for Egyptian Christians to turn that record on its head indicates the pressures of syncretism in that context. The second historical example is the segregation of Jews from Christians as a result of the Fourth Lateran Council in 1215. Tillich says, "All authoritarian systems are filled with this kind of fear. They feel secure as long as those who recognize their authority are cut off from every other tradition. But as soon as other possibilities appear, the unity of consciousness, and thereby the security of authority, is threatened. The Jews represented another tradition, and on this tradition not only Christianity but also Islam was dependent. That is the background of the segregation laws which were passed by Innocent III and his successors."[44] For Tillich, the threat of syncretism was manifest in the "fear" of other religious possibilities, specifically Judaism and Islam. This led to the abuse of political authority, on religious grounds, to eliminate those possibilities.

The third example comes from the Protestant Reformation. According to Tillich, Luther believed that if the Christian Church could be purged of pagan elements, then it would have been possible for Jews to enter the Christian church. Allegedly, what the Jews found most objectionable were the pagan elements of Roman Catholicism, in particular the 'demonic monstrosity' of Catholic sacramentalism.[45] According to Tillich, Luther's theological presuppositions were similar to the "Jewish prophetic consciousness," as reflected in his condemnation of the Mass.[46] However, Tillich argues that the failure of the Jews to convert to Christianity ran afoul of Luther's apocalypticism, leading Luther to pen his infamous tract *On the Jews and Their Lies*.[47] Tillich does not cite Luther's

---

42 *Judenfrage* lectures, 429.
43 Ibid., 429–431.
44 Ibid., 429–431.
45 "For the Jews, Catholic sacramentalism, including its christological presuppositions, was idolatry and a demonic monstrosity. It was the Mass especially which was the basis of this judgment. Nothing could contradict more the Jewish, prophetic consciousness that the priestly transformation of bread and wine into the body and blood of the incarnate God" (ibid., 432).
46 Ibid.
47 A standard reading of Luther's anti-Judaism begins with his initial "positive" assessment of Jews in his 1523 *Jesus Christ Was Born a Jew*. After twenty years of religious strife, sectarian violence and imperial politics, Luther become bitter that the Jews had not converted, leading him to vent his frustrations in the infamous 1543 pamphlet *On the Jews and their Lies*. Luther, Renais-

work directly, for it was well known, but he does observe that Luther engaged in "angry attacks against the stubbornness of the Jews, from which Christian anti-Judaism gained a foothold also in the churches of the Reformation."[48]

4.3.2 The Churches under Hitler: The Struggle for Life and Death

Tillich closes this lecture with a discussion of the Christian churches under Hitler. In doing so, he raises key ideas that represent his mature understanding of the relationship of Judaism to Christianity, some of which will recur in the remaining three lectures. Tillich's first observation is that the Christian churches were initially "bewildered" at Hitler's anti-Semitism, but eventually came to the realization that attacks upon Judaism were always a precursor to attacks on Christianity.[49] Tillich's argument proceeds by reviving the analogy between Nazism and ancient Gnosticism, which he first developed in *The Socialist Decision*, as reviewed in the preceding section, and in Chapter Three. Tillich boldly asserts that the biggest threat to Christianity in the ancient world was not persecution by Rome, but syncretism with "gnostic-syncretistic religions of late antiquity."[50] In Roman antiquity, the Christian church fought a "struggle for life and death"[51] against paganism, and decisively retained the Old Testament

---

sance humanism, the Protestant Reformation, anti-Judaism, and anti-Semitism receive a nuanced treatment by Heiko A. Oberman in *The Roots of Anti-Semitism in the Age of Renaissance and Reformation*, trans. James I. Porter (Philadelphia, PA: Fortress Press, 1984).

48 *Judenfrage* lectures, 433.

49 Ibid., 436.

50 Ibid. This is a perceptive observation, in light of the anti-Semitic uses of the history of religions as described by Heschel.

51 Tillich uses this phrase numerous times in his works – *History of Christian Thought*, *Systematic Theology*, *The Socialist Decision* – and always to describe the conflict between some form of paganism and prophetism or Christianity. In ST II, in a discussion of the symbol "Christ," its historical and transhistorical meaning, Tillich writes: "The receding of the eschatological consciousness of early Christianity led to an almost exclusive emphasis on individual salvation. This is already visible in Paul, whose Christ-mysticism and doctrine of the Spirit provided an important bridge across which the non-historical type could enter Christianity. Under these circumstance it is not astonishing that that the horizontal line, derived from the Old Testament, was in danger from annihilation by the vertical line, derived from Hellenism. In the Gnostic mixture of religious motifs the danger became reality. The two interdependent symbols of creation and consummation were obliterated. In this situation Christianity was forced into a life-and-death struggle to preserve the Old Testament within the church, the historical type of the expectation of the New Being. The church made the decision and saved the historical character of Christianity. This must be defended in all periods, but in such a way that the universal significance of Christianity

to preserve the historical roots of Christianity. According to Tillich, this was especially important to preserve the witness of the Jewish prophets, who warned against idolatrous religious nationalism.[52]

According to Tillich, without the Old Testament, the New Testament cannot exist, and to detach Christ from Old Testament prophetism is to render him "one pagan mystery god among many."[53] Here Tillich clearly draws upon the analogy between gnosticism and Nazism, as he does elsewhere. However, he seems to suggest that ancient gnosticism was also plagued by religious nationalism, not just a dualistic cosmology that deprecated the material world as evil, and the Old Testament God as evil: "That is what the gnostic movement was about and what National Socialism was about, as well as all religious nationalism, which is by no means limited to Germany. In order to transform Jesus into a cult-god among others or a national leader and prophet, one must take him out of his connection with Old Testament prophetism, for that prophetism was always a continual struggle against the religious nationalisms of its time."[54] This is problematic from a historical point of view, since in the late second century and third century, when the ancient Marcionites and Gnostics appeared as opponents of emerging Catholic orthodoxy,[55] Christianity was a vulnerable minority religion within the Roman Empire. During that period, the later coalescing of church and state under Constantine and Theodosius was something scarcely imaginable.

Tillich concludes this lecture by echoing *The Socialist Decision* on the spirit of prophetic Judaism: "In the decision against National Socialism the church experiences again what it had experienced in the decision against Gnosticism in the third century: that the spirit of prophetic Judaism is the spirit alone which

---

is not lost and replaced by the conditioned validity of a contingent historical movement." ST II, 89–90. Also, in a discussion of early church authority, over against Gnosticism: "The problem which the Gnostics posed for the church was in the realm of authority, the question whether the Holy Scriptures were decisive as over against the secret teachings of the Gnostics. The gnostic teachers said that Jesus had passed on secret insights to them during the forty days after his resurrection when he was together with his disciples. These insights formed the content of gnostic theology and philosophy. Against this notion the anti-gnostic fathers had to establish a doctrine of Scripture....The Holy Scripture is given by the Logos through the divine Spirit. Therefore, it became necessary to fix the canon....Thus, the decision to fix the canon arose out the life-and-death struggle with gnosticism;" *History of Christian Thought*, 38.

52 *Judenfrage* lectures, 436.

53 Ibid. This is like the Aryan Jesus referred to in Chapter One above.

54 Ibid., 437.

55 A rich overview is provided by Jaroslav Pelikan, *The Christian Tradition: A History of the Development of Doctrine; The Emergence of the Catholic Tradition (100–600)*; Chicago: The University of Chicago Press, 1971; 72–97.

can guard the church from sinking back into a national religion, that is, to paganism."[56] For Tillich, the key aspect of paganism appears to be religious nationalism, although he acknowledges other factors.

4.4 Second Lecture: The Mirror of Jewish Prophetism

In the second lecture Tillich adds two qualitatively new dimensions to his analysis, a psychological and a sociological aspect. Tillich was surprised to learn that, even after the Holocaust, there remained among German Jewish émigrés a deep longing for the Germany that existed before the Nazis came to power, as he would have expected the opposite. Reflecting on the nineteenth century, he was compelled to conclude: "It is astonishing how quickly after Emancipation[57] Jews lent to German culture their creative powers and how there occurred, on the basis of a deep affinity, a fruitful reciprocal permeation. It is difficult to find an explanation for this without referring to similarities in the spiritual structure of both cultures."[58] As a result, Tillich devotes most of the lecture responding to the question, "Are there structural analogies between the Jewish and German character?" [59] He concludes that there are two, although there are important differences as well as similarities. Tillich observes that the structural similarities of the German and Jewish people, which I am designating "corporate personalities," have caused them to be in a peculiar relationship of attraction and repulsion, suggesting another form of dialectical relationship. Tillich tries to demonstrate that both Germans and Jews are affected by, or exhibit, these social-psychological features, to an equal degree, if not in an identical manner. The main limitation of Tillich's analysis is that the discussion is shaped more by what Tillich sees as deficiencies in the German corporate personality, than what can be empirically supported by examining Judaism, as it exists in its cultural, geographical and theological diversity. Nevertheless, there is considerable explanatory power.

---

56 *Judenfrage* lectures, 437.

57 Starting in the Kingdom of Prussia in 1812, with periodic progress and regress, until full emancipation in 1918. See decree by Emperor Frederick William III from March 11, 1812, in *The Jew in the Modern World: A Documentary History*, 2nd edn; ed. Paul Mendes-Flohr and Jehuda Reinharz (New York: Oxford University Press, 1995), 141 ff. However, Rosemary Radford Ruether observes, "All disabilities were not dropped in Germany until the Weimar Republic!" *Faith and Fratricide*, 214.

58 *Judenfrage* lectures, 439. Tillich means, implicitly, "German" and "Jewish" cultures.

59 Ibid. 438–439. The term "structural analogies" recurs in the occasional lectures referred to in Chapter Six below.

The lecture can be divided into three parts. The first two parts discuss the two structural analogies, and the third part discusses their social and political implications, with a particular focus on the development of anti-Semitism. The analysis of both structural analogies employs psychological categories. The discussion of the second structural analogy includes an excursus on German history which reflects back to the dictum from *The Socialist Decision*, "justice is the true power of being." In the third part, Tillich takes a sociological approach, in his discussion of anti-Judaism and anti-Semitism, concluding that Jewish prophetism serves as a critical "mirror" to hold against the German corporate personality. While Tillich believes that the two structural analogies are more decisive than the factors discussed in the third part,[60] the analogy of the mirror is yet another instance of the ongoing importance of the prophetic aspect of Judaism, and the inseparability of Judaism from (German) Christianity.

4.4.1 The First Structural Analogy: Space, Territorial Insecurity and Anxiety

The first structural analogy is the metaphysical problem of space. Both the Jews and the German people have experienced a prophetic-reform movement in their history – the Jews with the prophets culminating with the Babylonian exile, and Germany with the Protestant Reformation. For Tillich, they are similar insofar as both events ended periods of idolatry.[61] Both events caused a "break" in the history and national self-consciousness of each, and the fact that much later both in Germany, in the nineteenth century, and for the Jews in 1948, when political unity failed to heal that break.[62] For Germany, it created a "territorial insecurity," which sought relief in the deification of space and national self-realization. In this lecture, Tillich appears to assign a different function for the Protestant Ref-

60 "I believe, however, that the relation of both peoples to each other can be better understood through this analysis than from the causes of which I will next speak and, which though certainly effective, were perhaps not in the final analysis decisive" (ibid., 448).

61 A difficulty emerges here. While a common theological interpretation of the Babylonian Exile is that it was punishment for the idolatry of the Davidic kingship, the problem of religious nationalism does not have an exact parallel in pre-Reformation Germany. It is more complex to interpret the German Reformation as political liberation from the "bondage" to Roman Catholic dominance, as the Holy Roman Empire was an assemblage of Imperial cities and semi-autonomous political entities under an Emperor allied with Rome. One could argue that German unification in the 19th century laid the groundwork for Nazism in the 20th century, which Tillich in fact argues later on in these lectures.

62 Ibid., 440: "In both cases, the national self-actualization has never succeeded in healing the break."

ormation than in the first lecture, where it served to critique the paganism of the Roman Catholic sacrifice of the Mass. In this lecture, Tillich says the Reformation caused a delay in the emergence of German nationalism, which occurred in the nineteenth century: "The break which the Reformation brought to the German people created a territorial insecurity and the world-historical late arrival of the Germans to territorial self-actualization."[63] The idea of something "insecure" about the corporate German personality recurs in the second structural analogy below, in the discussion of self-hate and despair.

For the Jews, the similarity with the Germans is that they, since the Babylonian Exile, have remained the "people of time," in a prolonged *diaspora*. This theme of the Jews as the people of time was first introduced in Tillich's *Interpretation of History*, but became fully developed in *The Socialist Decision*, as discussed in Chapter Three. In the latter work, Jewish monotheism and prophetism serve to critique pagan polytheism and the idolatry of religious nationalism, which in Tillich's Weimar context were embodied in National Socialism. In this lecture, despite the discussion of space as a metaphysical problem, and consequently "time" as some kind of metaphysical solution, there is no discussion of justice, as an outgrowth of this analysis of space and time. In the next (third) lecture, Tillich will revisit the concept of justice, as part of a theological interpretation of history.

4.4.2 The Second Structural Analogy: The Psychic Split, Despair, Mutual Attraction and Repulsion

The second structural analogy is the "psychic split" between self-hate and self-aggrandizement, or an inflated sense of importance, which Tillich calls "over self-valuation," or "(false) vocation consciousness."[64] With respect to self-hate, Tillich says that Germans are ruthlessly critical of themselves and of their own people, well beyond a healthy, self-correcting criticism: "The great Germans who have exerted this critique have not done it in the hope to change the German character; rather, their critique had the character of despair."[65] Here Tillich does not say who the great Germans are, but further on he refers to Nietzsche and Goethe.[66] As for Jews, Tillich says that the Judaism of his time possessed a strong

---

63 Ibid.

64 Ibid., 440–442.

65 Ibid., 441.

66 "In Germany the great have always been lonely. The masses have never understood them as the expression of their own consciousness. Hence the despair of so many great Germans, as well

strain of anti-Semitism, "even with the most intelligently and analytically trained Jews," exemplified in Karl Marx's essay, "On the Jewish Question."[67]

German History, False Vocation-Consciousness, and the Split between Power and Being

For Tillich, the other pole of the psychic split is a sense of being set apart, a feeling of "vocation consciousness,"[68] something that all peoples have, but which is more pronounced in Germans and Jews.[69] Tillich's application of the idea of vocation-consciousness to Germans contains a brief but revealing historical analysis, which echoes his analysis of being, power and justice in *The Socialist Decision*, but with a different emphasis. According to Tillich, the history of Germany's vocation-consciousness has two periods, with the first period manifesting a genuine vocation-consciousness, and the second period devoid of it. The first period is the Middle Ages, when Germanic peoples maintained "the consciousness of being the national center of unified Christianity," under the German emperors.[70] Tillich does not develop this idea here, but in *History of Christian Thought*, he discusses how the German feudal kings were willing to submit to a council of bishops, in opposition to the centralized power of the Holy Roman Emperor, or in opposition to the Roman Pope.[71] For Tillich, this first phase was not characterized by German nationalism, and he does not condemn it for being nationalistic or pagan. As noted above, this provides a difficulty for Tillich's position

---

as the inclination of the great bearers of culture in Germany to seclude themselves and set themselves over against the average. I am thinking, for example, of all the German classicists, above all Goethe, of the revolutionary groups in the of middle of the nineteenth century, and of the despair of the prophetic spirits of the nineteenth century, for example, Nietzsche." Ibid., 446.

67 Ibid., 441.

68 Ibid., 442.

69 Ibid., 441–442.

70 Ibid., 443.

71 In the *History of Christian Thought* he acknowledges that Germanic political influence went through different phases, none of which approximated the nationalism of the Wilhelmine Reich of the nineteenth century. The first phase was during the late Roman Empire, during the time of Augustine, "when the Roman Empire, and later the Germanic-Romanic kingdoms, were realms of non-Christian power" (150). However, according to Tillich, during the Middle Ages the Germanic kings resisted the Catholic bishops' newly found political power, which ultimately led to the conflict between Pope Gregory VII and Emperor Henry IV (151). A third phase occurs later, in the time of William of Ockham, placing the Germanic kings on the side of "conciliarism," in which a council of bishops is the ultimate authority of the church, versus the authority the Pope and Holy Roman Emperor (153).

implied in the prior section, that the Protestant Reformation ended a period of idolatry rooted in German nationalism.

The second period is the modern period, during which Germany either manifested raw power, which was not informed by a true sense of calling, or the opposite problem of having a sense of being set apart, but lacking power. Tillich first alludes to the Second Reich, beginning under Bismarck in the late nineteenth century, and ending under Kaiser Wilhelm II at the end of World War I, a period dominated by "Realpolitik," which exposed the ugliness and brutality of nationalistic power-politics.[72] Tillich believes this was one of the causes of World War I. This was followed by the political "vacuum" of the Weimar Republic, which Tillich previously criticized in the 1920s and 1930s as ambivalent and powerless. The failure of both regimes was the inability to manifest both power and vocation-consciousness at the same time:

> When power and vocation-consciousness are combined, power ceases to be brutal power. There exists a unity which goes back to the deepest roots of Being, to the unity of Being and value in the Ground of Being itself. Where this unity is lost, there occurs on the one hand self-contempt and on the other, the brutal, unideological Will-to-Power.[73]

Where the unity of being and power is lost, the result is either self-contempt, as described above, or brutality.[74]

Tillich's normative position, in which there is a "unity of Being and value," is reminiscent of the dialectical balance that he sought in his maxim, "justice is the true power of being," which was prominently displayed in *The Socialist Decision.* Tillich's concept of justice from the Weimar period, in which the "ought" of equality is derived from the "is" of being, drew upon certain elements of the collective unconscious as it unfolded in the history of religion, especially in the Jewish people of the ancient Near East. In the third lecture, discussed below, Tillich links this concept of justice to a deeper, overtly theological understanding of reality. This unity of being and value represents a dialectical balance, and is an instance of the ontological dialectic of balance.

Above I observed that Tillich's analysis of these "corporate types," of Germans and Jews, is influenced more by the psychological and sociological peculiarities of Weimar and Nazi Germany, and less so by what could have been empirically determined by analyzing real communities of Jews. This is evident in the

72 *Judenfrage* lectures, 443.

73 Ibid.

74 Tillich discusses the concept of "vocational consciousness" in *Love, Power and Justice*, in a similar fashion (102–104).

imbalance that Tillich employs in this phase of his analysis. Tillich has a lot to say about Germans and despair. He says this is rooted in their "yearning for the foreign," in which Germans willingly forfeit their identity when they encounter what they perceive to be a superior culture, whether it is ancient Greece, or Renaissance Italy, or even other modern European cultures.[75] For Tillich, this is the manifestation of "a secret wish of the Germans to negate themselves as Germans."[76] In addition, Tillich's use of corporate types as analytical categories is similar to his use of types elsewhere in this book.

The Inner Split and Despair

In an attempt to underscore the comparison between Germans and Jews, Tillich proceeds to claim that Jews also manifest a kind of self-negation, in particular their ability to adapt to any situation.[77] He does not elaborate, but he probably means that Jews can be found around the world, in many cultures, in *diaspora*. However, instead of praising Jews for their resilience, he argues that "the deepest root of this adaptability is a lack of self-affirmation."[78] Tillich gives several examples, the most important and most convincing of which are Christian theologians of Jewish origin. According to Tillich, they are more critical of Judaism than any Christian would be:

> After their conversion to Christianity, they are more radical in their critique of Judaism than any Christian theologian. They negate that from which they came. Often they are of the greatest value for Christian theologians, because they see things which the theologian who was born as a Christian does not see. They, themselves, however, are in a bind: they must repress something in themselves and become for that reason fanatical. Here too we find analogies between Jewish and German existence. In both cases, self-negation searches for ways to realize itself.[79]

---

75 "Despair is the expression of an insurmountable split. Out of this despair comes the wish to be rid of oneself. One of the most harmless and most curious forms of this wish to be rid of oneself is the yearning for the foreign. This we find in Germans more than any other well-known people. We all know of the yearning of Germans in the classical period for Greece, of the always alive yearning for Italy, the wish to do the same as the French or English, and the hope for Russia and Asia. As soon as the yearning is fulfilled and the German settles with one of these peoples, he blends in with them more quickly than would a representative of any other people" (ibid., 444).
76 Ibid.
77 Ibid., 445.
78 Ibid.
79 Ibid.

Tillich may be remiss in not acknowledging the resiliency of Jews worldwide. But he is correct about the hyper-critical posture of Jewish converts to Christianity that become theologians. More than one convert became an aggressive interlocutor in high profile disputations between Christians and Jews in the Middle Ages, and Reformation, such as Nicholas Donin, Pablo Christiani, Hieronymus Santa Fe and Anthonius Margaritha.[80]

Tillich concludes this section by observing that this "prophetic break," which both peoples have experienced in their collective, ethnic, and national self-actualization, has not only psychological consequences, which have just been discussed, but sociological consequences, to be discussed below. According to Tillich, Germans and Jews are unique because they have experienced this prophetic break. For those national groups that have not experienced it, their leaders come from "the substance of the people."[81] The sociological consequences derive from a "gap" between great individuals and the ordinary masses. Tillich observes, "In Germany the great have always been lonely," as "the masses have never understood them as the expression of their own consciousness."[82] For Tillich, this gap between the great and the masses causes the masses to remain "unformed," making them vulnerable to other influences, especially Nazism.[83] For Tillich, the Jewish people express something similar, in the pro-

80 In the Middle Ages it was not uncommon for Christians to have Jewish converts serve as interlocutors in theological disputations with Jews. Three prominent examples are Nicholas Donin at the Paris Disputation of 1240, Pablo Christiani at the Barcelona Disputation of 1263, and Hieronymus de Santa Fe at the Tortosa Disputation of 1413–1414. The literature on this is vast, but a useful introduction is Hyam Maccoby's *Judaism on Trial: Jewish–Christian Disputations in the Middle Ages* (London: Littman Library of Jewish Civilization, 1996). Another example, from the Reformation period in Germany, is Anthonius Margaritha's *The Entire Jewish Faith* of 1530. According to R. Pochia Hsia, this work, written by the son of Rabbi Jacob Margolis of Regensburg (who was consulted by the German humanist Johannes Reuchlin concerning the *Kabbalah*), became an "encyclopedia of Judaism" for Germans of the early sixteenth century, and it intended to "expose" the "false beliefs" of the Jews. See Hsia's *The Myth of Ritual Murder: Jews and Magic in Reformation Germany* (New Haven, CT: Yale University Press, 1988), 148–151.

81 *Judenfrage* lectures, 446.

82 Ibid. Tillich elaborates: "Hence the despair of so many great Germans, as well as the inclination of the great bearers of culture in Germany to seclude themselves and set themselves over against the average. I am thinking, for example, of all the German classicists, above all of Goethe, of the revolutionary groups of the middle of the nineteenth century, and of the despair of the prophetic spirits of the nineteenth century, for example, Nietzsche. If, however, the leading individuals are not symbolic for what is happening in the masses, and if they do not represent what the unconscious wishes of the average people, then the masses themselves remain unformed."

83 Tillich comments on other European cultures, such as the "gentleman-ideal" in England, the "citizen-ideal" in France, and the ideal of human rights in America. In Germany, there were sev-

phetic personality, which is "the individual carrier of the prophetic spirit and of the highest cultural form."[84] Similar to what Tillich argued in *The Socialist Decision*, the prophetic spirit is that which seeks to promote justice, especially the equality of persons. According to Tillich, "the average Jew" never measures up to the prophetic ideal, and in fact, "The entire history of the Jewish people shows that it is impossible to make a whole people serve the ideal of the prophetic message."[85] Tillich concludes this presentation of the two structural analogies between the German and Jewish corporate personalities, by asserting that Germans and Jews "lead to both the strongest attraction and the strongest repulsion [between the two peoples]."[86]

4.4.3 Typological Thinking, Objectification, Dehumanization and the "Mirror"

In the final section of the second lecture, despite the fact that Tillich believes it is of lesser importance, he discusses how religious (theological) anti-Judaism causes political anti-Judaism, with the latter laying the foundation for political anti-Semitism. Tillich discussed the factors causing religious anti-Judaism in the first lecture (the New Testament, patristic and medieval background), and here he deepens his historical analysis by introducing a distinction between "diversionary" anti-Judaism and "systematic" anti-Semitism. Diversionary anti-Judaism was practiced throughout pre-modern Europe, which was expressed in periodic, opportunistic persecutions of Jews, "to divert criticism from the ruling classes onto a minority."[87]

Systematic anti-Semitism is a later development, based upon two fundamental factors. The first factor is the creation of stereotypes, which have an illogical and a pseudo-scientific basis. By the nineteenth century, Tillich observes that pseudo-scientific theories of biology and race came together, which were used in a "dilettantish and distorted way for political ends," by totalitarian dictatorships, which were needed to create an "absolute enemy."[88] For Tillich, the creation of "stereotypes" assigned guilt to a group because of its very identity, with

eral relationship types, including the "bureaucrat-ideal," the "officer-ideal," but they each failed to bridge the gap the between the leaders and the masses, and to express the consciousness of the masses. Ibid., 446–447.

84 Ibid., 448.

85 Ibid.

86 Ibid.

87 Ibid., 450.

88 Ibid.

absolutely no assessment of personal responsibility of any kind.[89] For Tillich, this phenomenon is a logical absurdity, and it demonstrates the abandonment of "universal reason," and the related predilection to objectify and dehumanize persons, a hallmark of modern industrial society:

> In the Middle Ages, one accused a collective which existed as such, the Ghetto, in most cases unjustly, but yet still with a semblance of reason. Today one accuses a type, not a collective or an individual. This is connected with the naturalistic dehumanization of persons and with the progressive objectification of the personal in industrial society.[90]

In the above passage, Tillich picks up a thread from *The Religious Situation* and *The Socialist Decision*, the reductionist anthropology implicit in modern capitalist society. For Tillich, the problem has not gone away, since he originally diagnosed it in the 1920s and 1930s. Therefore, he deepens his analysis with psychological and sociological considerations. The addition of psychological and sociological analyses is Tillich's way of acknowledging the depth and complexity of the problem of anti-Semitism.

According to Tillich, anti-Semitic stereotyping received additional legitimacy from its appeal to pseudo-science, especially by appealing to a form of biological determinism. Tillich observes that anti-Semites persist in the dogma that " 'the Jew' is a type," despite the evidence provided by depth psychology that acquired characteristics are not inherited, but are the result of specific sociological conditions.[91] This effectively dehumanizes Jews: "A type stands against history, nature, and personality; the inherited stands against the acquired. But when type is given priority over history, the human being is no longer valued as a human being."[92]

---

89 Ibid., 451.

90 Tillich continues to describe the "exterminationist logic" (my phrase) of stereotyping: "The absurdity of the whole thing becomes especially clear when an antisemite meets an actual Jew. The actual Jew is always viewed as the exception to the rule. In the encounter with the real Jew, the stereotype breaks down, since it cannot be verified. The antisemite, however, wants it to be true, and therefore views the individual Jew as the exception. This typological thinking is unhistorical, for it does not recognize that personalities are subject to historical transformation. Typological thinking cannot believe that the type which it attacks can change; therefore it must be exterminated" (ibid., 451–452). However, despite a certain a-historical character, Jewish prophetism is not a stereotype. In addition, this "typological thinking" seems to have no relation to the "types" referred to by Stone, who believed that Tillich borrowed this concept from Max Weber, as discussed in Chapter Three above.

91 Ibid., 452.

92 Ibid.

Tillich concludes the third part of this lecture by circling back to psychological categories, particularly the concept of "anxiety," as manifested by Germans. According to Tillich, anti-Semites create anxiety by appealing to the concept of "the unwelcome alien," meaning something that cannot be incorporated into the whole.[93] Tillich extends this reasoning to the phenomenon of German anxiety over "the alien" and the phenomenon of anti-Semitism. Germans are attracted to the external alien, but threatened by the internal alien, in this case the Jews:

> We have seen that the Germans like that which is alien, in part because they want to get rid of themselves and lose themselves in the alien. But the alien which they have among them they cannot tolerate because it wrenches them from the certainty of their self-affirmation and because this self-affirmation is so weak that it cannot bring anything alien into itself. From this comes a feeling of anxiety ... Perhaps one can say: for the German self-consciousness, the Jew is too close to be considered a welcome alien and not close enough to be experienced as one of their own.[94]

Tillich ends the lecture by observing that anti-Semitism, as a social psychological phenomenon, is an expression of the German corporate personality's self-loathing. In developing this, Tillich introduces the image of the mirror:

> antisemitism creates in ideality and reality that against which it fights. Indeed, it must create it, since it cannot find it in reality. The antisemite ... is terrified by the mirror which the Jew holds before him. There are moments – when we look at ourselves in the mirror – in which we have a dislike, indeed a loathing, of ourselves. The mirror tells what we are for others who look at us. In many remarks of the Jewish bearers of culture there is something which for Germans is a mirror.[95] The German knows that the mirror says the truth, but cannot bear the image, and therefore reacts against those who hold it before him.[96]

Tillich says that the particular kind of mirror that Judaism holds up to the German people is the prophetic tradition,[97] something that he initially developed twenty years ago in *The Socialist Decision*, which serves as a segue into the theological discussion in the third lecture.

93 Tillich says that there are welcome and unwelcome aliens. Ibid., 453.
94 Ibid.
95 Marion Pauck translates this sentence as: "In many utterances of cultured Jews, there is something that the Germans regard as a 'mirror'. " *Die Judenfrage – ein christliches und ein deutsches Problem*, by Paul Tillich, trans. Marion Pauck, *BNAPTS* 30/3 (Summer 2004): 14.
96 *Judenfrage* lectures, 454.
97 Ibid.

4.5 Third Lecture: The Dialectic of the Holy and Judaism as a Perpetual "Thorn in the Flesh"[98]

Tillich's argument climaxes in the third lecture. All of the categories that have emerged concerning Judaism, theological anti-Judaism, and anti-Semitism are found here, in their most mature form.[99] In this brief lecture, Tillich analyzes the Jewish question from a theological standpoint. For Tillich, it is ultimately "a religious (i.e. theological) problem," since the "prophetic break" in the histories of both Jews and Germans necessarily leads beyond sociological and social-psychological analyses, into a theological analysis.[100] This logical move is not entirely clear. Yet, it seems that the "prophetic break" can only be explained by "the new," which was first understood by Tillich in relation to the Exile, one of the pivotal theological concepts for Tillich's appropriation of the history of religion. In *The Socialist Decision*, this was expressed as eschatological expectation.[101] After raising the issue of the prophetic break, Tillich initiates his analysis by asking the question, "why could there be such a history?," questioning how the theological problem arose in the first place.[102]

---

98 The image of "thorn in the flesh" recurs in a fundamentally methodological comment in the Introduction to ST I: "The perennial question has been: Can the Christian message be adapted to the modern mind without losing its essential and unique character? Most theologians have believed that it is possible; some have deemed it impossible either in the name of the Christian message or in the name of the modern mind. No doubt the voices of those who have emphasized the contrast, the *diastasis*, have been have been louder and more impressive – men usually are more powerful in their negations than in their affirmations. But the continuous toil of those who have tried to find a union, a 'synthesis,' has kept theology alive. Without them traditional Christianity would have become narrow and superstitious, and the general cultural movement would have proceeded without the 'thorn in the flesh' which it needed, namely, an honest theology of cultural high standing;" *ST I*, 7.

99 An exception is Tillich's view of Zionism, which is treated in his 1959 address: "My Changing Thoughts on Zionism," unpublished manuscript of an address given to a Christian-Jewish Colloquy on "Israel's Rebirth in the Middle East," Chicago IL, January 21, 1959. In GW XIII, 403–408, and Harvard Tillich Archive, bMS 649/45 (4).

100 *Judenfrage* lectures, 455.

101 In particular, Tillich, *Socialist Decision*, 102–105, "Elements of the Socialist Principle" and "Expectation and Action."

102 Tillich asks two related questions: "For though it is possible to apply all the well-known sociological categories to the history of the Jewish people, after this history is given, a more deeply penetrating discussion of the question 'why could there be such a history?,' is still needed. Surely a group such as the Jews – once they are there and have survived through a 3,000 year history – can be used as a mechanism of diversion. Judaism can be typologically caricatured, and psychological conflicts can originate within it. But the decisive question is: how does it come about that such a group is there? We have spoken of Christian anti-Judaism

4.5.1 "The Holy" as the Foundation of Reality

Tillich begins his answer by positing "the Holy" as the starting point for any theological analysis. Echoing Rudolf Otto, Tillich introduced his idea of the Holy in a major work in the first volume of the *Systematic Theology*, in 1951, a year before the *Judenfrage* lectures were delivered.[103] In the *Judenfrage* lectures, the Holy is something that "concerns us unconditionally," which possesses "the ground and meaning of our Being," is not limited by time or space, has an irresistible quality, and presents to us "an unconditional demand," similar to what was described in Chapter Three.[104] In addition, the Holy has two sides, or poles, which exist in perpetual tension, the priestly and the prophetic, a clear instance of the ontological dialectic of balance. The priestly side manifests "that which is, that which is present, as what grasps us, as what precedes all acting and thinking."[105] The prophetic side is never completed, always demands, requires perfection and promises fulfillment.[106] These poles are similar to what was discussed in Chapter Three, in the analysis of the dictum, "justice is the true power of being."[107] According to Tillich, the tension between the two poles is the framework that undergirds all of reality:

> The Holy contains within itself the tension between that which is and that which should be, a tension which reaches to the deepest roots of being. This tension of both elements in the Holy has a polar character. One pole conditions the other. As soon as this reciprocal dependence is called into question conflicts originate ... The "is" and the "ought" struggle with each other. To be sure, this struggle can never lead to a total separation, since the sphere of the Holy would itself cease to be if one of the poles would completely disappear.[108]

Tillich completes this subsection by underscoring that if the priestly dimension obscures the prophetic, then the sacramental becomes magic, and if the prophet-

---

which runs from the New Testament through all of Church history. But there is no satisfactory explanation for this fundamental fact. Christianity also fought against other minorities. In no case, however, did something originate which would be at all comparable to Christian anti-Judaism." *Judenfrage* lectures, 455–456.

103 *ST* I, 215–218, 271–272. The *Systematic Theology* will be discussed in Chapter Five.

104 *Judenfrage* lectures, 456. This language is used elsewhere by Tillich to characterize God, as in *ST* I, 155–157.

105 *Judenfrage* lectures, 456. In terms of the "is–ought" polarity, this can be assigned to the "is."

106 *Judenfrage* lectures, 457. In terms of the "is–ought" polarity, this can be assigned to the "ought."

107 See Chapter Three, 93–95.

108 *Judenfrage* lectures, 457.

ic dimension obscures the priestly, then legalism results.[109] For the Holy to be present, neither pole is obliterated. Therefore, only if both poles are in some way effective is the Holy real.[110] For Tillich, this polarity fundamentally characterizes the optimal relationship between Judaism and Christianity, and the relationship of both to Germany.[111]

4.5.2 The Continuity of Priestly and Prophetic through the Covenant

Prior to Tillich's application of his metaphysical framework to the patterns of Abraham and Amos, he engages in a deeper analysis of the ontological polarities of priestly/prophetic and space/time, in order to show how they can be applicable to the historical phenomenon of the church. For Tillich, the priestly dimension of the Holy is "sacramental," in the sense of being "consecrated," referring to that which "concerns us unconditionally."[112] The latter phrase is characteristic of Tillich's expression of the human relation to the divine. In language reminiscent of *The Socialist Decision*, for Tillich, the priestly side of the Holy has three main features: (i) it is the generative aspect of reality, as "the mother precedes the child,"[113] (ii) it is dependent upon tradition and authority;[114] and (iii) it exhibits a hierarchical structure, and therefore levels of authority.[115] For Tillich, the perfect concrete illustration of such a sacramental system is the Roman Catholic church, although he underscores that such a system does not lack the prophetic 'demand', which is mediated through the hierarchy, from within.[116]

109 Ibid.

110 Ibid., 457 – 458.

111 Ibid., 458.

112 Ibid., 458 – 459.

113 Ibid., 458. The matriarchal analogy is also cited in *Socialist Decision*, 15, and in the 1910 Dissertation, 81 – 82.

114 "The sacramental type of religion is dependent upon tradition, through which the *material substance* is passed on from generation to generation. One is born into this tradition, into this *substance*, and the priestly bearers of this tradition are the mediators of the Holy for everyone who belongs to this tradition. This gives authority to the bearers of *substance* of such a religious group. Priestly authority is the authority of those in whom the Holy is at the same time *substantially* embodied" (*Judenfrage* lectures, 459; emphases mine).

115 "There are levels of authority in the Holy; the bearers of religious authority are hierarchically organized. There are levels of holiness: the sacramental power of the higher levels is greater than the lower, quite apart from the personal quality of the bearer" (ibid.).

116 "But in the sacramental system the demand moves within the system. It can never be directed against the system as such" (ibid.).

The prophetic pole issues the "demand" from outside the system, but an important element of continuity remains, as the prophet criticizes the system, but *in the name of the system itself:* "The prophet does not criticize from the outside as the enlightener, but rather from within as the representative of the will of God against the fixed priestly sacramental system."[117] The essence of the prophetic critique is objecting to what conflicts with the unconditional demand, when that is done in the name of the Holy.[118] Using the language of "substance" emphasized above, the prophetic seeks to establish a "reformed sacramental piety:"

> It does not belong to the essence of prophetism to negate priestly piety. For indeed the prophet comes out of the sacramental substance of the church, and from the prophetic message, if it is successful, follows a reformed sacramental piety.[119]

If the sacramental elevates itself to an absolute and therefore idolatrous status, then it can be negated by the prophet.[120] Otherwise, there is an essential continuity between the priestly and the prophetic, and this is due to God's covenantal relationship with humanity:

> The prophet criticizes all who want to hide themselves behind the sacramental taboo. And yet even here the presence of the Holy is not obliterated. The prophet raises his or her demand not on the basis of an abstract moral law, but rather on the basis of the covenant which God made with his people or on the basis of the events on which the church is founded.[121]

As will be shown below, this aspect of the covenantal relationship between God and humanity is what enabled the Jews to survive the Exile, and to remain the people of God. The idea of covenant is a new addition to Tillich's understanding of the Exile.[122]

---

117 Ibid., 460.
118 Ibid.
119 Ibid.
120 Ibid., 461.
121 Ibid.
122 In the 1910 Dissertation there is no discussion of the Exile and no discussion of the Old Testament prophets warning of Israel's destruction. Prophetism is a transitional period from the particularity of Israel to the universality of revelation. Also in the 1910 Dissertation, particularity and universality are not assigned any political implications. In *The Socialist Decision*, Tillich's interpretation of the Exile dominates his understanding of prophetism, because it provides the basis for something truly "new," generated from "the origin." Here he is thinking of a new social order built upon religious humanistic principles, with an eschatological posture. While something is destroyed something new appears, as God's people are subject to the "uncondi-

4.5.3 Sacramental Space: Polytheism, Imperialism and Sacral Injustice

According to Tillich, each polar dimension of the Holy, the priestly and the prophetic, is uniquely related to space and time.[123] In a section linking the discussion of the priestly and prophetic to the covenant, and the discussions of Abraham and Amos, is a discussion of polytheism and sacral injustice. Tillich initially draws upon what he said about polytheism in *The Socialist Decision*,[124] that each localized deity possesses a universalizing impulse, which inevitably causes conflict. Tillich elaborates on this considerably, noting that such a "political imperialism" has three additional features, including: (i) the paradoxical combination of absolute power and the limits of a particular geographic space; (ii) the passion and impetus behind will-to-power; and (iii) the "full weight of economic interests."[125] However, such a drive for absolute power by the different gods results in earthly conflict: "From this structure results the conflicts of the gods and with it the conflicts of the empires and their mutual destruction."[126] In addition, this drive for absolute power, combined with divine sanction, is the basis for all social and political injustice:

> From this primeval polytheistic conflict comes the justification of social and political injustice. Sacral injustice is the background of all other injustice, for it provides injustice with a religious consecration. This holds as well for oppression of one nation or race by another, which places itself at the top of the polytheistic world-order. That is the world against which the prophets had to fight and against which the prophetic spirit in all ages must fight.[127]

Any idolatry tied to space, as expressed in the spirit of polytheism, can be fully offset by the monotheism and prophetism of Abraham and Amos, to be discussed below.

4.5.4 Prophetic Time: Abraham and the Pattern of Exodus, Exile and Diaspora

Thus far, Tillich has developed the metaphysical foundations for his theological interpretation of history, which are indispensible for understanding the phenomenon

tional demand." Also in *The Socialist Decision*, Tillich's view of Jewish prophetism acknowledges the potential problem of Jewish religious nationalism (22–23).

123 *Judenfrage* lectures, 461

124 Tillich, *Socialist Decision*, 18–20.

125 *Judenfrage* lectures, 463.

126 Ibid.

127 Ibid., 464.

of theological anti-Judaism, and the later permutations of political and racial/scientific anti-Semitism. In addition, these metaphysical foundations are illustrated by Tillich's use of two biblical characters, the patriarch Abraham and the prophet Amos. Up until this point in Tillich's career, 1952, Tillich has had very little to say about Abraham. In the 1910 Dissertation, Tillich interprets God's command for Abraham to sacrifice Isaac as the paradigm for pagan substance and revelational form, with pagan substance referring to the practice of human sacrifice, and revelational form referring to the personal God, Jehovah. However, there is no other mention of Abraham, nor a discussion of the metaphysical problem of space. In addition, with the exception of two references in *The Systematic Theology*, one of which will be discussed in Chapter Five below,[128] Abraham is not mentioned in the other major works that are discussed here.

Tillich elaborates upon the prophetic dimension of the Holy ("Ought"), and observes that the future is the decisive mode of apprehending time.[129] This recalls the importance of maintaining an eschatological orientation, as discussed in *The Socialist Decision*. Tillich makes three theological observations about Abraham. First, his call by God is the foundational example of breaking away from the limitations of space, and moving towards a new kind of space, the undetermined "space of the future:" "There is no story more characteristic of this situation than the story of the call of Abraham. Here is found, in classical symbols, all that we have said about the struggle between time and space. Abraham was called out of the space-boundedness in which he stood, out of the social, cultural, and religious conditions which gave him his existence."[130] Second, the experience which Abraham's call symbolizes has been repeated in Israel's history, in the pattern of Exodus, Exile and *diaspora*, resulting in a perpetual inhabitation of "an insecure guest-space," which can be taken away at any time.[131] According to Tillich, this means the Jewish people were transformed from "being bound to space to being imprisoned in time."[132]

Third, this spatial insecurity and transience has a threefold consequence. The first two are based on Abraham's example, and the third is based on the ex-

128 In *ST* III, 310, "The Bearers of History," Tillich discusses the concept of vocation-consciousness, which clearly corresponds to the idea of vocation-consciousness discussed above. The other reference to Abraham is incidental, occurring in *ST* II, 159.

129 *Judenfrage* lectures, 464.

130 Ibid., 464–465. "He was called from space into time ... This does not mean that space as space is negated. Indeed he is supposed to go to the land which God will show him. But this space of the future is left undetermined. It is a space of the future, and the future is the mode of time, its decisive mode." For Tillich, the future is the mode of decision (465).

131 Ibid., 465.

132 Ibid., 465–466.

ample of Amos, to be discussed after Abraham. The first consequence is that true history is linear, and non-repeatable, meaning that the future is always "open," the realm of "the new."[133] Just as Tillich previously made reference to a new kind of space, a space of the future, here he refers to a new sense of time, historical time versus physical time. Whereas physical time is mere chronology, historical time is imbued with theological meaning.

> Therefore history is always the history of the struggle against the demands of the gods of space, and the people who represent time against space are necessarily the enemy of all space-bound nationalisms and imperialism. There was already a Roman anti-Judaism before there was a Christian anti-Judaism.[134]

Three observations can me made here. First, this understanding of history as the vehicle for "the new," as opposed to mere chronology, was clearly seen in Tillich's discussion of Judaism "breaking" the myth of origin, found in *The Socialist Decision*, and discussed in Chapter Three. This distinction between chronology and a theological interpretation of time is also a major theme of Tillich's *Interpretation of History.* Second, the comment about Roman anti-Judaism points to another of Tillich's distinctions, between "monotheism" and "polytheism." This is the second consequence of the transformation of the Jewish people from space bound to time bound. Third, given Tillich's distinction of polytheism and monotheism, and the metaphysical importance of space and time for each, anti-Judaism is perennial problem. This is because the temptation to deify space, in the form of religious nationalism, is a perennial problem.

Contrary to what might be implied from this analysis thus far, that anti-Judaism is unique to Christian antiquity, Tillich observes that Roman anti-Judaism existed first. According to Tillich, the Roman empire permitted the worship of many gods, including gods deriving from conquered lands of the empire, but insisted that those gods be subordinated to the supreme god of the empire, the emperor. Since the Jews refused to worship the emperor, they were deemed to be politically subversive:

> In the Roman pantheon the gods of all spaces were gathered together but subordinated to the god of Roman space. And the Romans felt that the Jews attacked the space of the em-

---

133 "History goes toward something, something undetermined, something new, something other than that which one comes. History does not repeat itself. In it the new is created. Therefore historical time is not reversible. Physical time is reversible, but not historical time" (ibid., 466). This is in direct contrast to the pagan eternal cycle of birth, growth, development and death, characteristic of paganism.

134 Ibid.

> pire through the God of time, whom they served. The imperial space was not for the Jews the ultimate and unconditional that it was for the Romans and what they required it to be for their subject peoples.[135]

This observation about pagan imperial Rome carries a different emphasis from the concept of "mythical-political imperialism," first discussed in *The Socialist Decision*. The latter posits that polytheistic cultures inevitably experience conflict because the individual gods each have a universalizing impulse, discussed above in Chapter Three.[136] Here Tillich says that polytheism ultimately means subjection to the gods of space, and monotheism ultimately means subjection the gods of time. Therefore, an ostensibly monotheistic religion can assume a polytheistic posture:

> Rather, polytheism is subjection to gods of space, and monotheism is subjection to the God of time. As long as the Jewish God stands against other national gods as a Jewish national god, he is a space-bound polytheistic god as all the others, even if it is only one. Only when the narrow association of Yahweh to his people was cut through by prophetic critique, did the God of Israel become the God of monotheism. He became the God of monotheism when he became the God of time.[137]

4.5.5 Amos: The Exile and the Preservation of the Covenant

The third consequence of spatial insecurity and transience is that it provides a basis for universality, which is an essential feature of justice, over against cultural and ethnic particularity. Whereas for Tillich nationalistic religion was "space bound" because of its national or ethnic exclusivity, to be free of those limitations was to be "time bound," and universal. For Tillich, national or ethnic boundaries prevented the establishment of justice. Contrariwise, he claims, "The universality of the God of time is the universality of the God of justice."[138]

Whereas the figure of Abraham symbolized for Tillich the virtue of breaking away from space bound idolatry, Amos underscores the importance of the Exile, and the possibility of a remnant of God's people enduring the loss of their sacred space. For Tillich, Amos was important in five ways: (i) he was the first prophet to warn Israel of its destruction for breaking "the covenant," presumably the Mosaic law, which was the basis for divine justice; (ii) this forced a break between

---

135 Ibid.

136 Chapter Three, 37. Mythical-political imperialism is discussed in Tillich, *Socialist Decision*, 19.

137 *Judenfrage* lectures, 467.

138 Ibid.

the divine and a national/ethnic boundary, which had devolved into the idolatry of space; (iii) the priestly cult was deprived of any automatic, unquestioned revelatory power, with the office of the prophet becoming the vehicle for God's revelation, another expression of the shift of revelatory capacity from space to time; (iv) the shift from space to time was an expression of true monotheism, described above as subjection to the God of time; and (v) the destruction of God's people was not a nullification of the covenant, because a righteous remnant was preserved as a testimony to God's faithfulness.

> It was one of the greatest moments in the history of humanity when Amos, the first of the great prophets, threatened Israel with destruction and severed the connection between God and the space with which he was associated ... The God of whom Amos speaks declares that every summons to election and priestly cult is in vain when justice is destroyed. The message of Amos, which was taken up by all the prophets, was the hour of the birth of genuine monotheism ... The God of monotheism stands against every sacrally consecrated injustice. He negates all sacrally grounded privileges; he places the bearers of the Holy under the "ought," under judgment and under the promise which reaches into the future. He is the God of history and time.[139]

According to Tillich, the history of Judaism illustrates a balance of the two poles of space and time, the dialectic of the Holy, as the proper basis to convey revelation:

> On the one side stands the closing of the covenant, the election of Israel, the presence of God in Israel, the gift of the Law, and the intimate connection between land and people. On the other side stands the breaking of the covenant by Israel, the split between God and the people, the judgment and the rejection. There is always a remnant which remains obedient to the God of time and carries forth the function of Israel to be the people of time. For this reason, Judaism remains for all time a thorn in the flesh of all deification of space, all nationalism, and all imperialism.[140]

Two important themes are present in this passage. First, it illustrates the ontological dialectic of balance between space and time as constitutive of the Holy. Second, the image of Judaism enduring as a perpetual "thorn in the flesh," against all space-bound idolatry, underscores the permanent theological importance of Judaism for Tillich.

---

139 Ibid., 467–468.
140 Ibid., 468.

4.5.6 The Cross and the Prophetic Spirit in Christianity

Tillich completes this lecture by applying his dialectical analysis of the Holy to Christianity. He makes three points about Christianity: (i) the Cross critiques all absolutes and idolatry; (ii) Christianity exists not only within a tension between the sacramental and priestly, like Judaism, it also exists in tension between the "already" and the "not yet;" and (iii) the history of Christianity yields repeated examples of prophetic reactions against sacramental hierarchy. First, Tillich begins by observing that Christianity had a prophetic origin in John the Baptist, and that early Christians sought universality and justice by transcending the ethnic and national boundaries of Judaism.[141] However, Tillich warns that the belief that the Messiah had already come could lead to a new idolatry of space.[142] Second, Tillich counters by asserting that the Cross should be the permanent critique for Christians against all space-bound idolatry, occupying the optimal relation between space and time, priestly and prophetic expressions: "Neither the mountain of Sinai or Zion but Golgotha is the middle space for Christian thinking. What happened on this mountain around the year 30 … determined the whole future. In this event the Holy has appeared, achieving presence and sacramental reality."[143]

Third, Tillich's interpretation of the history of Christianity hinges on the prophetic critique of idolatrous sacramental tendencies. He begins with a general observation that the prophetic often emerged within sects, were often persecuted by the existing churches and the state, but ultimately expressed what the prophets had begun: "they kept the Holy as a living demand and directed the new toward the future."[144] For Tillich, the Protestant Reformation is the model for prophetic critique within Christianity, and this provides the inspiration for Tillich's "Protestant principle," which was introduced in Chapter One as one of Tillich's key organizing principles. For Tillich, the Protestant principle, like the Cross, calls every absolute into question, and bears a resemblance to prophetic Judaism:[145]

---

141 Ibid., 468–469.

142 Ibid., 469. There are some supersessionist aspects of Tillich's theology, which will be discussed in Chapter Seven. However, this point anticipates one of Rosemary Radford Ruether's criticisms of Christian theology, the assumption of "realized eschatology," that the Messiah had come, with all of that which is entailed by that.

143 Ibid.

144 Ibid., 471.

145 Earley points out that Jewish prophetism and the Protestant principle are effectively the same thing, as discussed in Chapter One above.

> The Protestant principle is the prophetic principle, namely, the negation of every attempt of something infinite to take God's place through sacramental consecration ... .Thus there exists a close relationship between Protestantism and Judaism. Luther believed, therefore, that it was possible, on the basis of the community of the prophetic protest, to take Judaism into the Protestant movement. Thus he was deeply disappointed when this did not happen.[146]

For Tillich, the prophetic spirit could exist within ostensibly secular movements, as long as the target of critique was some form of absolutism and idolatry.[147] Specifically, this includes the Enlightenment critique of the tyranny of the churches, the eighteenth-century bourgeois revolution, and the anti-bourgeois revolutions of the nineteenth and twentieth centuries, which all had their inspiration in the Protestant Reformation, which ultimately had its roots in Jewish prophetism.[148]

Tillich concludes this lecture by claiming that the dialectical relationship of the priestly and sacramental is fundamental to the diagnosis and solution to the Jewish problem.[149] He further argues that this dialectical relationship provides an appropriate framework to understand the related problems of Zionism, Judaism and national self-actualization, the relationship of Judaism to Christianity, and the ongoing importance of Judaism as a critical, prophetic force: "Its function is to keep awake the spirit of prophetism, against itself, against national

---

146 *Judenfrage* lectures, 471–472. According to Tillich, "The Protestant principle (which is a manifestation of the prophetic Spirit) is not restricted to the churches of the Reformation or to any other church; it transcends every particular church, being an expression of the Spiritual Community. It has been betrayed by every church, including the churches of the Reformation, but it is also effective in every church as the power which prevents profanization and demonization from destroying the Christian churches completely. It alone is not enough; it needs the 'Catholic substance' " (*ST* III, 245). Catholic Substance is the dialectical partner of the Protestant Principle, which is not tied to Roman Catholicism, but expresses the sacramental aspects of religion, and relates to the "is" in the "is–ought polarity." Tillich also describes it as the "concrete embodiment of the Spiritual Presence" (*ST* III, 245).

147 "There are prophetic and quasi-prophetic movements not only in the religious sphere but in the cultural as well ... The sects of the Reformation period are the fathers of many modern revolutions and behind these sects stand the sects of the Middle Ages, early Christianity, and Jewish prophetism. This holds for revolutions which use anti-Christian and anti-religious slogans. They were driven to this position by the fact that the sacramental churches were bound to the ruling groups and gave political injustice sacramental consecration. In spite of their secular, anti-religious character, and the total perversions to which some of the revolutionary movements have been led, the prophetic spirit was originally effective in them" (*Judenfrage* lectures, 472).

148 Ibid.

149 Ibid.

groups, and against the Christian churches when they fall into bondage to space. The Jews are and must remain the people of time."[150]

4.6 Fourth Lecture and Conclusion: Theological Answers and the Search for Reconciliation

The fourth lecture seeks to answer the opening question of the Jewish problem as it relates to the German people and Christians, through the theological insights presented in the third lecture. Tillich provides specific recommendations to provide a basis for reconciliation. He achieves this in three parts, in consecutive discussions of Judaism, the German people and Christianity. He initially observes that the traditional sociological categories are inadequate to describe Judaism, and Judaism occupies a unique position within Christendom.[151] On the one hand, Judaism is a religious community, but on the other hand it is a national entity.[152] Echoing the language of the prophet Hosea 1:9, Tillich argues that the Jews are both "a people and not a people,"[153] in whom "history has expressed its mystery."[154] For Tillich, the ability of the Jews to endure despite not having a dedicated geographical space, a homeland, underscores the importance of their survival in *diaspora*.[155] Tillich employs the idea introduced in the third lecture, that territorial insecurity and *diaspora* existence for Judaism is theologically vital, as it avoids the idolatry of space: "Seen in terms of space, Judaism lives necessarily in dispersion ... for which *diaspora* is a genuine destiny."[156] For Tillich, the difficult tension of a *diaspora* existence entails preserving religious distinctiveness, but in the context of geographical transience, always living potentially on the run. This tension can be eliminated in two ways. The first way is by assimilation, which involves giving up religious community and distinctiveness, which "foundered" in Europe, but arguably was having some success in America.[157]

150 Ibid., 473.
151 Ibid., 474.
152 Ibid., 474–475.
153 Ibid., 475.
154 Ibid.
155 Ibid.
156 Ibid.
157 Tillich grants a qualified legitimacy to assimilation: "In assimilation one avoids the condition of the diaspora by giving up that side of Jewish existence according to which it is a people. One identifies oneself with the alien space in which one lives, not only geographically, sociologically, and culturally. The giving up of the ethnic-elements does not necessarily mean giving up the religious elements of Judaism. One can assimilate without becoming a Christian. I am thinking of certain

The other alternative is Zionism, in which religious distinctiveness can be maintained through obtaining a religiously dedicated geographical space. Tillich specifically refers to the creation of a Jewish state in Palestine. Tillich observes, on the one hand, that this can lead to the end of the sociological problem of territorial insecurity and the psychological problem of despair.[158] On the other hand, this brings back all of the problems that go with religious nationalism, which were the target of prophetic critique by the Old Testament prophets, which Tillich describes as the problem of theocracy.[159] For Tillich, "Every attempt to identify a nation with the Kingdom of God must run aground (*scheitern*). This was the problem with which all the leading men of the Old Testament wrestled."[160] Tillich ends his application of theological concepts as applied to Judaism in an inconclusive, open-ended manner. Here Tillich condemns religious nationalism, as he has consistently since 1933 in *The Socialist Decision*. However, he wonders whether the State of Israel can generate "new embodiments of the prophetic spirit, and that from there new impulses will come for Israel and the diaspora?"[161]

Having reflected upon Judaism, Tillich now turns to the implications of his theological analysis for the German people. He responds to the problems he raised in the second lecture, and recommends that Germans avoid stereotypes, avoid misplaced self-hate and aggression with "philosemitism," which has the

groups in American Judaism, in particular the liberals. Here an astonishingly extensive cultural assimilation has taken place, without the corresponding groups giving up their particular religious existence. The religious element is not destroyed through assimilation in a Christian culture. However, where assimilation succeeds, the meaning of the diaspora has been lost, namely, the special mission which Judaism has in the dispersion. Then the religious particularity is often also lost, and a total immersion in Christian culture takes place" (ibid., 476).

158 Ibid., 477.

159 Tillich distinguishes between "theocracy" and "hierocracy:" "Hierocracy is priesthood; theocracy is the lordship of God, executed through laypersons and theologians. A secular state can be theocratic but not hierocratic. It is theocratic when the law of its existence–the laws of family, school and rights–are subjected to fundamental religious law. In a theocracy the will of God is the foundation of the political structure. It is however, quite questionable whether it is possible to build a modern state on a theocratic foundation. The development of Israel up to this point doubtless speaks against this possibility" (ibid., 477–478).

160 Ibid., 478.

161 "Speaking for this is the fact that this space (the State of Israel) is psychologically and sociologically completely filled with the Jewish spirit. Against this speaks the dangers which are given with the space-boundedness of every nation. History can never be calculated. My question is a question to the future and a hope in the future" (ibid., 480). See Chapter Seven below, and also Tillich, "My Changing Thoughts on Zionism."

same source as anti-Semitism.[162] For Tillich, the phenomenon of German anti-Semitism cannot be undone simply through education, and having Germans interact with real Jews, although both are necessary. Tillich identifies the fifth type of guilt from the first lecture, in which Germans believed they had suffered enough in the war, as particularly pernicious. Because of the deep-rooted nature of this problem, a solution with equal "depth" will be needed, Tillich's call for "collective (psycho) analysis:" "Such a collective analysis would uncover the irrational and perverted structures which lay at the basis of the antisemitism of the most recent period in the history of the German people. I can scarcely believe that without such a collective analysis of the problem that the problem of 'Germans and Jews' can be solved."[163] While Tillich acknowledges that not every German should, or could, undergo such an analysis, it would apply to those who form "the public consciousness."[164] The main focus of this analysis would be to un-do the psychological problems of "over self-valuation," arrogance, self-hate and inferiority that Germans had suffered from.[165] The end result would be that Germany should re-inculcate the spirit of true German humanism, which it previously embodied during the Reformation, and in other periods, but had been tragically forfeited, especially in northern and northwest Germany.[166] He concludes: "The German people can gain an understanding of the prophetic-humanistic character of Judaism only when they themselves take part in the Christian-humanistic character of the West."[167]

Third, having discussed Judaism and the German people, Tillich makes three recommendations about how his theological "solution" in the third lecture must inform the relationship of Christianity to Judaism. The first recommendation is that Christianity must affirm that the Old Testament is an essential part of its own Scriptures, which serves two functions. The first function requires affirming

---

162 Ibid., 481–482.
163 Ibid., 484.
164 Ibid., 485.
165 Ibid., 485–486.
166 "the unity of Christian-humanistic culture is deeply threatened, perhaps more than we know. I am here not so much thinking of the contemporary political constellation as of the events of the German past which have hindered Germany from fully opening itself to Christian humanism. The first event was the failure of the Romans to conquer middle and northern Germany, which would have meant bringing with them the values of Greek–Roman antiquity. The second event ... is the way that north-west Germany turned against Christianity and was converted by force by Charlemagne, and thereby never opened itself to Christian values to the same extent as south and west Germany. Therefore northwest Germany was the best soil for the pagan elements of National Socialism" (ibid., 487).
167 Ibid.

the God of time, creation, justice, judgment and promise, over against the paganism found in the ancient world.[168] The second function is to relate political forms to religion: "The Old Testament, in particular the prophetic message, speaks of peoples, social classes, and political forms in relation to the religious message. In the New Testament we find very little about this."[169] The second recommendation is that the Christian church must fight its own anti-Judaism, part of which involves diagnosing its own legalism. For example, Tillich says that the ostensibly anti-Jewish passages in John's Gospel need to be interpreted "typologically," meaning that the legalism exhibited by Jesus' opponents needs to be identified wherever it is found, and that legalism is not the exclusive property of Judaism.[170] The third recommendation is that Christianity must permit the prophetic dimension of Judaism to serve as a perpetual critique of its own tendencies toward paganism: "It belongs to the function of Judaism to hold before Christianity the mirror of its own regression into paganism."[171] Here the image of the mirror from the third lecture recurs. According to Tillich, Judaism and Christianity converge in some ways, but ultimately diverge over the question of the Messiah, who for Christians has come in Jesus as the Christ.[172] This image supports the reciprocal relation of Judaism and Christianity. Tillich concludes the *Judenfrage* lectures with the assumption that when Christians and Jews diverge, Christians can no longer argue, but must resort to preaching, to explain that the coming of the Christ has indeed ushered in a new reality.[173]

---

168 Ibid., 488.

169 Ibid.

170 "The anti-Jewish expressions go all the way back to the latest books of the New Testament and from there comes the anti-Judaism in all periods of church history. In order to fight against this tendency, church instruction should show that in the fourth Gospel individuals always have at the same time a typological-symbolic meaning. The Jews in the fourth Gospel with whom Jesus fights represent a type of piety which occurs in all religions and recurs in Christianity. It is the piety of the law, which claims for itself possession of the absolute truth and in this basis rejects the Christ again and again. If the church said it more clearly, it would have turned the anti-Jewish critique not only against the Jews, but applied it also to itself. And if the church turns anti-Jewish critique against itself, then its anti-Judaism cannot degenerate into anti-Semitism" (ibid., 489). This "typological-symbolic" meaning is to be distinguished from the "typological thinking" discussed above, which is stereotyping, and the vehicle for anti-Semitism.

171 Ibid., 489–490.

172 Ibid., 490.

173 "This Christian answer is not an arguing answer. It is a pointing answer. It is an answer of being. Perhaps the hope is not unjustified that from the Christian Being [namely, Jesus Christ as the New Being] the power will come forth which will break the demon of antisemitism and create a new community between Christianity and Judaism, not only in the German people, but among all peoples" (ibid., 491).

In this chapter I have illustrated how Tillich sought to understand the causes of the Holocaust and also to recommend measures for reconciliation between Christians and Jews. Drawing upon lectures he drafted during World War II, perhaps at the instruction of the U.S. Office of War Information,[174] in the first lecture Tillich made the connection between patristic and medieval Christian theology and modern anti-Semitism. This topic of the theological contribution to the *ideology* of modern anti-Semtism will be elaborated upon in Chapter Seven.

In the second and third lectures, Tillich creates various dialectical structures to maintain continuity between Judaism and Christianity. In the second lecture, Tillich uses the image of the mirror to illustrate that prophetic Judaism must always serve a critical function for Christianity. More emphatically, in the third lecture, Tillich's analyses of the theological importance of space and time, priestly and prophetic, Is and Ought, are applied to the biblical characters Abraham and Amos. Tillich identifies Amos as the bearer of the single most important development in the history of religion. Tillich argues that Jewish prophetism, and any truly prophetic spirit, cannot be constrained by the limits of geographical space, or it could lapse into idolatry. Tillich goes beyond the imagery of the mirror, and says that Judaism must remain a permanent "thorn in the flesh" of Christianity. To sever the dialectical relation between Christianity and Judaism would be unthinkable for Tillich, for they must maintain a reciprocal relationship, suggesting an ontological dialectic of balance.

In the next chapter, the goal will be to analyze how the related ideas of Judaism and Jewish prophetism function within Tillich's three volume *Systematic Theology.* All of the most important concepts have been introduced, such as the transformation of the particular to the universal within the history of religion (the 1910 Dissertation on Schelling), the metaphysical importance of time, the critique of scientific rationalism, the emergence of eschatological expectation, and possibility of "the new" within history, and justice as the true power of being (*The Socialist Decision*) and the dialectic of the Holy (the *Judenfrage* lectures). In the *Systematic Theology,* Tillich's use of Judaism and Jewish prophetism appear at key points, underscoring the thesis that Tillich believes that Christianity is theologically inseparable from Judaism.

---

174 See Note 35 above.

Chapter Five: A Rational Dialectic in the *Systematic Theology*

This chapter will analyze Tillich's *Systematic Theology*, which was written in three volumes, and in five parts, with volume I (*ST* I) being published in 1951, volume II (*ST* II) being published in 1957 and volume III (*ST* III) being published in 1963. This chapter will underscore the importance of the history of religion for Tillich's theological method, and it will present in greater detail the two kinds of dialectical relation between Judaism and Christianity, the historical dialectic of progression, and the ontological dialectic of balance.

In *ST* I, Tillich presents his typological method, which is used to compare one religion to another, and he also describes the history of religion in terms of a dialectical, and rational quest for balance. Tillich's paradoxical understanding of the Exile in the Old Testament provides a unique foundation for the paradox of the Cross found in the New Testament, and both provide the basis for Tillich's critique of idolatry. In *ST* II, Tillich's Christology is grounded in the historical background of the Old Testament, and was saved from Gnosticism by a "life and death struggle." In *ST* III, Tillich's understanding of the Kingdom of God is based upon the transition from immaturity to maturity, with the Old Testament again playing an indispensable role.

In *ST* I, there are two sections that directly discuss the relationship between Judaism and Christianity. The first section is I.II.B.7., "The History of Revelation." The second section is II.II.A.2, "Typological Considerations," which relates to the history of religion. Because the latter section on typology provides key concepts employed in the former section on revelation, the section on typology will be discussed first.

5.1.1 ST Volume I: Typological Method

To fully appreciate what Tillich attempts to achieve in *ST* I, it is important to realize that he is saying that Judaism is not simply the historical predecessor to Christianity, but that the "inner logic" of Jewish prophetism enables it to be the basis for the final revelation in the appearance and reception of Jesus as the Christ. This process initiates in the movement from polytheism to trinitarian monotheism, which will be explained below in section 5.1.3. The inner logic, or dialectic, of the history of religions, is a very complex historical process. He believes that his typological method can meaningfully compare one religion to another, avoiding the problem of seeing each religion as *sui generis* and therefore incommensurable with other religions.

In Chapter Three it was noted that Ron Stone believed that Tillich's writings on socialism were pervaded by Max Weber's methodology, in particular Weber's theory of "ideal types."[1] It appears that this theory influences Tillich in his section in *ST* I on "Typological Considerations." While it may be too much to say that Tillich fully adopts Weber's theory in every detail, and with all of its implications, the broad outlines, and the intent behind using the theory, will be evident.

Weber articulates his theory of ideal types in a 1904 essay, " 'Objectivity' in Social Science and Social Policy," in which he provides introductory methodological principles, as a new editor for a prestigious social science journal.[2] Weber was addressing methodological problems in the social sciences that arose in the 19th century. One problem concerned how the scientific method could manage and interpret a vast array of empirical data, and arrive at meaningful conclusions: "The stream of immeasurable events flows unendingly towards eternity."[3] One the one hand, if concepts are too general, such as trying to explain capitalism or Protestantism by using more general concepts of economics or religion, the risk is that what is distinctive is obscured. On the other hand, if the analytical concepts are too specific, in the attempt to capture what is distinctive, the risk is that no meaningful comparative analysis can be made with any other phenomenon.[4]

To manage the potentially limitless detail, Weber created a conceptual "utopia," arrived at by highlighting ("analytical accentuation") certain aspects of the phenomenon being examined:

> An ideal type is formed by the one-sided accentuation of one or more points of view and by the synthesis of a great many diffuse, discrete, more or less present and occasionally absent *concrete individual* phenomena, which are arranged according to those one-sidedly emphasized viewpoints into a unified analytical construct (*Gedankenbild*). In its conceptual purity, this mental construct (*Gedankenbild*) cannot be found empirically anywhere in reality. It is a *utopia.*[5]

---

1 See Chapter Three, 73–74 and Notes 38–39.

2 In 1904, Weber, along with Werner Sombart and Edgar Jaffé, assumed the editorship of the *Archiv für Sozialwissenschaft und Sozialpolitik*, a position he held until the journal was suspended in 1933. Max Weber; *The Methodology of the Social Sciences*; trans., eds. Edward A. Shils and Henry A. Finch; New York: The Free Press, 1949; iii – iv ("Weber, *Methodology*").

3 Weber, *Methodology*, 84.

4 Lewis A. Coser, *Masters of Sociological Thought: Ideas in Historical and Social Context* (New York: Harcourt Brace Jovanovich, 1971, 223.

5 Weber, *Methodology*, 90.

The task of historical research determines to what degree the ideal-type approximates to, or diverges from, the concrete phenomenon under investigation.[6] Tillich's language in *ST* I echoes this: "Types are ideal structures which are approximated by concrete things or events without ever being attained. Nothing historical completely represents a particular type, but everything historical is nearer to or farther away from a particular type."[7]

Tillich believes that the typological method is appropriate for understanding and analyzing the history of religion because it enables analogies to be drawn between one religion and another, to determine how each participates in universal preparatory revelation. For Tillich, universal preparatory revelation refers to the foundational symbols, categories, forms and religious experiences without which the final revelation could never be understood.[8] The final revelation is the event of the reception of Jesus as the Christ, which is based on a variety of foundational symbols, which are mostly found in the Old Testament and historic Judaism, as will be seen later on in this chapter. The history of revelation assumes a period of "preparation" and a period of "reception," with universal preparatory revelation being logically and chronologically prior to the period in which revelation is "received." The paradigmatic sense of "universal(ity)" is seen in the doctrine of the Logos becoming flesh in the event of Jesus as the Christ, which is the simultaneous manifestation of concreteness and universality.[9]

---

6 Weber, *Methodology*, 90.

7 "Historical understanding oscillates between the intuition of the special and the analysis of the typical. The special cannot be described without reference to the type. The type is unreal without the special event in which it appears. Typology cannot replace historiography; historiography cannot describe anything without typology." Tillich, *ST* I, 219.

8 *ST* I, 139.

9 For Tillich, "universal" appears to carry two different senses, of "always and everywhere" and, of something that pervades all of reality (*ST* I, 16). Other uses of "universal" in the *Systematic Theology* support this claim. First, Tillich says that the story of Pentecost has five elements, the fifth of which is its universality. This is expressed in "the missionary drive of those grasped by the Spiritual Presence:" It was impossible that they should not give the message of what had happened to them to everybody, because the New Being would not be the New Being were not mankind as a whole and even the universe itself included in it. In light of the element of universality in the story of Pentecost we must say that there is no Spiritual Community without openness to all individuals, groups, and things and the drive to take them into itself" (*ST* III, 151–152). Second, in Tillich's analysis of the ambiguities of religion within the Spiritual Presence, he argues that the churches are paradoxical in three ways, the third of which is the paradox of universality. For Tillich, the churches exhibit "extensive" universality, which is implied in Jesus as the bearer of the New Being, which is valid for all nations, social groups, races, tribes and cultures (*ST* III, 171). Third, in Tillich's discussion of the uniqueness and universality of the appearance of Jesus as the Christ, his fundamental question is, in what way does the unique

In addition, typological analysis can determine how each religion compares to "the final revelation," which is the appearance and reception of Jesus as the Christ.[10] This occurs by using "typical structures" common to each religion, and comparing them to the final revelation. Tillich does not illustrate this specific point, but he probably means that Judaism, Christianity and Islam have similar, typical structures, insofar as they are each monotheistic. However, each has its own unique cultural and historical form, which makes them identifiable as Judaism, Christianity and Islam. Tillich argues that to over-emphasize a religion's uniqueness is to prevent any meaningful comparison between different religions:

> Theological interpretations of the history of religion often are misguided by the unique picture which every religion presents – a picture which can easily be criticized in light of final revelation. The criticism is much more difficult and much more serious if the typical structures within the unique form of a non-Christian historical religion are elaborated and compared with the typical structures appearing in Christianity as a historical religion. This is the only fair and methodologically adequate way of dealing systematically with the history of religion.[11]

For Tillich, the definitive measure would be to compare each religion to the "criterion of the final revelation."[12] How the final revelation fits into Tillich's history of revelation will be seen in greater detail below.

---

event of Jesus as the Christ have universal significance for every human being and, indirectly, for the universe? (*ST* II, 150–151). Fourth, in Tillich's discussion of the historical and non-historical expectations of the New Being, he argues that the quest for the New Being is universal, appearing in all religions, because the human predicament is universal: "The quest for the New Being is universal because the human predicament and its ambiguous conquest are universal. It appears in all religions" (*ST* II, 86).

10 *ST* I, 132.

11 Ibid., 220–221. The method avoids what a reductionist view of comparative religion, which relies upon a "lowest common denominator" approach. In the *Judenfrage* lectures, Tillich notes that liberal Protestants and liberal Jews work together in many areas, and create an "astonishingly rich experience from the standpoint of human community and mutual understanding." However, he warns that this is no solution to the Jewish- Christian problem: "The presupposition is that both religions would have to give up so much of their concrete customs and doctrines, that something relatively thin and unsatisfyingly moralistic would remain. The problem of the different religions and their relation to each other can in no case be solved by subtraction." 434–435.

12 Ibid.

5.1.2 The Rational Quest for Balance

Tillich's history of religion exhibits a tension between the concrete and the absolute on two levels, within God and within human history. Tillich uses the metaphor of "quest," reminiscent of the method of correlation, in which the questions of existence are raised, and answers are sought, depending on what form ultimate concern takes. The historical progression moves in this sequence: (i) "polytheism" confronts two forms of monotheism, "monarchical monotheism" and "mystical monotheism," to create "exclusive monotheism;" (ii) exclusive monotheism is uniquely based upon certain aspects of Judaism; and (iii) exclusive monotheism is transformed into "trinitarian monotheism" through the appearance of various mediating figures that foreshadow the Christian Logos.[13] In this way, Judaism is not only the historical predecessor of Christianity, but by its own "inner logic" it serves as the unique basis for Christianity. This sequence will be discussed in greater detail below, in Section 5.1.3.

For Tillich, this inner logic is driven by the quest for an optimal relationship between the "absolutely universal" and the "absolutely concrete." The optimal balance between the absolutely concrete and the absolutely universal is the Christian Logos, or "the Word made flesh." This tension seeks resolution in the optimal balance of trinitarian monotheism:

> The general outline of the typological analysis of the history of religion follows from the tension of the elements in the idea of God. The concreteness of man's ultimate concern drives him toward polytheistic structures; the reaction of the absolute element against these drives him toward monotheistic structures; and the need for a balance between the concrete and the absolute drives him toward Trinitarian structures.[14]

The above passage indicates that Tillich's view of the history of religion can be traced to his conception of the divine.

A key element here is the notion of "balance," implying that there is an optimal contribution from each pole to a third, new entity, a unity of the two poles. In this instance, the two poles are polytheism and monotheism, with the optimal contribution from polytheism being "concreteness" and the optimal contribution from monotheism being "the absolute", or "the ultimate." In this context, "absolute" is another way of expressing "ultimate concern," which is the only proper object of worship, since to worship anything preliminary would be idolatry. For Tillich, concreteness is generally that which is preliminary and transitory,

13 Ibid., 218 – 235.
14 Ibid., 221.

and is manifest in human history.[15] It is also that quality which is associated with a "personal God."[16] For Tillich, polytheism is not a quantitative concept, but a qualitative concept. The main problem with polytheism is not that it represents a "plurality of gods," but that each instance lacks a "uniting and transcending ultimate."[17] What is implied in Tillich's scheme is that an optimal contribution from the history of polytheism, and from the history of monotheism, should endure in the manifestation of a new, third, divine expression, trinitarian monotheism. This is the paradigmatic instance of the ontological dialectic of balance, because the optimal relationship itself is thought of as a "new unity," the teleological goal of the rational striving of the participants in the dialectic.

5.1.3 Volume I: Judaism and Trinitarian Monotheism

Due to space limitations, the full development of trinitarian monotheism will not be traced, but the essential enduring aspects of polytheism and monotheism channeled through Judaism will be summarized. For Tillich, there are two types of monotheism that contribute to exclusive monotheism. The first is "monarchic monotheism," which occupies a "boundary line" between monotheism and polytheism, in that a "god-monarch" rules over a hierarchy of inferior gods and god-like beings.[18] Tillich uses the biblical image of "the Lord of Hosts," as found in the Old Testament and Christian liturgy, as an example of a heavenly monarch who rules over heavenly beings, angels and spirits.[19] The enduring element in this is the concept of a being that has sovereignty over all. The second type is "mystical monotheism," in which all beings, and any distinctions, are swallowed up in "the divine ground and abyss from which they come and in which they disappear."[20] However, according to Tillich, the quest for concreteness can never be completely eradicated, with one example being polytheism in India: "Yet even this most radical negation of the concrete element

15 "The ultimate can become actual only through the concrete, through that which is preliminary and transitory. This is the reason why the idea of God has a history, and why this history is the basic element in the history of religion, simultaneously determining it and being determined by it" (ibid., 218).
16 Ibid., 223.
17 Ibid., 222. This problem was noted in Tillich's analysis of polytheism in *The Socialist Decision*, 18–19, discussed in Chapter 4 above.
18 *ST* I, 226.
19 Ibid., 226.
20 Ibid.

in the idea of God is not able to suppress the quest for concreteness."[21] Therefore, for Tillich, one aspect of mystical monotheism survives to make an enduring contribution to exclusive monotheism, the quest for concreteness.

In order to accommodate the ineradicable quest for concreteness by the human religious consciousness, Tillich argues that a third form of monotheism emerged in history, "exclusive monotheism." According to Tillich, this form of monotheism posits a god that is ultimate and universal, a god who is not demonic, destructive or idolatrous, and yet is concrete and personal.[22] These are features that became manifest in the Christian Logos, in perfect balance. Tillich says this form of monotheism emerged *uniquely* with Judaism, and he emphasizes that certain unprecedented elements emerged for the first time: "Such a possibility contradicts every expectation which can be derived from the history of religion. It is the result of an astounding constellation of objective and subjective factors in Israel, especially in the prophetic line of religion."[23] Therefore, for Tillich, the God of Israel has two characteristics that are not only new to the history of religion, but they also inform the enduring possibility of exclusive monotheism, which in turn is the only basis for trinitarian monotheism. First, the God of Israel is concrete, the one who led his people out of Egypt, the "God of Abraham, Isaac and Jacob."[24] Second, this God is absolute, who judges the other gods of the nations, and who is a "jealous God" that cannot permit any competing divine claim.[25] However, the absolute and jealous God does not become the object of idolatry because this God is the God of justice, who requires the keeping of the Ten Commandments, and relates to Israel through a covenant:

> Yahweh does not claim universality in the name of a particular quality or in the name of his nation and its particular qualities. His claim is not imperialistic, for it is made in the name of that principle which implies ultimacy and universality – the principle of justice. The relation of the God of Israel to his nation is based on a covenant. The covenant demands justice, namely, the keeping of the Commandments, and it threatens the violation of justice and destruction ... He proves his universality by destroying his nation in the name of principles which are valid for all nations – the principles of justice. This undercuts the basis of polytheism.[26]

21 Ibid.
22 Ibid., 227.
23 "Theologically speaking, exclusive monotheism belongs to the final revelation, for it is a direct preparation" (ibid.). Tillich uses the metaphor "constellation" frequently. For example, he argues that a certain "constellation of conditions" must be present for the organic to appear in the inorganic realm. *ST III*, 25.
24 Ibid.
25 Ibid.
26 Ibid.

This understanding of justice is similar to what was expressed in *The Socialist Decision* and the *Judenfrage* lectures. For Tillich, exclusive monotheism needs an expression of "the concrete element in humanity's ultimate concern," and this provides the basis for the trinitarian problem.[27] How this occurs will be explained below, but Tillich is clear that exclusive monotheism was first expressed in Judaism, and that it provided *the only historical basis* for Christianity.

The progression beyond exclusive monotheism to trinitarian monotheism is bridged by the idea of God as "living:" "It is an attempt to speak of the living God, the God in whom the ultimate and concrete are united."[28] For Tillich, trinitarian monotheism, like polytheism, is not concerned with quantity, but with a qualitative characterization of God: "The trinitarian problem is the problem of the unity between ultimacy and concreteness in the living God. Trinitarian monotheism is concrete monotheism, the affirmation of the living God."[29] Each type of monotheism, monarchic, mystical and exclusive, yields implicit or explicit answers to the quest for a unity of ultimacy and concreteness.[30] According to Tillich, monarchic monotheism, with its hierarchy of divinities as found in the mystery cults of late antiquity, anticipated trinitarian thinking through the suffering and death of a divine figure, demonstrating that this divine figure fully participated in human destiny.[31] Mystical monotheism, in a different way, anticipated trinitarian thinking. Tillich uses the example of the distinction between the god Brahma and the Brahman principle, arguing that this is analogous to Origen's "Logos theology," which sought to clarify the ambiguous ontological standing of the pre-existent Christ.[32] There is no indication here on Tillich's part, to use these pre-Christian, non-Jewish, contributions to the development of trinitarian monotheism, as an occasion to deny the Jewish roots of Christianity, as in Aryan Christianity.

According to Tillich, exclusive monotheism gives rise to the trinitarian problem because of the conflict between "abstract transcendence" and the irrepressible demand for concreteness. Tillich says that abstract transcendence is expressed in any *absolute* divine command, which appears to override, overwhelm or nullify any recipient of the command, because of the absolute

27 Ibid., 228.
28 Ibid.
29 Ibid.
30 Ibid.
31 Ibid.
32 Ibid., 229.

power of the divinity.[33] Using a peculiar turn of phrase, Tillich describes the ineradicable quest for concreteness as a personal "demand:" "But since the concrete element *demands its rights*, mediating powers of a threefold character appear and posit the trinitarian problem."[34] To resolve this conflict between the overpowering absolute divine command, and the ineradicable "demand" for concreteness, three levels of mediating beings are posited, a hierarchy with a pure divinity at the "top" and a divine-human figure at the "bottom." The mediating powers with a threefold character are:

> The first group of these mediators is made up of hypostasized divine qualities, like Wisdom, Word, Glory. The second group is the angels, the divine messengers who represent special functions. The third is the divine-human figure through which God works the fulfillment of history, the Messiah. In all these the God who had become absolutely transcendent and unapproachable now becomes concrete in time and space.[35]

Tillich concludes that there is a Christian solution to the optimal relation, or balance, between the concrete and the absolute. This balance is found in the paradox that the Messiah, the mediator between God and man, is identical with a historical, individual, personal life, who carries the name of Jesus of Nazareth.[36] But this balance could not exist without the contribution of exclusive monotheism, which was uniquely expressed in Judaism.

5.1.4 The Prophetic Struggle

In the preceding section, Tillich's history of religion demonstrates that Judaism, as presented in the Old Testament, manifests a combination of absoluteness and concreteness that provided a unique basis for the final revelation in Jesus as the Christ. The God of the Old Testament is absolute, the one, "jealous" God, who is also the God of justice. At the same time, the God of the Old Testament is concrete, historically and culturally specific, and personal. These two factors unite in "the living God," and this bridges the historical transition from exclusive monotheism to trinitarian monotheism. For Tillich, the history of religion is interpret-

33 "In exclusive monotheism an abstract transcendence of the divine develops. It is not the transcendence of the infinite abyss in which everything concrete disappears, as in mystical monotheism; rather it is the transcendence of the absolute command which empties all concrete manifestations of the divine" (ibid.).

34 Ibid.; emphasis mine.

35 Ibid.

36 Ibid., 229 – 230.

ed theologically, taking a selection of empirical facts, and discerning a unique combination of symbols serving as the basis for the "final revelation." This section provides the conceptual framework for understanding the inextricable relationship between the Old Testament/Judaism and the New Testament/Christianity, in the history of revelation.

For Tillich, the appearance and reception of Jesus as the Christ is the final revelation.[37] Tillich underscores that this complex historical and theological process is not an isolated event, and it is divided into two periods.[38] The first is the period of "preparation," which starts with the beginnings of religious consciousness in ancient paganism, and includes the emergence of monotheistic and prophetic Judaism, as discussed above in the history of religion. The second is the period of "reception," which is effectively the history of the Christian church. This discussion will focus on the period of preparation, because that is the period that involves the relationship between Judaism and the Old Testament, and Christianity and the New Testament.

According to Tillich, the period of preparation must include two things: (i) the element of expectation or anticipation, and (ii) prior revelations, which had become distorted. Therefore, the final revelation had a "revelatory history:"

> It [i.e. the final revelation] could not have occurred without having been expected, and it could not have been expected if it had not been preceded by other revelations which had become distorted. It would not have been the final revelation if it had not been received as such, and it would lose its character as final revelation if it were not able to make itself available to every group in every place. The history of the preparation and reception of the final revelation can be called the "history of revelation."[39]

Two issues emerge here that must be developed. First, according to Tillich there were other, preceding revelations that became distorted.[40] For Tillich, "universal

---

37 "Christianity claims to be based on the revelation in Jesus as the Christ as the final revelation" (ibid., 132). "The final revelation, like every revelation, occurs in a correlation of ecstasy and miracle. The revelatory event is Jesus as the Christ ... Jesus as the Christ, the miracle of the final revelation, and the church, receiving him as the Christ or the final revelation, belong to each other. The Christ is not the Christ without the church, and the church is not the church without the Christ. The final revelation, like every revelation, is correlative" (ibid., 136–137).
38 "The final revelation of Jesus as the Christ divides the history of revelation into a period of preparation and a period of reception. In addition, the event of the final revelation establishes itself as the center, aim and origin of the revelatory events which occur in the period of preparation and the period of reception" (ibid., 138).
39 Ibid., 137.
40 For example, in the 1912 Dissertation, both paganism and Judaism "go to ruin" because of their "one-sidedness;" 123.

revelation" contributed the symbols, categories, forms and religious experiences without which the final revelation could never be understood, as "the biblical terminology is full of words whose meaning would be strange if there had been no preceding revelations in Judaism as well as in paganism."[41] This parallels the observation above in the preceding section that Judaism made an essential contribution to the emergence of exclusive monotheism. Second, the final revelation, by definition, must become "available to every group in every place," having the quality of universality.

The period of preparation involves a three-phase process that Tillich characterizes as "the prophetic struggle,"[42] which is the purification of the religious consciousness. Tillich uses as many as four three-phase constructs to describe essentially the same process.[43] The first phase is the priestly function, which tries to "keep alive the power of the original revelation" by enabling new individuals and groups to enter into the revelatory situation. This process risks idolatry, which would be a confusion between the medium and content of revelation.[44] This idolatrous impulse, or "distorted sacramentalism,"[45] is opposed by the second, critical phase, which appears in prophetic form, and is decisive for the development of universal revelation.[46] Like the first phase, the critical phase appears in all phases of history, whether it is Old Testament prophetism, Christian monasticism, the Protestant Reformation, evangelical radicalism, or even movements in Islam and Zoroastrianism.[47] For Tillich, however, the common feature to each critical phase is the *concrete* foundation of their attack on the dominant sacramental system, through "the judgment of the divine law."[48] Tillich does not give an example here, but his terminology suggests that the Mosaic Law would be the prototype. The third phase, of anticipation, is not descri-

---

41 Ibid., 139.
42 Ibid., 143.
43 (i) conservation, criticism, anticipation (ibid., 139 ff.); (ii) reception, development, transformation (143); (iii) acceptance, rejection, transformation (143); and (iv) reception, rejection and transformation (143). These all appear to be ways to describe "the prophetic struggle."
44 Ibid., 140.
45 Ibid., 141.
46 The critical phase also has rational and mystical forms, but the prophetic form is most important here. Ibid., 140 – 141. In addition, Tillich argues, "The prophetic attack on distorted sacramentalism is decisive for the development of universal revelation" (ibid., 141).
47 Ibid.
48 "They subject the concrete mediums of revelation and the concrete sacramental symbols and priestly systems to the divine judgment of the divine law, to that which ought to be because it is the law of God" (ibid., 142).

bed generically, but is illustrated solely by the uniqueness of the prophets of Israel, which for Tillich extends from Moses to John the Baptist.[49]

What kind of dialectic is this? While Tillich's history of religion is utterly pervaded by tensions, polarities and movement, he seldom reflects on the features of the dialectic itself. It is something that he assumes, and has done so since the Schelling dissertations. Yet in Tillich's discussion of the prophetic struggle of reception, rejection and transformation there are traces of spatial imagery, with reference to "sides:"

> Reception, rejection and transformation – that is the movement from the side of the Old Testament toward universal revelation, and from the side of the New Testament toward the universal revelation *and* the Old Testament. The dynamics of the history of revelation exclude the mechanistic-supernatural theories of revelation.[50]

This is the only spatial language describing the poles of the dialectic up to this point in this survey of Tillich's works, and it is not elaborated upon. The spatial language may be an indication of a polar relation. Below it will be seen that Tillich employs the concept of "the center of history," but this does not characterize the relationship of the poles, and does not effect whether the optimal relationship between the poles is one of balance, or movement beyond a contradiction to a new unity. Only in the Bampton Lectures,[51] to be discussed later in this chapter, will Tillich describe his dialectical history of religion in spatial terms.

5.1.5. Volume I: The Paradoxes of Prophetism and of the Cross

Volume I, part I, II.A.7, "The History of Revelation," contains the clearest and most comprehensive articulation of the relationship between the Old and New Testament in the entire *Systematic Theology*. In four respects, the Old Testament prophetic revelation cannot be severed from the final revelation of Jesus as the Christ. In all four instances, a progression or advancement from Judaism to Christianity is evident. However, Judaism is not denigrated, but has a profound influence on its successor religion, Christianity. First, the Old Testament prophetic tradition, which extends from Moses to John the Baptist, is uniquely and inseparably related to the final revelation in Jesus as the Christ in the New Testa-

49 Ibid.
50 Ibid., 143.
51 Published in Paul Tillich, *Christianity and the Encounter of World Religions*, Fortress Texts in Modern Theology, foreword by Krister Stendahl (Minneapolis, MN: Fortress Press, 1994), 34–35.

ment because it is "the direct concrete preparation" for the final revelation in the event of Jesus as the Christ.[52] While there are other forms of prophetic criticism in other religions, such as in Islam or in the Greek mystery religions, they bear no direct relation to the final revelation of Jesus as the Christ. The Old Testament prophetic revelation is concrete, in the sense that it is historically and culturally specific. It was in the lands of present-day Palestine and Israel that the prophets spoke, and it was in these same lands that the Christ event occurred. This historical and cultural uniqueness is the primary reason that the Old Testament prophetic tradition is inseparable from the revelation of Jesus as the Christ.

Second, the Old Testament prophetic revelation informs New Testament revelation through a threefold process of prophetic struggle, in this case the process of reception, rejection and transformation.[53] Here and in other places (see *ST* II, 89–90), Tillich shows the influence of Schelling's view of the history of religion, as displayed in the 1910 Dissertation. This analyzes Christianity as emerging from a complex historical and cultural context that included late Judaism, Oriental eschatology, and Greek mystery religions.[54] Specifically, Tillich says that the early church extracted criteria from Second Isaiah and applied them to Jesus of Nazareth, as the Christ. There are two personal figures in Second Isaiah, chapters 40 through 55. One is the "Servant of the Lord," who brings justice to the nations, as in 42:1–4.[55] The other is the "Suffering Servant," who "was wounded for our transgressions,"[56] found in Isaiah 53:3–5. According to Tillich, both the establishment of justice by the Servant of the Lord, and the redemptive power of suffering by the Suffering Servant, were both attributed to Jesus of Nazareth, as "the Christ."

> When the early church accepted Jesus as the Christ, it was guided by criteria such as those given by Second Isaiah. Without a group of people who were indoctrinated by the paradoxes of Jewish prophetism, the paradox of the Cross could not have been understood and accepted. It is, therefore, not surprising that those who separated the New from the Old Testament – from early gnosticism to recent nazism – lost the christological paradox, the center of the New Testament ... they denounced the religion of the Old Testament as one of the lower forms of paganism ... But this is a complete misunderstanding.[57]

52 *ST* I, 141.
53 Ibid., 143. Referred to above as "the prophetic struggle."
54 Unlike the Aryan Christians discussed in Chapter One, Tillich does not take the concepts from this milieu and move in an anti-Jewish or anti-Semitic direction.
55 Is. 42:1–4 NRSV.
56 Is. 53:3 NRSV
57 *ST* I, 142.

Third, the Suffering Servant is one aspect of the "paradox of Jewish prophetism" referred to above, which serves as a unique preparation for the later paradox of the Cross. Tillich acknowledges that the Old Testament is full of Jewish nationalism, which is one reason it was denounced by the Nazis. However, he argues that the election of Israel by God is not an expression of national arrogance, because election carries with it the permanent threat of destruction.[58] For Tillich, in a paradoxical way, the threat of destruction is what prevents any nation, ethnic group or individual from becoming ultimate or idolatrous, and it also preserves the covenant of election. This understanding of election and Exile is similar to what Tillich says in *The Socialist Decision*[59] and in the *Judenfrage* lectures.[60] In the following passage, we can see how Tillich ties the paradox of Old Testament prophetism to the paradox of the Cross, as referred to above:

> Election and destruction are bound together so that no finite being, group, or individual may consider himself as more than a medium of the mystery of being. If, however, a group or single individuals endure this tension, their destruction is their fulfillment. This is the meaning of the prophetic promise which transcends the prophetic threat.[61]

This is what Tillich means by the paradox of Old Testament prophetism serving as concrete preparation for Jesus as the Christ. For Tillich, the suffering servant as applied to Jesus as the Christ is the most radical *transformation* of the Messiah symbol.[62]

Fourth, it is the final revelation in Jesus as the Christ that confirms the authenticity of the Old Testament prophetic revelation, selecting it from other forms of universal, yet non-concrete forms of prophetic revelation.[63] This would explain what Tillich means when he says that it is "impossible and absurd to interpret the Old Testament not as the concrete and unique preparation of the final revelation but as a document of the final revelation itself, as a kind of anticipated New Testament."[64] For Tillich, the absurdity would be to conclude that the Suffering Servant figure as portrayed in Isaiah 53 is to be *identified with* Jesus of Nazareth, in the sense of "Jesus is what Isaiah 53 is *really* referring to." Yet, it is the *balance* of absolute concreteness and absolute universality in the Logos made flesh in Jesus as the Christ that provides the criteria for selecting which

58 Ibid., 142–143.
59 Tillich, *Socialist Decision*, 20.
60 *Judenfrage* lectures, 465, 467–468.
61 *ST* I, 143.
62 *ST* II, 111.
63 *ST* I, 143.
64 Ibid.

religions provide an essential basis for the final revelation. Also, it is this balance of absolute concreteness and absolute universality that represents the logical culmination of the rational quest of the religious consciousness.

5.2 ST Volume II: The Life and Death Struggle to Save the Old Testament

When Volume I of Tillich's *Systematic Theology* appeared in 1951, the president of Union Theological Seminary, Henry Sloane Coffin, is said to have fallen into a state of outrage, as his worst suspicions were confirmed, that Tillich was not Christian, but a Greek mystic who held heretical views of Plotinian dualism, Hegel and Schelling.[65] Whether or not Tillich was a heretic in the sense that Coffin describes is outside the scope of this analysis, but Tillich repeatedly affirms the importance of the Old Testament, for Christian theology, in contrast to various types of Gnosticism and Marcionism, as traditionally understood.

The inextricable relationship between the Old and New Testaments is also reflected in Tillich's Christology, particularly in volume II, III.1.E.4. "The Symbol of 'Christ', Its Historical and Transhistorical Meaning." In this analysis, Tillich again engages in a historical and theological analysis of religious symbols. Tillich's view of how historical, religious symbols are appropriated and transformed is similar to his views in Volume I, as discussed above. This is similar to Tillich's understanding of the history of revelation, since there is a dialectic of progression from Judaism to Christianity, with Judaism exercising a profound influence on Christianity. In this section, there is another example of how the history of religion exhibits rationality. Specifically, this will be found in the optimal balance between, or mutual affirmation of, the "historical type" and "transhistorical type" of the expectation of the New Being. For Tillich, the New Being is that reality in which the self-estrangement of our existence is overcome, what Paul calls the "new creation," which is found in "Jesus the Christ."[66]

For Tillich, the symbol Messiah, which refers to a king who conquers enemies and ushers in peace and justice, has an origin that transcends both Judaism and Christianity: "When Christianity used this symbol for what it believed to be the central event in history, it accepted – as the religion of the Old Testament had done before – a large amount of symbolic material from the social organization of the Semitic and Egyptian world, especially from the political institution of

---

65 Pauck, Pauck, *Tillich*, 176.
66 Ibid., 49.

kingship".[67] This suggests the initial form of universality, meaning the symbols can be found "always and everywhere," although in different historical forms. The next phase of the development of the symbol Messiah occurs with the addition of mythological attributes that characterize a cosmic redeemer who transforms historical existence.[68] Here the second sense of universality emerges. This transition from a primarily political figure of a conquering king, within a culturally and historically specific setting, to that of a cosmic redeemer has cross-cultural origins, and therefore universality, in both senses of "always and everywhere," and "cosmic." In addition, despite the accretion of mythological traits attributed to a cosmic redeemer, these messiah figures are still *rooted in history* in so far as they serve *particular peoples*, giving meaning to their origins, predicaments and destinies. Despite the shared methodological assumption with the Aryan Christians, Tillich comes to opposite conclusions concerning Judaism and its relation to Christianity.

For Tillich, the "strictly historical" dimension of the Messiah symbol possessed three benefits. First, it could be applied to groups, ethnicities, and social classes, such as the proletariat, and nations, such as the remnant of Israel.[69] Second, the symbol Messiah could be combined with other redeemer or cosmic figures, such as the "Servant of Jahweh," the "Son of Man," or the "Man from Above."[70] Third, and for Tillich the most important, was that the "historical type of the expectation of the New Being" could encompass the "non-historical type (of the expectation of the New Being)".[71] Tillich's assumption here is that any non-historical religion is intrinsically unable to manifest the features, and corresponding benefits, of a historical religion, as "the non-historical is unable to embrace the historical type."[72]

For Tillich, the *quest* for the New Being is universal, appearing in all religions although in different historical forms, because the ambiguous *conquest* of the human predicament is also universal, appearing always and everywhere.[73] For Tillich, there are cultural variations to the quest for the New Being, the rational unfolding of divine revelation in history. Yet, there are two main types of "quest for the New

67 *ST* II, 88.
68 *ST* II, 88.
69 Ibid., 88–89.
70 Ibid., 89.
71 Ibid.
72 "Christianity must show–and has always tried to show–that the historical type of the expectation of the New Being embraces itself and the non-historical type, while the non-historical is unable to embrace the historical" (ibid.).
73 Ibid., 86.

Being" that exist in polar relation, partly in conflict and partly in unity, the historical and non-historical.[74] No religion is "purely" historical or non-historical, but they are "predominantly" historical or non-historical. In predominantly *non-historical religions*, the New Being is expected in a vertical direction,[75] as they are unable to create anything "new," exhibiting a circular view of history. For Tillich, most polytheistic religions, "Brahmanism," Buddhism and anti-mystical classical Greek humanism are predominantly non-historical.[76] This is clearly similar to Schelling's view of the history of religion as found in the 1910 Dissertation, and also the "myth of origin," political romanticism and polytheism as discussed in *The Socialist Decision*. Predominantly non-historical religions are able to illuminate or enlighten individuals, but they are unable to transform groups, communities, and entire societies: "A group, whether a family or mankind as a whole, does not participate in the effects of the New Being. The misery of mankind in history is not to be changed, but individuals may transcend the whole sphere of existence ... This is the root of the difference in the East and West in the feeling for life."[77] This is in keeping with Tillich's assessments of paganism and Gnosticism, which have been discussed in prior chapters.

For Tillich, predominantly *historical religions* are Zoroastrianism, Judaism, Christianity, Islam and some forms of modern humanism, the latter in secularized form.[78] In contrast to predominantly non-historical religions, predominantly historical religions, "expect the New Being" in a horizontal direction, meaning that salvation can be attained *in the realm of history*. This also means that the "whole of reality," including nature and the physical world, is deemed "good," and worthy of redemption.[79] The transformation of all reality occurs through a historical process in a unique, unrepeatable and irreversible process, mediated through groups, such as families, nations or the church.[80] According to Tillich, the "decisive event" for Christianity, the appearance of Jesus as the Christ who is the bearer of the New Being, occurs at the center of history, giving history a "center."[81] This is an important assumption for the next step in his use of the history of religion.

---

74 Ibid., 86–87.
75 This is the opposite of what Tillich says about a predominantly historical religion, as stated below.
76 Ibid., 87.
77 Ibid.
78 Ibid.
79 Ibid.
80 Ibid.
81 Ibid.

Tillich observes that Christianity employed the conceptual tools provided by late, post-exilic, Judaism in order to be universally valid, uniting the "horizontal" (historical) and "vertical" (transhistorical) expectations of the New Being. The Messiah was attributed cosmic significance, the law was declared to have eternal validity, and divine Wisdom, a divine being equal with God, was determined to be the one who both creates and brings creation to its consummation.[82] As the "the eschatological consciousness" (the horizontal/historical dimension) began to fade with the delay of the Parousia, Paul's Christ mysticism enabled the transhistorical type to enter Christianity.[83] At the same time, Gnosticism, which negated the Old Testament, entered the picture, threatening the historical element:

> Under these circumstances it is not astonishing that the horizontal line, derived from the Old Testament, was in danger of annihilation by the vertical line, derived from Hellenism ... In this situation Christianity was forced into a life-and-death struggle to preserve the Old Testament within the church, the historical type of the expectation of the New Being. The church made this decision and saved the historical character of Christianity.[84]

For Tillich, therefore, the historical type of the expectation of the New Being and the transhistorical type of the expectation of the New Being both need to be affirmed, without sacrificing one for the other.[85] For Tillich, this mutual affirmation is the result of a rational, historical dialectic. Tillich concludes that the church must defend the historical basis for Christianity *in all periods*, without sacrificing its universality.[86]

5.3 Volume III: The Purification of the Religious Consciousness

In section V.II.A.2. of volume III, "The Central Manifestation of the Kingdom of God in History," the prophetic witness of the Old Testament once again underscores its foundational relationship to the New Testament. Tillich observes that there is a clear distinction between the Jewish and Christian interpretations of history, since Juda-

---

82 Ibid., 89.
83 Ibid. See Albert Schweitzer's *The Mysticism of the Apostle Paul* (Baltimore, MD: Johns Hopkins University Press, 1998).
84 *ST* II, 89 – 90. Tillich also refers to the "life or death struggle" numerous times in his writings. For example, in *BRSUR* the Church's "life or death struggle" against the Gnostics maintains "the Old Testament as its own presupposition" (35). In addition, in the first lecture of the *Judenfrage* lectures, this image is also used.
85 *ST* II, 104, cited by J. Heywood Thomas, *Tillich* (New York: Continuum, 2000), 107 – 108.
86 *ST* II, 90.

ism remains in a mode of continual prophetic and apocalyptic expectation (the "Ought"), while Christianity has experienced a degree of "inner-historical" fulfillment (the "Is").[87] Whereas the center of history for Judaism is the Exodus,[88] the center of history for Christianity is the appearance of Jesus as the Christ.[89] This movement to the center of history is a complex process, one that assumes an organic relationship between the Old and the New Testaments.

For Tillich, the concept of "the center of history" is a metaphor for that moment in history "before which everything is preparation," and "after which everything is reception."[90] The center of history is both the criterion and source of the saving power of history, and is therefore a fundamental component of Tillich's doctrine of revelation.[91] The center of history is not a chronological center, and there is no progress beyond the center. History does not move in an equal rhythm but is a dynamic force with its ups and downs.[92] There is a progressive dimension to the movement of history, but it is not inevitable. Using a metaphor reminiscent of that used by Clement of Alexandria,[93] for Tillich the only progressive dimension of history is the movement from immaturity to maturity, which involves the purification of the religious consciousness.[94] The immature stage belongs to the universal history of religion, prior to its transformation by prophetic criticism.[95]

> This maturing process is working in all history, but a particular development was necessary in order to prepare for Him in whom the final revelation would occur. This is the function of the development of which the Old Testament is the document. The Old Testament manifestations of the Kingdom of God produced the direct preconditions for its final manifestations in the Christ ... And every missionary activity, inside and outside Christian culture, must follow the Old Testament's purification of the religious consciousness. Without the Old Testament, Christianity relapses into the immaturities of the universal history of religion – including the history of the Jewish religion (which was the main object of criticism and purification by the Old Testament prophets).[96]

---

87 *ST* III, 368.
88 Ibid.
89 Ibid., 368 – 369.
90 Ibid., 364.
91 Ibid., 365.
92 Ibid., 371.
93 J. N. D. Kelly, *Early Christian Doctrine*, rev. edn (San Francisco: Harper & Row, 1978), 179. For Clement, Adam as a historical individual and as representative of all humanity was born into an innocent and childlike state. Although weakened by sin, he could advance to a more perfect state through the exercise of free will.
94 *ST* III, 365.
95 Ibid.
96 Ibid

Three additional observations can be made about this passage. First, as with the prior passages on revelation and Christology, the Old Testament plays an essential, preparatory role. The historical particularity of the times, places and persons of the Old Testament provided the necessary and direct preconditions for the revelation of Jesus as the Christ. Second, the process of maturing is best exemplified by the prophetic critique and transformation of religion. For Tillich, similar transformations could occur within other religions in other cultures that participate in the New Being, both before and after the Christ event, referred to as the "transtemporal presence of the Christ in every period."[97] This process of critique and transformation is an outworking of the rational, historical dialectic. Third, there is also a distinction between "the Jewish religion" and the Old Testament prophetic consciousness. For Tillich, the purely historical expression of Judaism, with instances of legalism and nationalism, must be challenged and purified by the prophetic dimension. Tillich has consistently maintained a distinction between "empirical Judaism," and "Jewish prophetism," the latter being the precursor to the Protestant principle.

This chapter has analyzed several themes that were developed in Tillich's theological history of religion, which consistently portrays Judaism as providing an indispensable basis for Christianity. In ST I, Tillich draws upon Max Weber's theory of ideal types to compare different religions using his typological method, by taking into account what they have in common, and by what is distinctive to each. This is to avoid the paralysis that would occur if each tradition were completely diffused by its historical particularity, making meaningful comparisons impossible. Tillich has struggled with the problem of historical particularity since *The Socialist Decision.* In ST I, II and III, Tillich employs the history of religion as the context to develop a doctrine of revelation (Volume I), a Christology (Volume II), and an ecclesiology (Volume III). In all three volumes, Tillich develops various theological-historical schemes to describe how the Christian revelation emerged from the complex history of religion, although he never uses that complexity to diminish or eliminate, the role of Judaism as the precursor to Christianity.

In Chapter Six, the final change to Tillich's method of dealing with historical particularity will be discussed. In addition, how he establishes an "inclusive" history of religion will be observed, and also how he subordinates Judeo-Christian monotheism, indeed any and every religion, to "the religion of the concrete spirit."

97 Ibid., 390, cited by Thomas in *Tillich*, 170.

Chapter Six: An Inclusive Dialectic

Introduction

Thus far, five works have been analyzed in detail, the 1910 Dissertation, the 1912 Dissertation, *The Socialist Decision*, the *Judenfrage* lectures, and the *Systematic Theology*. Three out of the five works, the two Schelling dissertations, and *The Socialist Decision*, have short but distinct sections dedicated to the meaning of Judaism. Four out of the five works have a dialectical structure. The fourth work analyzed, the *Judenfrage* lectures, does not have a dialectical structure, but discusses in considerable detail the roots of anti-Semitism and anti-Judaism within Christian history and thought, and relates directly to the thesis of this book.

However, these are not the only written works on Tillich's view of Judaism and its relation to Christianity, or the topics of anti-Semitism and anti-Judaism. For example, in Chapter Four it was noted that two lectures written in the early 1940s provided the background for the *Judenfrage* lectures, "Catholicism and Anti-Judaism"[1] and "Protestantism and Anti-Semitism."[2] During the post World War II period of the 1940s and 1950s, Tillich wrote or drafted several more lectures on these topics.[3] He never wrote a systematic analysis of Judaism, its relationship to Christianity, anti-Semitism and anti-Judaism, other than the *Judenfrage* lectures. Nevertheless, he committed enough to print to enable an analysis and summary of his views on these topics. It is outside the scope of this book to analyze each of these pieces,

1 Tillich, Harvard Archives, bMS 649/62(6).

2 Tillich, Harvard Archives, bMS 649/62(7).

3 Many of these lectures are found in the Harvard Tillich Archives. 1: bMS 649/62 (5) "Can the Jew Return to Germany?," handwritten, n.d.; 2: bMS 649/28 (11) "Anti-Semitism and the Christian Church," handwritten, in German, n.d.; 3: bMS 649/28 (15) "Gespräch über Earl Mayer's theses on Anti-Judaism," typescript, in German, 1941; 4: bMS 649/45 (1) "The Role of Judaism in Post-War World Reconstruction," address, typescript, n.d.; 5: bMS 649/45 (2) "The Relevance of Judaism and Christianity in Face of the Secular Systems of Life," handwritten, n.d.; 6: bMS 649/45 (3) "The Search for Truth and Unity in the Judaic-Christian Tradition," Cooper Union University, New York, handwritten, February 14, 1955; 7: bMS 649/46 (3) "The Concept of Faith in the Jewish-Christian Tradition," article, handwritten, n.d.; 8: bMS 649/62 (5) "Can the Jew Return to Germany?," handwritten, n.d.; 9: bMS 649/62 (8) "The Religious Relation Between Christianity and Judaism In the Future," handwritten and typescript, n.d.; 10: bMS 649/81 (5) "Is there a Judeo-Christian Religion?" three versions of a presentation at the Jewish Theological Seminary of America, handwritten and typescript, December 10, 1947; 11: bMS 649/87 (5) "The Religious and Philosophical Presuppositions of the National Socialist Attack on Judaism," in 'The Interpretation of History', typescript, 1936; in Chapter Seven, this will be referred to as "Two Types of Historical Vision," for the reasons discussed there.

but eight lectures emerge as directly related to Jewish-Christian relations: (i) "The Religious Relation Between Christianity and Judaism in the Future;"[4] (ii) "Is There a Judeo-Christian Religion?," from 1947;[5] (iii) "The Relevance of Judaism and Christianity in the Face of the Secular Systems of Life;"[6] (iv) "The Concept of Faith in the Jewish-Christian Tradition;"[7] (v) "Jewish Influences on Contemporary Christian Theology,"[8] (vi) "The Search for Truth and Unity in the Judaic-Christian Tradition;"[9] (vii) the four-part 1961 Bampton lectures at Columbia University, and (viii) the final lecture Tillich gave ten days before he died in October of 1965, "The Significance of the History of religion for the Systematic Theologian."[10] The final two works, the Bampton Lectures and "The Significance of the History of religion for the systematic theologian" ("Significance"), were published and became the most important of these. In both works, the influence of Tillich's "dialectic of the Holy" is apparent.

The following analysis intends to demonstrate the following: (i) that the history of religion remained fundamentally important for Tillich throughout his entire career;[11] (ii) that Tillich's history of religion has an inclusive dialectical structure, meaning that conflicting elements make enduring contributions to new creative unities; and (iii) that this inclusive dialectic provides a philosophical

4 Handwritten and typescript; undated. Tillich, Harvard Archive, bMS 649/62(8) – Tillich, "Future."

5 Handwritten and typescript. Presented at the Jewish Theological Seminary of America, 10 December 1947; Tillich, Harvard Archive, bMS 649/81(5) – Tillich, "Judeo-Christian."

6 Handwritten and undated. Tillich, Harvard Archive, bMS 649/45(3) – Tillich, "Relevance."

7 Handwritten and undated. Tillich, Harvard Archive, bMS 649/46(3) – Tillich, "Faith."

8 Transcript of a lecture given as one of the Milton Steinberg Lectures in Jewish Theology at the Park Avenue Synagogue in New York City, published in *Cross Currents* 2/3 (1952): 35–42 – Tillich, "Jewish Influences."

9 Handwritten lecture delivered at Cooper Union University, New York, February 15, 1955. Tillich, Harvard Archive, bMS 649/45(3) – Tillich, "Search."

10 The Fortress Press edition of Tillich, *Encounter* has added an appendix to the Bampton lectures, with Tillich's final public lecture, "The Significance of the History of religion for the Systematic Theologian." Editor Stendahl notes that this lecture was recorded on tape, was delivered from ten pages of carefully outlined notes, and was transcribed and edited by Jerald C. Brauer in its final form. The Brauer edition, which was reprinted in the Fortress volume, first appeared in Brauer's *The Future of Religions* (New York: Harper & Row, 1966.). This will be noted as Tillich, "Significance."

11 In the eighth Lecture, "Significance," Tillich acknowledges his debt to the German "History of Religions School:" "I am still grateful, looking back on my own formative period of study and the time after it, to what in German is called the *religiongeshichtliche Schule*, the School of the History of Religions in biblical and church historical studies. These studies opened our eyes and demonstrated the degree to which the biblical tradition participates in the Asia Minor and Mediterranean traditions. I remember the liberating effect of the understanding of universal, human motives in the stories of Genesis or in Hellenistic existentialism and Persian eschatology, as they appeared in the late periods of the Old and New Testament" (ibid., 68).

and theological basis for Tillich to promote a permanent importance of Judaism, until the *eschaton.*

6.1 The Bampton Lectures

Tillich visited Japan in 1960, and his first-hand encounter with Buddhism, as prototypical of non-western religions, had profoundly influenced how he understood the relation of religion to secular society. This influence was expressed in the four Bampton Lectures delivered in the fall of 1961 at the Low Memorial Library of Columbia University. In the Foreword to the Bampton Lectures editor Krister Stendahl observes that Tillich believed that he should start his theological work "all over again," even though he was nearing the completion of the third volume of the *Systematic Theology,* which was published in 1963.[12] Whereas Tillich's primary goal in the *Systematic Theology* was to provide a theological response to secular culture, in the Bampton Lectures he adds a new aspect to this discussion.

For Tillich, since the Enlightenment, secularism generated "quasi-religions," which are cultural and political movements that are objects of ultimate concern, which is in keeping with Tillich's theological interpretation culture.[13] In the Bampton lectures, Tillich analyzes the encounter of the major world religions and the quasi-religions brought on by modernity: liberal humanism, nationalism, socialism, Fascism (the radicalized form of nationalism) and Communism (the radicalized form of socialism). There are four lectures in the series: (i) the encounter of religions and quasi-religions with the present situation; (ii) the principles that Christianity uses to judge non-Christian religions; (iii) a Christian-Buddhist conversation; and (iv) how Christianity judges itself in light of its encounter with the world religions.

---

12 Tillich, *Bampton Lectures*, foreword, vii.

13 Tillich's expansive concept of "religion" in the Bampton Lectures is similar to that used in *The Religious Situation:* "Religion is the state of being grasped by an ultimate concern, a concern which qualifies all other concerns as preliminary and which itself contains the answer to the question of the meaning of our life. Therefore this concern is unconditionally serious and shows a willingness to sacrifice any finite concern which is in conflict with it. The predominant religious name for the content of such concern is God–a god or gods. In nontheistic religions divine qualities are ascribed to a sacred object or an all-pervading power or a highest principle such as the Brahma or the One. In secular quasi-religions the ultimate concern is directed towards objects like nation, science, a particular form or stage of society, or a highest ideal of humanity, which are then considered divine" (Tillich, Bampton Lectures, 3).

The relationship of Judaism to Christianity within the history of religion is most directly discussed in the first and third Bampton lectures, with the relevant sections to be discussed below. In the first Bampton lecture, Tillich discusses "Christian universalism," which provides a model for how Christianity ought to relate to non-Christian religions, and concludes that the prophetic concept of justice provides the basis for judging the theological value of all other religions.[14] In addition, in the third Bampton lecture on the Christian-Buddhist conversation, Tillich modifies his typological method from what was presented in the *Systematic Theology*. In this discussion, he presents an "inclusive" dialectical history of religion.

6.1.1 First Bampton Lecture: The Emergence of an Exclusive Self-Consciousness

For Tillich, Christianity has historically related to other religions with a posture of "indefiniteness," characterized by openness and mutual influence, especially within antiquity and in the modern period. According to Tillich, in the ancient world Christianity experienced major conflict only internally. This is far from conclusive, given the emergence of the Apologists in the pre-Nicene period and the transition from Christianity as a persecuted religion under Diocletian to Christianity as a dominant religion under Constantine.[15] Nevertheless, Tillich also claims that during the middle ages, this posture of indefiniteness, or relative openness in the West, was interrupted by a long period of exclusivism because of the rise of Islam, which caused Christianity to become defensive.[16] Tillich's view of the rise of Islam appears virtually unchanged from his view in the 1910 Dissertation:

> The first outside encounter took place with the rise of Islam, a new and passionate faith, fanatically carried over the known world, invading, subjecting, and reducing eastern Christianity and threatening all Christendom ... The victorious wars of the Islamic tribes and nations forced Christianity to become aware of itself as one religion confronted with another against which it had to defend itself. According to the law that defense narrows down the defender, Christianity at this point became radically exclusive. The Crusades were the ex-

14 James M. Kitagawa uses the term "theological history of religions" in an article titled, "Tillich, Kraemer, and the Encounter of Religions," in *The Thought of Paul Tillich*, ed. James Luther Adams (San Francisco: Harper & Row, 1985), 197–217.
15 In addition, Ruether's view of the Theodosian and Justinian Codes, which mandated a degree of legal subordination of Jews to Christians, was not simply motivated by economic considerations, but was the outworking of a Christian theocratic world view. See Chapter Seven, Section 7.3.
16 Tillich, Bampton Lectures, 24.

> pression of this new self-consciousness. They were the result of the first encounter of Christianity with a new world religion.[17]

This led to an adversarial posture toward the Jews:

> The irrational character of the crusading spirit was confirmed by the fact that the narrowed self-consciousness, created by the encounter of Christianity with Islam, produced also a changed self-consciousness with respect to the Jews... But after the shock of the encounter with Islam the Church became conscious of Judaism as another religion and anti-Judaism became fanatical. Only after this was it possible for governments to use the Jews as political scapegoats to cover up their own political and economic failures, and only since the end of the nineteenth century did religious anti-Judaism become racial anti-Semitism, which was – and still is – one of the many ingredients in the radicalized nationalistic quasi-religion.[18]

For Tillich, Christianity historically permitted itself to be influenced by other religions that it came into contact with. Therefore, in "the present situation," Christianity should maintain a posture of relative openness in its encounters with other religions and quasi-religions. Tillich's historical framework employs "a dialectical union of rejection and acceptance" between Christianity and the other religions, which often involves tension and uncertainty.[19] His brief historical analysis applies this mixture of rejection and acceptance in the following periods: (i) the Old Testament in the religion of Israel versus paganism; (ii) the ministry of Jesus, especially in the story of the Good Samaritan and John's story of the Samaritan woman (in John 4); (iii) in Paul's polemic against "the legalism of Christianized Jews and against the libertinism of Christianized pagans;"[20] (iv) the universal presence of the Logos as described by many Church Fathers;[21]

---

17 Ibid., 23–25.
18 Ibid., 24–25.
19 Tillich, Bampton Lectures, 19.
20 Ibid., 21.
21 Tillich's portrayal of the patristic period is consonant with his dialectical method: "In early Christianity the judgment of other religions was determined by the idea of the Logos. The Church Fathers emphasized the universal presence of the Logos, the Word, the principle of divine self-manifestation, in all religions and cultures. The Logos is present everywhere, like the seed on the land, and this presence is a preparation for the central appearance of the Logos in a historical person, the Christ. In light of these ideas Augustine could say that the true religion had existed always and was called Christian only after the appearance of the Christ. Accordingly, his dealing with other religions was dialectical as was that of his predecessors. They did not reject them unambiguously and, of course, they did not accept them unambiguously. But in their apologetic writings they acknowledged the preparatory character of these religions and tried to show how their inner dynamics drives them toward questions whose answer is given in the central

(v) the return of this mediating position with Nicholas of Cusa in the Renaissance (after the long period of reaction to the threat from Islam), and Christian humanism under Erasmus, and into the Enlightenment.[22]

A. The Universal Importance of Justice

Tillich's portrayal of the history of Christianity as the dialectic of acceptance and rejection illustrates his dedication to dialectical structures. Also, his use of typological analysis combines analyzing the general features of a religion, in addition to its "inner drive," as will be seen in the next section of this chapter. However, for the purposes of this argument, Tillich's portrayal of the Old Testament and its relation to paganism contains a critical detail. He underscores the importance of justice, as rooted in the Hebrew prophets, as the *condition* by which all subsequent expressions of religion have enduring value. Similar to the *Judenfrage* lectures, Tillich identifies the prophet Amos as the starting point of the universality of justice, insofar as the chosen people of Israel became subject to a divine standard that existed independently of their king, temple and cult.

Specifically, Jewish prophetism is the paradigmatic instance of "exclusive monotheism," which was noted as a critical transitional stage from polytheism to trinitarian monotheism, as discussed in *ST* I, 218–230. It is worth quoting Tillich at some length:

> Since Amos, prophecy threatened Israel, the nation of Jahweh, with destruction by Jahweh because of its injustice. The covenant between Jahweh and the nation does not give the nation a claim to Jahweh's championship; he will turn against them if they violate justice. The exclusive monotheism of the prophetic religion is not due to the absoluteness of one particular god as against the others, but it is the universal validity of justice which produces the exclusive monotheism of the God of justice. This, of course, implies that justice is a principle which transcends every particular religion and makes the exclusiveness of any particular religion conditional. It is this principle of conditional exclusiveness which will guide our further inquiry into the attitude of Christianity to the world religions.[23]

Once again the principle of justice, which is uniquely rooted in the prophets of the Old Testament, plays an indispensible role in Tillich's theology.

---

event on which Christianity is based. They tried to show the convergent lines between the Christian message and the intrinsic quests of pagan religions" (ibid., 21–22).

22 Ibid., 25–27.

23 Ibid., 20.

6.1.2 The Third Bampton Lecture: "The Holy" within an Inclusive Dialectic

In the third Bampton lecture, one of Tillich's goals is to discuss the encounter of Christianity with "one of the greatest, strangest, and at the same time one of the most competitive of the religions proper – Buddhism."[24] In this lecture, Tillich does not say anything about the relationship between Christianity and Judaism, but he clearly states *what kind* of dialectic his history of religion scheme employs. First, his method of "dynamic typology" employs the concept of "inner drive," which identifies that which is distinctive and enduring for any particular religion. Second, in contrast to Hegel, Tillich explicitly refers to the history of religion as "inclusive," which helps provide a theoretical basis for continuity between Judaism and Christianity. Specifically, Tillich's dialectical history of religion assumes that individual religions represent contrasting poles within one structure, with each pole making an enduring contribution to a new unity within the single structure. This sounds very similar to what he described in the 1910 and 1912 Dissertations.

A. Dynamic Typology and Inner Drive

Tillich's typological method becomes more refined over time. Specifically, his use of "particularity and universality" in the 1910 Dissertation, his application of "principle" in *The Socialist Decision*, his use of "structural analogies" in the *Judenfrage* lectures, and his use of "typological analysis" in the *Systematic Theology* and, and his final modification to "dynamic typology" in his two final occasional lectures on the topic, are all ways that Tillich extracts meaning from diverse historical phenomena.[25] In creating these analytical concepts, he is not being naïve about the diversity of historical phenomena, but astute in seeking ways to manage that diversity and assign relative priority to its elements.

Similar to his approach in the *Systematic Theology*, in the Bampton Lectures Tillich attempts to make sense of historical multiplicity through the use of "types." Types identify the general characteristics of each religion and help articulate how one religion relates to another, in order to make sense of "the seemingly incomprehensible jungle which the history of religion presents to the investigating mind."[26] In the Bampton Lectures, Tillich modifies his "typological analysis," as seen in ST I, in opposition to what he understands to be Hegel's use of "static"

24 Ibid., 34–35.

25 In *Interpretation of History*, Tillich tries out the concept of "phenomenological intuition" (266–269), although this bears no relation to the relationship of Judaism and Christianity, and is outside the scope of this book.

26 Ibid., 34.

types. First, the practice of hermeneutical "oscillation" between "intuition of the special" and "analysis of the typical," as expressed in ST I, is replaced by a clear description of a polar relation between independent elements, "*each of which is necessary for the other and for the whole*" (italics mine), with the corresponding tension between the independent elements being assigned a potentially transformative role.[27] Second, instead of the binary distinction of special/typical being assigned dynamic/static features, respectively, Tillich redefines the term "type" to increase its flexibility within his dialectical framework.

In his revised view, "types" have two features, the first being a "static" and "spatial" character that distinguishes one type from another.[28] Second, types also have a "dynamic" aspect, or inner drive, which reflects how they relate to one another, and also characterizes how one type can be *transformed into* another. This dynamic quality of types allows individual phenomena, expressed as types, to exist in creative tension with one another. Therefore, individual types could persist in a relation of *mutual interdependence:*

> The kind of dialectics which, I believe, is most adequate to typological inquiries is the description of contrasting poles within one structure. A polar relation is a relation of interdependent elements, each of which is necessary for the other one and for the whole, although it is in tension with the opposite element. The tension drives both to conflicts and beyond the conflicts to possible unions of the polar elements. Described in this way, types lose their static rigidity, and the individual things and persons can transcend the type to which they belong without losing their definite character.[29]

B. Creative Tension and the Holy

Thus far, Tillich's emphases on the importance of "creative tension" and "mutual interdependence" between phenomena, *all within one structure*, are intended to provide a basis for dialogue between Christianity and Buddhism. However, this can also be applied to support the continuity between Judaism and Christianity.

At this point, Tillich addresses the critical question concerning the fate of religions that no longer participate in this dialectical history of religion, but rather "die off." Tillich's response to this question contains the kernel of how his understanding of the history of religion can be applied to *any* historical or religious phenomenon: not only does a religion come into conflict with one or more religions, and is either enhanced or diminished through that conflict, but each religion has an ongoing inner conflict *within itself.* Therefore, in principle, no reli-

27 Ibid., 34–35.
28 Ibid., 34.
29 Ibid., 34–35.

gion *must* die off, but if it responds *creatively* and *critically* within any given context, it will endure by providing one or more elements to *the new union* resulting from the tension of two *prior* polar elements:

> While specific religions, as well as specific cultures, do grow and die, the forces which brought them into being, the type-determining elements, belong to the nature of the holy and with it to the nature of man, and with it to the nature of the universe and the revelatory self-manifestation of the divine. Therefore the decisive point in a dialogue between two religions is not the historically determined, contingent *embodiment of* the typological elements, but these elements themselves. Under the method of dynamic typology every dialogue between religions is accompanied by a silent dialogue *within* the representatives of each of the participating religions.[30]

For Tillich the idea of the "silent dialogue" appears to be an extension of what occurred in the emergence of the Christian Logos. Given the context, he is most likely referring to the tension occurring *within* a religious tradition, which could result in the creation of a new unity. For example, as discussed in the prior chapter on the *Systematic Theology*, Tillich viewed polytheism as predominantly concrete with some absolute features, and he viewed monotheism as predominantly absolute with some concrete features.[31] He believed that an optimal balance was achieved between the two poles of monotheism and polytheism, or more specifically, when trinitarian monotheism emerged. For Tillich, this occurred at "the right time," when the Christian Logos became manifest, in the appearance and reception of Jesus as the Christ, the bearer of the New Being.

When Tillich applies this framework to the relationship between Christianity and Buddhism, he is only willing to venture a preliminary statement that Christianity and Buddhism occupy opposite poles within a single polarity, and that each has maintained a sacramental basis, but also moved beyond it, in one of two possible directions.[32] For Tillich, one direction is towards a mystical expression, "the experience of the holy as being," which is predominantly seen in the religions of India.[33] The other possible direction is towards an ethical expression, "the experience of the holy as what ought to be," predominantly seen in the religion of Israel.[34] This is similar to the Is/Ought, mysticism/prophetic, Christian-

30 Ibid., 35–36.

31 For example, "Polytheism could not exist unless it included monotheistic elements....However, just as there no absolute polytheism, so there is no absolute monotheism;" ST I, 225.

32 Tillich cites an example of a Christian theologian arguing for the relative priority of "the ethical" over "the mystical" in a dialogue with a Buddhist priest, and at a minimum the Christian concedes that he struggles with the same tension *within* his own tradition. Bampton Lectures, 36–37.

33 Ibid.

34 Ibid.

ity/Judaism set of polarities that have been discussed in prior chapters, but Tillich is extending how they can be used to encompass non-theistic religions. This is revealing because it shows how he attempts to simultaneously retain his theological dialectic of the history of religion,[35] yet modify its concepts to expand the scope such that it could encompass any religion. Tillich concludes this brief methodological statement by acknowledging that it is a preliminary instance of dialogue between religions, but that it also illustrates the encounter and conflict of elements of "the Holy" within every particular religion.[36]

C. An Inclusive Dialectic

For Tillich, this dialectical history of religion is superior to Hegelian dialectics, which pushes "into the past that which is dialectically left behind."[37] Tillich gives a specific example, that of the relation of Christianity and Buddhism: "For example, in the problem of the relation of Christianity to Buddhism, Hegelian dialectics considers Buddhism as an early stage of the religious development which is now totally abandoned by history. It still exists, but the World-Spirit is no longer creatively in it."[38] It is outside the scope of this book to address Hegel's view of the relation of eastern religions to Christianity, but it is clear that Tillich's alternative is inclusive by contrast. In principle, Tillich's dialectical history of religion tends to "gather up" not "leave behind," providing a framework for maintaining continuity between Judaism and Christianity, not to mention continuity between Christianity and other religions.

Tillich never refers to his dialectic as "inclusive," but he does use this term to characterize his view of the history of religion. In the above discussion of the first Bampton lecture, Tillich observed the alternating manner by which Christianity accepted and rejected other religions in antiquity. When this posture of acceptance and rejection is applied to the modern encounter of Christianity and the world religions, especially non-western religions, Tillich invokes Jesus' command in Matthew 5:48: "You must be all-inclusive as your heavenly Father is all-inclusive."[39]

35 James M. Kitagawa uses the term "theological history of religions" in an article titled, "Tillich, Kraemer, and the Encounter of Religions," in *The Thought of Paul Tillich*, ed. James Luther Adams (San Francisco: Harper & Row, 1985), 197–217.

36 Tillich, Bampton Lectures, 37.

37 Ibid., 35.

38 Ibid.

39 Commenting upon early Christianity and its implications for Christianity and the world religions, Tillich says: "All these are well-known facts, but it is important to see them in the new light of the present encounter of the world religions, for they show that early Christianity did not consider itself as a radical-exclusive, but as the all-inclusive religion in the sense of the say-

6.2 The Significance of the History of Religion

Right up until ten days before his death from a heart attack in October of 1965, Tillich was pondering the theological significance of the history of religion. As mentioned above, in the 1961 Bampton Lectures and just prior to his completion of Volume Three of the *Systematic Theology* in 1963, Tillich began to seriously consider the importance of non-western religions for Christian theology. Tillich's final lecture, "The Significance of the History of religion for the Systematic Theologian," establishes a method for integrating all religions, especially non-western religions, into a theological and revelatory framework.

"Significance" possesses three characteristics that relate to the argument of this chapter. First, he maintains a dialectical history of religion as the underlying framework of his comparative analysis of Christianity and non-Christian religions. Second, he employs the principle of justice, as derived from the Hebrew prophets Amos and Hosea, as an essential critical principle within his dialectical framework. Third, his dialectical framework provides criteria that, to the extent they emerge in one phenomenon, will constitute his optimal, non-Christocentric, form of religion, "the religion of the concrete spirit."

At the very beginning of this final public lecture, Tillich remains committed to maintaining an "existential" dimension to his method of inquiry. He argues that any theologian who believes in the importance of the history of religion has made "two basic decisions," by rejecting two distinct, yet related, ways of doing theology, the "orthodox-exclusive" approach, and the "secular-rejective" approach. The notion of making a "decision" as part of the method of inquiry is not new for Tillich, as he developed an eschatological view of socialism in *The Socialist Decision*. Tillich, in keeping with numerous prior works, says that these alternatives have a long history, and his solution serves to mediate between them.

For Tillich, one way of doing theology, the "orthodox-exclusive" approach, was revived by Karl Barth in the 20th century. This view concludes that Christianity manifests the one true revelation of God, and that all other religions are false, merely human attempts to reach God. Under this view, "religion" is a theologically substandard concept, because all religions are "merely human," without any revelatory content.[40] In order to reject this view, Tillich says that one must adopt these five presuppositions: (i) that revelatory experiences are universally

ing, 'All that is true anywhere in the world belongs to us, the Christians.' And it is significant that the famous words of Jesus, 'You, therefore, must be perfect, as your heavenly Father is perfect' (which was always an exegetic riddle), would, according to recent research, be better translated, 'You must be all-inclusive as your heavenly Father is all-inclusive' " (ibid., 22).

40 Tillich, "Significance;" 63 – 64.

human; (ii) that revelation is received within the limitations of human finitude; (iii) that there is a revelatory process that is subject to mystical, prophetic and secular criticism; (iv) that there may be a central event in the history of religion that is the basis for a concrete theology with universal significance; and (v) that the sacred is the "depth" of the secular, in which the former is the critic and creative ground of the latter.[41] As will be shown below, the fifth presupposition is distinctive in its use of "depth" and "creative ground, which employs spatial imagery to characterize a phenomenon's inner drive: "The sacred does not lie beside the secular, but it is its depths. The sacred is the creative ground and at the same time a critical judgment of the secular. But the religious can be this only if it is at the same time a judgment on itself, a judgment which must use the secular as a tool of its own religious self-criticism." [42]

The other way of doing theology has precedence in 19th century liberal theology, which emphasizes the primacy of the ethical, and is also found in the 20th century, the "God is dead" theology. Unlike the orthodox-exclusive view in which revelation is expressed in historically traditional language, this "secular-rejective" approach assumes that the sacred has been "fully absorbed by the secular."[43] Similar to the orthodox-exclusive view, the secular-rejective view dismisses religious symbols, rites and institutions, not as "purely human," as if there were things that could be of divine origin, but as non-empirical phenomena that are excluded in principle.[44] To deny the secular-rejective view requires adherence to only one presupposition: that even the most apparently secularized culture maintains myths and rites that express relation to the divine, even if those myths and rites possess much different *content* than that which is suggested by *traditional forms*.[45] For Tillich, traditional myths, rites and language must have some origin in the divine, and cannot be completely "collapsed into" or "identified with" the secular.[46]

---

41 Ibid., 64–65.

42 Ibid., 65.

43 Ibid., 65.

44 Ibid., 65–66.

45 "He must assume that religion as a structure of symbols of intuition and action – that is, myths and rites within a social group – has lasting necessity for even the most secularized culture and the most demythologized theology. I derive this lasting necessity, the lasting necessity of religion, from the fact that spirit requires embodiment to become real and effective. It is quite well to say that the Holy, or the Ultimate, or the Word is within the secular realm, and I myself have done so innumerable times. But in order to say that something is *in* something, it must have at least the possibility of being *outside* of it. " Ibid., 66.

46 Tillich provides the following illustration: "Let me say the same thing in a well-known, popular form. The reformers were right when they said that every day is the Lord's Day and there-

Tillich argues that both approaches are reductionistic, and exhibit a "Jesus-centered alliance" in the sense that each eliminates everything from Christianity except the figure of Jesus of Nazareth. The orthodox do this by making him the exclusive bearer of revelation, and the secular do this by limiting his significance to ethical principles.[47]

6.2.1 Dynamic Typology and the Religion of the Concrete Spirit

In response to the twin problems of the orthodox-exclusive and secular-rejective approaches, Tillich develops a *theology* of the history of religion, which intends to draw upon the richness of the tradition, but must balance a positive valuation of universal revelation with a critical assessment.[48] Tillich's theology of the history of religion employs a dynamic-typological approach, which is the fourth time that Tillich has used "type" or "typological" to interpret religious phenomena.[49] Due to limits of space, Tillich refrained from going into detail on what he meant by typological, except that it encompasses periodic manifestations of the Holy: "My approach is dynamic-typological. There is no progressive development which goes on and on, but there are elements in the experience of the Holy which are always there, if the Holy is experienced. These elements, if they are predominant in one religion, create a particular religious type."[50] If the optimal relations are achieved, then the "religion of the concrete spirit" is present.

Specifically, there are three elements that, if they unite, would constitute the religion of the concrete spirit. The first element of any religion is its sacramental basis, in which there is an experience of the Holy expressed within the finite, which is apprehensible despite having a mysterious character.[51] Against the

---

fore, devaluated the sacredness of the seventh day. But in order to say this, there must have been a Lord's Day, and that not only once upon a time but continuously in counterbalance against the overwhelming weight of the secular. This is what makes God-language necessary, however, untraditional that language may be. This makes a serious affirmation in the history of religion possible." Ibid., 66.

47 Ibid., 67.

48 Ibid., 68.

49 The first time was in the *Judenfrage* lectures, where typological was explained as the creation of and fostering of stereotypes. The second time was a much more involved understanding in *ST* I, II.II.A.2, "Typological Considerations," which described the process of how typical events are related to special events. The third time was the third Bampton lecture on the conversation between Christianity and Buddhism discussed above.

50 Ibid., 70.

51 Ibid., 70–71.

first element a critical movement emerges that seeks to prevent the sacramental element from being reduced to mere objects, which requires adding a dimension of "depth."[52] Against these two elements, a third element emerges, the prophetic/ethical element, the element of "ought to be," which is based upon Jewish prophetism and maintains the principle of justice:

> Here the sacramental is criticized because of demonic consequences like the denial of justice in the name of holiness. This is the whole fight of the Jewish prophets against sacramental religion. In some of the words of Amos and Hosea the fight is carried so far that the whole cult is abrogated. This criticism is decisive for Judaism and is one element of Christianity.[53]

For Tillich, if religious experience does not exhibit both the sacramental and the mystical/critical elements, then moralism and ultimately secularization occur. However, for Tillich, the history of religion will endure, and that the religion of the concrete spirit will always be present at some point, however fleetingly and fragmentarily, because "the inner aim of the history of religions is to become the religion of the concrete spirit."[54] The history of religions is "a living tradition" and is "a fight for the religion of the concrete spirit, a fight of God against religion within religion."[55] For Tillich, this fight is the key for interpreting the otherwise chaotic array of events that is the history of religions.[56] The manifestation has been, and will only be, actualized fragmentarily, only to "happen here and there."[57] Despite the non-Christocentric character of the religion of the concrete spirit, Tillich retains the fundamentally Christian symbol of "Christus Victor," a patristic era interpretation of Christ on the cross, as a definitive criticism of any demonic claim, any idolatrous claim to the absolute.[58] This is Tillich's mediating position against the reductionist, Jesus-centric orthodox-exclusive and secular-rejective approaches to theology.

Tillich's observation about the abrogation of the cult is very similar to his position in *The Socialist Decision,* the *Judenfrage* lectures, and in the Bampton Lectures. Each of these posed critiques of Jewish idolatry of temple cult, king and nation, with the threat of destruction being in keeping with God's faithfulness to the covenant. In addition, the foundation of justice has been a consistent theme since *The Socialist*

52 Tillich refers to this as the "demonization of the sacramental;" Ibid., 71.
53 Ibid., 71.
54 Ibid., 72.
55 Ibid., 72–73.
56 Ibid., 72–73.
57 Ibid., 73.
58 Ibid., 73.

Decision. For Tillich, to the extent that these three elements of sacramental, mystical and prophetic can occur in a unified form, then the "religion of the concrete spirit" is present. Tillich refrains from identifying this with Christianity, as he has fully relativized and subordinated Christianity, and every other religion, to "the religion of the concrete spirit." However, he claims that Paul's doctrine of the Spirit is the best expression of this.[59] For the purposes of this book, the prophetic dimension of Judaism is an essential component of Tillich's highest and best form of religion, the religion of the concrete spirit.

By the end of his life, Tillich had articulated a highly adaptive framework, as he responded to momentous challenges. The main examples discussed in this book are the Holocaust and the problems of anti-Judaism and anti-Semitism. These led him away from what appears to be Christian exclusivism in the 1910 and 1912 Dissertations, to an emerging view of Judaism and Christianity as equals (a "Judeo-Christianity"), developed during the decades of the 1930s into the 1960s. There also appears to be another shift, which occurred after Tillich's visit to Japan in 1960. While Tillich maintains his dialectical structure that is charged with theological meaning, he casts aside any distinctively Christian terminology, in favor of the universally applicable religion of the concrete spirit, which retains the dialectic of the Holy. The adaptability of the religion of the concrete spirit reflects its ability to accommodate the tension between critical and creative aspects, as contrasing poles, within one structure.

Chapters Two through Six have made a solid case for how Tillich avoided the sub-Christian position of the Aryan Christians. This meets the original goal of providing a descriptive, historical and developmental treatment of Tillich's theological interpretation of Judaism, within his historical context. The final chapter will assess Tillich's view from a normative position, what it might mean for current Jewish-Christian relations, and what is enduring for his legacy on this issue.

59 Ibid., 72.

Chapter Seven: The Importance of Historical Consciousness

Beginning with the Preface, this analysis has intended to be a work of historical theology, not a work of inter-faith dialogue. I have attempted to draw out the clearly positive manner in which Tillich's theological method views Judaism, albeit in a specialized way. Chapter One demonstrates Tillich's ongoing concern with anti-Semitism, and it also characterizes some of the complicated ways that anti-Judaism is deeply embedded in Western thought (Nirenberg). It also recalls the overt and shameless Christian anti-Judaism and anti-Semitism of the Nazi period (Heschel). This served to set up a stark contrast between those views and Tillich's view, which was developed in the following chapters. Tillich's spirit of Judaism is positive relative to some other thinkers, for example, prominent German philosophers such as Kant, Fichte and Hegel, as portrayed by Nirenberg. In addition, he identifies the theological roots of anti-Jewish and anti-Semitic *ideology.* In doing so, he takes the vital first step in making a positive contribution to Jewish-Christian relations.

The primary source analyses performed in Chapters Two through Six portray a "positive trajectory" in terms of how Tillich uses Judaism within his theological framework, even if his view is not fully faithful to Jewish self-understanding. Within Tillich's mature thought, meaning his later works over earlier works, four concepts stand out. The first three are the dialectic of the Holy, the related universality of justice as the criterion to judge the legitimacy of religions, and the purportedly anti-Hegelian inclusive history of religion, citing Matthew 5:48. These are still important concepts in the Bampton Lectures from 1961, as Tillich is deeply pondering the importance of non-Western, non-theistic religions such as Buddhism. The fourth concept is Tillich's non-theistic religion of the concrete spirit, which he develops in his final public lecture in 1965. Tillich illustrates a key aspect of the latter with a reference to Amos and Hosea, two Jewish prophets. The enduring importance of the Jewish prophets in the religion of the concrete spirit parallels anything appropriated from the Christian tradition at this late stage in Tillich's career.

While this historical description and analysis should put Tillich's view in a comparatively favorable light, additional work could be done in several areas to provide a broader and deeper context for the core argument contained in the previous chapters. First, the provocative analysis by Susannah Heschel indicted several high-profile mainstream theologians, meaning those not typically understood to be anti-Jewish, anti-Semitic, or supporters of German National Socialism. More work needs to be done on the use of the history of religions method by other theologians, to determine whether Tillich was an exception to a pattern of systemic anti-Jewish ideas, or whether there was an anti-Jewish pattern. Second, if a more informed perspective can be obtained on how Tillich compares to other theologians who use the history of religions method, then it can be determined whether Tillich was on the way to establishing a new theological paradigm for the relationship of Judaism and Christianity. In other ways, Tillich represented a significant departure from 19th century Protestant liberalism, due to his critique of rationalist trends within theology.[1] A recent article has concluded that Friedrich Schleiermacher was openly a Marcionite.[2] Schleiermacher lamented that Marcion was misunderstood, incorrectly denounced as a heretic, and that the Old Testament was the source of "evil" within Christian theology.[3] This leaves open the possibility that Protestant liberalism needs to be further examined for anti-Jewish dimensions, over and above what Heschel and Marchand have already done. Third, more work needs to be done on Tillich and Islam, or perhaps on Tillich and Orientalism,[4] and/or Tillich and "German Orientalism,"[5] from a historical and contemporary perspective.

In addition, some consideration should be given to more distinctly normative questions. In what ways could Tillich's spirit of Judaism be constructive today, in terms of Jewish-Christian relations? Tillich no doubt proposed these views in order to improve Jewish-Christian relations, and he believed that the two faiths would ideally be engaged in an "eternal conversation,"[6] until the *eschaton*. As a result, Tillich's spirit of Judaism should be assessed from a norma-

1 James C. Livingston, *Modern Christian Thought: From the Enlightenment to Vatican II* (New York: MacMillan Publishing Co., Inc., 1971), "Christian Existentialism," 345–384.

2 Samuel Loncar, "Marcion's Child: Friedrich Schleiermacher, Anti-Judaism, and the Birth of Protestant Liberalism;" Loncar, "Marcion's Child." This paper is currently being reviewed by a major academic journal.

3 The epigraph to the article quotes directly from Schleiermacher, in a letter: "As soon as it is left as a matter of religious taste I have nothing against it; but we owe a dreadful amount of evil in our theology to the dogmatic use of Old Testament. And if Marcion had been properly understood and not hereticized, our doctrine of God would have remained far purer. I consider this necessary to say with the utmost strength, and for me it is a matter of conscience [...]" Friedrich Schleiermacher to Ludwig Gottfried Blanc, April 23, 1830, in Schleiermacher, *Aus Schleiermachers Leben: In Briefen*, ed. Ludwig Jonas and Wilhelm Dilthey (Berlin: Reimer, 1858–1863), 4:496; Loncar, "Marcion's Child."

4 See Edward W. Said, *Orientalism* (New York: Vintage Books, 1979).

5 See Suzanne L. Marchand, *German Orientalism in the Age of Empire: Religion, Race and Scholarship* (New York: German Historical Institute and Cambridge University Press, 2009).

6 One of the epigraphs to the Earley Dissertation; cf. from Tillich's "My Changing Thoughts on Zionism;" unpublished manuscript of address given to a Christian-Jewish Colloquy on "Israel's Rebirth in the Middle East," Chicago, IL, January 21, 1959. In *GW* XIII, 403–408, and Harvard Tillich Archive, bMS 649/45 (4).

tive standpoint. On prior occasions, notably in *The Socialist Decision* and the *Judenfrage* lectures, Tillich explicitly stated the need for "existential participation" to properly address the problems at hand.

In this final chapter, I want to discuss four topics, with the first two being substantive criticisms of Tillich. The first is a brief summary of the most pointed, and extensive, critique of Tillich's view of Judaism, the Earley Dissertation. Second, in a similar vein, Tillich and supersessionism will be examined. Both of these criticisms ought to be evaluated from an inter-faith standpoint. However, they fail to capture the weightiness of Tillich's position, which will be taken up in sections 7.3 and 7.4.

Third, the origin and development of anti-Jewish ideology, and its contribution to Christian theology, will be examined. One of the most penetrating analyses regarding the influence of Christian theology upon anti-Semitism is Rosemary Radford Ruether's *Faith and Fratricide,*[7] which identifies a pervasive dualistic trend within Christian theology that helped to make possible the denigration of Judaism as a religion and the demonization of Jews as a people. Ruether's analysis bears some similarities to Tillich's in the *Judenfrage* lectures, as both discuss the theological contribution to anti-Jewish and anti-Semitic ideology. Aspects of Tillich's inclusive, dialectical history of religion will be brought to bear on this.

Fourth, Tillich's most effective application of his spirit of Judaism was when he diagnosed the problems of German religious nationalism and anti-Semitism, as if it were a principle of historiography. His prophetic interpretation of history was succinctly articulated in a little known unpublished 1933 essay titled "Two Types of Historical Vision," which combines key elements of two larger works, *Interpretation of History* and *The Socialist Decision.* While Tillich was forced to flee Germany in 1933, his prophetic insights were unquestionably validated.

7.1 The Challenge of Real Jews

The only extended critique of Tillich's theology of Judaism is the Earley Dissertation. Earley concludes that Tillich's view is "utterly useless,"[8] and that Tillich is an heir of Marcion.[9] According to Earley, the fatal flaw with Tillich's theology

7 *Faith and Fratricide: The Theological Roots of Anti-Semitism* (Minneapolis, MN: The Seabury Press, 1974).

8 Earley Dissertation, 410–412.

9 Ibid.,, 357–358. This discussion will not address recent historical and textual analyses of Marcion, but refer to the traditional understanding of Marcion of Sinope (d. ca. 160), whose rejection of the Old Testament as Christian scripture, among other things, was determined to be

of Judaism, is that Tillich does not let Judaism "speak for itself," by identifying its own issues in its own terms.[10] Tillich imposes his own view, characterized by Jewish prophetism, and this imposition leads to other problems. Earley argues that it leads to a total misunderstanding of two fundamental aspects of Judaism, the law and the covenant.[11] Tillich's characterization of Jewish law as one form of the ever-present human tendency to seek "self-salvation," is a distinctively Protestant, and especially a Lutheran, distortion,[12] which appears to have its roots in the 1910 Dissertation. Much later in life, Tillich realized that Jewish law could be life-giving. During a 1963 trip to Israel, he and his wife Hannah were fully engaged in a Hasidic celebration of the giving of the Mosaic law, called *Simhat Torah.*[13] Nevertheless, this late-in-life realization did little to inform Tillich's theology, although it might have resulted in a more recognizably Jewish understanding of the law. This supports Earley's argument that Tillich was beholden to his system, to the point that any aspect of Jewish life and thought could be distorted, to serve non-Jewish ends.

While Tillich's deficient view of Jewish law is well-documented, I would not readily concede that Tillich has a similarly deficient view of the covenant, given his view of the fundamental importance of Amos. As noted in the analysis of the *Judenfrage* lectures, Amos's message warns of God's punishment for idolatry, but also of preservation *of God's covenant people*, albeit in exile. However, this phys-

---

heretical. For a recent, detailed textual and reconstructive study, see Judith M. Lieu, *Marcion and the Making of a Heretic: God and Scripture in the Second Century* (Cambridge: Cambridge University Press, 2015).

10 Earley's detailed critique of Tillich appears the final chapter of his Dissertation, 378–417.

11 This is part of van Buren's criticism of Tillich's essay, "Is There a Judeo-Christian Tradition?," cited above in Chapter Six, note 5.

12 Tillich, ST II, 79–81; cf. Earley Dissertation, 267–269. Charlotte Klein makes a similar observation about Tillich, in ST II, 93–94, *Anti-Judaism in Christian Theology*; translated by Edward Quinn, Philadelphia: Fortress Press, 1978, 54–55.

13 Hannah Tillich recalls: "At a pulpit in the center of the room stood a rabbi reading from the Torah in a singsong voice. The men bowed back and forth. They began to sing, forming a line around the Torah-reading rabbi. It was strange to see these men, in their modern suits and hats, moving around the room to such a wild rhythm (from old Chasidic melodies) and with such obviously unaccustomed ferocity....They seemed in a trance, their singing so powerful I imagined them in a fiery furnace killing flames with the power of their song. And, in shadowy vision, I saw the Jews of Germany condemned to die in the ovens of the concentration camps, knowing it, and bursting into song as powerfully as these people did now, dancing around the Torah....Paulus, wearing a skull-cap, had danced in the circle....It was impossible not to become involved. We returned exhausted to our motel." *From Place to Place* (New York: Stein and Day, 1976), 68; cf. Earley Dissertation, 98–99.

ical displacement, while drawing considerable rhetorical power from the time/space polarity, leads to a related problem.

Earley observed that Tillich limits the Jewish *people*, as a theological entity, to the "people of time," posing an obvious problem with the establishment of the State of Israel. How could Tillich, who consistently railed against the idolatry of "space" in the works discussed here, grant any theological legitimacy to Israel?[14] In January of 1959, Tillich publicly addressed this problem, arguing that Israel as a nation could not be considered a fulfillment of the Biblical promised land, but rather had to be assessed as other nations, who participated in the "historical ambiguities of justice and injustice."[15]

Earley also employs observations by his dissertation advisor, Paul van Buren.[16] The latter castigated Tillich for not understanding the importance of Jewish physical survival ("Jewish babies"), within their own nation-state ("Israel Defense Forces"), not only for their own sake, but for the sake of the Gentile church.[17] This assumes that Jews living in *diaspora* are not viable long-term, due to the long history of persecution and the failure of assimilation, leaving the only long-term sustainable option to be a Jewish state, the State of Israel. For this reason, van Buren and Earley see Tillich's idea of Judaism (which I have re-framed positively as Tillich's "spirit of Judaism") as thoroughly dis-embodied, a result of Tillich's neo-Platonism, Idealism and docetism.[18] Therefore, Tillich ends up unwittingly "singing Marcion's song," with the result that his views could not contribute to a constructive relationship between the church and the Jewish people.[19]

---

14 For example, Earley Dissertation, 357–358.

15 Stone, *Radical Social Thought*, 149. Tillich elaborates: "Today it (Israel) is a political reality with a definite space, with a very manifest structure of power, with the injustices of enforcing the law inside the country and the historical existence outside the country – partly, injustices against which the Jews stood always in foreign countries. Therefore, an identification of Israel as a nation with the nature and destiny of the people of time is wrong. There is only the hope that in Israel there will be Jews amongs (sic) the Israelis as there are Jews amongst the other nations, Jews meaning those who represent the prophetic principle of justice and hope for the historical and transhistorical unity of the Kingdom of God. For all this the Jew was and remains as long as there is history;" "My Changing Thoughts on Zionism," 9.

16 The other two readers of the Earley Dissertation were Gerhard Spiegler, at that time also of Temple University, and Franklin Littel, at that time of either Drew University or Temple, a pioneer in the study of Christian theological anti-Judaism.

17 Earley Dissertation, 358.

18 Ibid., 354.

19 Earley quotes van Buren: "I don't think Tillich could possibly have understood this at the time he wrote this essay. I doubt he ever understood it, for you see, it's not spiritual enough. Neo-Platonists have a tough time understanding Judaism. That's why they prefer the Ground of Being to the God of Israel. That's why, in spite of all the brave words spoken against Marcion, they end up singing Mar-

Despite the significance of Earley's criticisms, Tillich is not a Marcionite, in the fundamental sense that he would favor the elimination of the Old Testament from Christianity, and that he would posit two gods, an evil Demiurge that made the physical world, and God the Father. The traditional view of Marcionism is a complex phenomenon, generating several other dualisms, in addition to the aforementioned.[20] That Tillich avoids the former two should be abundantly clear from the primary source analysis of the previous chapters.

To the extent that Judaism and Christianity can be reconciled theologically, a careful analysis of the separation of the Church and synagogue in the first and second centuries would be required, based upon the scriptural and extra-biblical documents of the time.[21] It is clear that Tillich does not provide the tools to resolve this dilemma *to the satisfaction of Jews,* should any Jews care about what Christians think, as Tillich does not seriously engage Jewish *self-understanding.* At least, *from the Christian side,* Tillich does view Jewish prophetism as unique and indispensable, making Aryan Christianity and demonization of Jews impossible. As I will argue in sections 7.3 and 7.4 below, Tillich's response to the problems of anti-Semitism and Christian anti-Judaism, from metaphysical and historiographical standpoints, are the chief strengths of his view.

7.2 The Impasse of Supersessionism

Another critique of Tillich's theology of Judaism, is a 2010 article by Kayko Driedger Hesslein, who raises the issue of supersessionism.[22] Hesslein does

---

cion's song. That song, I am sure, is not only useless in 1982; it makes impossible any further development in a constructive relationship between the church and the Jewish people." Ibid., 358; cf. Paul van Buren, "Comments on Tillich," *The NICM Journal*, VII, 2 (Spring 1982), 20.

20 Pelikan lists the following: creation/salvation, law/gospel, the Creator (Demiurge)/God the Father, humanity/Christ, apostolic community/apostle Paul. Pelikan, 76. For example, the traditional view that is discussed in Jaroslav Pelikan, *The Emergence of the Catholic Tradition (100–600)*; series: *The Christian Tradition: A History of the Development of Doctrine*; Chicago: The University of Chicago Press, 1971; 68–81. "Pelikan, *Emergence of the Catholic Tradition.*" Pelikan also notes the curious relationship between the earliest Christian heresies and Judaism: "It is evident that certain forms of Judaism were the origin of the earliest forms of Christian heresy; to 'Judaize' was long a term for 'to teach false doctrine.' Nevertheless, the most important early heresies were not Jewish, but anti-Jewish in their inspiration." Pelikan, *Emergence*, 71.

21 For example, E.P. Sanders' *Paul and Palestinian Judaism* (Philadelphia, PA: Fortress Press, 1977).

22 Hesslein, "The (Dis)Integration of Judaism in Tillich's Theology of Universal Salvation," *Bulletin of the North American Paul Tillich Society*, vol. 36, 3, Summer 2010, 32–36; Hesslein, "(Dis)Integration."

not provide a definition of supersessionism, but she argues that Tillich puts forward a supersessionist theology of salvation history that ultimately invalidates the ability of contemporary Judaism bring salvation. Therefore, a reasonable working definition of supersessionism could be that Christianity is superior to Judaism because Judaism is inadequate to bring humanity into a complete relationship with God. This form of supersessionism is less adversarial to Judaism than "replacement theology," in which historic Judaism has no positive contribution to Christianity. A vivid form of replacement theology is found in the patristic period, and will be discussed in section 7.3 below, on theological anti-Judaism.

Hesslein concisely frames an important issue appearing in Tillich's *Systematic Theology*, asking how Judaism can be preserved, or "integrated," into Tillich's soteriological scheme. In doing so, she reminds us of the inherent difficulty for Christian theology, in general, of affirming the Jewish roots of Christianity and at the same time extending unique salvific status to Jesus Christ, who is not accepted as the Messiah by Jews.[23] She observes that Tillich's method, in particular his view of salvation history and his Christology, strives to meet the demands of affirming the revelatory importance of Judaism, but also seeks to uphold the unique role of the Christ-event. Despite his well-meaning attempts, Hesslein concludes that Tillich lapses into supersessionism, unable to resolve or transcend the fundamental problem referred to above.

Hesslein's analysis focuses primarily on passages within volumes I, II and III of the *Systematic Theology*,[24] and she acknowledges the ways Tillich seeks to maintain continuity between Judaism and Christianity. She concedes as much as possible, and observes three important aspects: 1) that Old Testament Judaism points to divine revelation; 2) that contemporary Judaism offers a prophetic voice to counter idolatry within Christianity; and 3) Tillich makes room for the salvation of Jews within his broad view of the salvation of the cosmos, or participation in the New Being.[25] Nevertheless, she concludes that Tillich does not offer a reason for Judaism to exist theologically on its own, on the basis of its own history of revelation.[26] In addition, she observes that Tillich persists in employing a chronological view of salvation history, in which Judaism is affirmed as historically antecedent to Christianity, and by implication, maintains a position of

23 There is a minority religious movemet that attempts to combine Judaism and Christianity, affirming that one can be Jewish and believe that Jesus is the Messiah, as Christians understand this. See: https://en.wikipedia.org/wiki/Messianic_Judaism [accessed October 14, 2015].

24 For example, ST I 133, 142–144, 147; ST II 97, 150 and 167; and ST III 273, 364–365 and 368–369.

25 Hesslein, "(Dis)Integration," 35.

26 Ibid., 35.

theological inferiority.[27] Based upon what I have demonstrated in the foregoing chapters, I beg to differ on the latter two points. Yet, she raises an additional criticism, to be discussed below.

Hesslein concludes that Tillich's dialectical christology, in which the historical particularity of Jesus and the universality of Christ, alternately preclude Jewish participation in *salvation*, and sever Christianity from Judaism:

> Emphasizing the historical nature of the Christ event particularizes Jesus and the nature of his salvific activity in such a way that Judaism's inability to incorporate that revelation leaves it outside of soteriological inclusion. Emphasizing the universal nature of Christ removes him from the historically located theological community – Judaism – that formed him, and severs Christianity from Judaism altogether.[28]

Hesslein is primarily critical of the manner in which Tillich attempts to relate *revelation* to *salvation*. This process of how Judaism contributes to divine revelation, according to Tillich, is described in detail in Chapter Five, the analysis of the *Systematic Theology.*

Tillich is abundantly clear about the revelatory capacity of historic and contemporary Judaism, which is exhibited in profound ways, as the dialectic of the Holy emerges from his ontology, via Schelling's dialectic of the potencies, and in "many and various ways" (Hebrews 1:1), through his theological and dialectical history of religion. However, I am willing to concede that that the next step of linking *revelation* to *salvati*on could be problematic, despite Tillich's creative attempt to do so through the concepts of particularity and universality, which play an important role in Tillich's modernized "Logos Christology."[29] Tillich's framework, as outlined in the *Systematic Theology*, while avoiding Marcionism and Aryan Christianity, appears inadequate to achieve the seemingly impossible task of preserving the historical and contemporary importance of Judaism for soteriological purposes, and upholding the uniqueness of Jesus Christ as the measure of participation in the New Being.

At the risk of taking the easy way out, I believe that by 1965 Tillich subordinates his heretofore "christo-centric" soteriology, and all forms of religion, to the religion of the concrete spirit, because of the latter's creative and critical capacities, and existential concreteness.

---

27 Ibid., 35.
28 Ibid., 35.
29 See Pelikan, *Emergence of the Catholic Tradition*, 184–200.

7.3 The Dualistic Metaphysics of Theological Anti-Judaism

Tillich argued in the *Judenfrage* lectures that modern political anti-Semitism which led to the genocide perpetrated against European Jews, did not arise in a vacuum but was nurtured by a long-standing tradition of anti-Jewish doctrines and attitudes maintained within Western Christianity, going back to the Gospel of John.[30] Oddly enough, Tillich does not use the term "ideology" anywhere in the *Judenfrage* lectures to describe this phenomenon, although this is exactly what it was, and he uses the term as early as 1933, as will be seen in section 7.4 below. While Tillich may have been one of the first major Christian theologians in the post-Holocaust period to make this connection, he would not be the last and others would expand considerably upon this topic. For example, one of the most provocative treatments of the theological origins of anti-Semitism is Rosemary Radford Ruether's *Faith and Fratricide: The Theological Roots of Anti-Semitism*,[31] which provides a helpful contrast to Tillich's view.

The Emergence of Anti-Jewish Essentialism[32]

Among the many important aspects of this work, Ruether provides a penetrating exposition of how Christian theology developed an anti-Jewish dimension, *at its core*. The first step in this process involved a core internal contradiction of Christian theology that she calls the "historicizing of the eschatological," or "fulfilled messianism."[33] More simply, this means that the historic Christian Christological claim that Jesus is the Messiah entails that the Kingdom of God had been *fully realized*, including the conquest of evil and death, because of Jesus's life, death and resurrection. Further, this perfected state of his divinity became conferred upon the Church, as the body of Christ. She observes that this interpretation was based upon (or perhaps assigned to!), a large body of passages from the

---

30 Tillich, Judenfrage lectures, 428–436.

31 Minneapolis, MN: Seabury, 1974. "Ruether, *Faith and Fratricide.*"

32 I am indebted to Matthew Hawk's reading of Ruether, in a 1992 Yale University Ph.D. dissertation titled, "Root, branch and rhetoric: Judaism and Christian self-understanding after the Holocaust;" 36–38; "Hawk Dissertation."

Ruether also uses the term supersessionism, arguing that early Christian self-understanding resulted in a "triple supersessionism," which had ontological, moral and historical dimensions. See Hawk Dissertation, 36–38; cf. Ruether, *Faith and Fratricide*, 164.

33 Ruether, *Faith and Fratricide*, 238, 248. Tillich also warns of the idolatry of space; see *Judenfrage* lectures, 469; Chapter Four, 4.5.6). This bears some resemblance to to what Heschel refers to as the racist aspect of "incarnational theology," as discussed in her essay "Race as Incarnational Theology," 231.

Jewish scriptures, which subsequently became the Christian Old Testament.[34] Therefore, this was a "revisionist" understanding of the Messiah, one who suffered death, but yet was resurrected, a clear departure from Jewish understandings of the Messiah at that time.[35] Ruether refers to this Christianized interpretation of the Jewish scriptures as a "christological midrash."[36]

As tension grew between the church and synagogue, this interpretive framework generated increasingly adversarial depictions of Jews, especially the Pharisees. Drawing upon the Gospel of John, the Jews *as a people* became associated with spiritual blindness and moral depravity.[37] In addition, drawing upon the epistle to the Hebrews, Jewish *religious practices* became cast as inferior, not just in the present, but *for all time.*[38] Ruether argues that a persistent and pervasive "dualistic" framework evolved, in which Jews were "essentialized," seen permanently in an a-historical, metaphysical, manner, as enemies of God. This view was developed by the Church Fathers, most notably Irenaeus (*Adversus Haeresis*), Tertullian (*Adversus Judaeos*), Justin Martyr (*Dialogue with Trypho*), Origen (*Contra Celsum*), Augustine (*Tractatus Adversus Judaeos*), and Chrysostom (*Demonstration to Jews and Greeks that Christ is God*). [39] This differs considerably to Tillich's reading of the patristic era in which Christianity assumed a posture of "indefiniteness" toward other religions, a "dialectical union of rejection and acceptance," which hardened to a political/religious monopoly only as a defensive measure in response to Islamic invasions.[40]

The above anti-Jewish ideas emerged, for theological and apologetic reasons, before the accession of Constantine and Theodosius, but then became the basis for a subordinated legal status of Jews within the Christian Roman empire, and also later within medieval Christendom.[41] Ruether underscores the *theological motivations* of the late antique Christian emperors in marginalizing Jews, as expressed in the Theodosian and Justinian Codes. She observes that these legal structures were intended to enforce in society the spiritual subordination of Jews to Christians. For example, according to Genesis 25:23, "the

---

34 Ibid., 124–137; 153–165.
35 Hawk Dissertation, 20–28.
36 For example, Ruether, *Faith and Fratricide*, 65.
37 Hawk Dissertation, 39–40.
38 Ibid., 41–42.
39 Ruether, *Faith and Fratricide*, 117–182; cf. Hawk Dissertation, 43–44.
40 Tillich, *Bampton Lectures*, 19, 23–25.
41 Ruether, *Faith and Fratricide*, 184–195.

elder shall serve the younger,"[42] meaning that the Jews are ordained by God to be subservient to Christians. This subordination endured into the modern period, with emancipation in the nineteenth century providing considerable improvement, only be lost in the disastrous first half of the twentieth century. Ruether claims that this ideology of "ecclesial triumphalism" resulted in the evils of imperialism, colonialism and genocide, as Christendom expanded around the world into the modern period.[43]

Ruether's analysis has been dismissed by some because it appears to say that Christian doctrine made the genocide against the Jews inevitable.[44] It is outside the scope of this book to assess the various criticisms of Ruether in this regard. However, her view of the relation between Christian theological anti-Judaism and racial anti-Semitism has been reasonably interpreted to have a less direct causal relation:

1. Anti-Judaic Christian self-understanding was expressed in Christendom through social policies that increasingly restricted the rights of Jews.
2. The limited social and economic roles open to them (e.g. medieval "royal userers") in turn fueled secular stereotypes (e.g. the Jew as money-grubbing conspirator).
3. These stereotypes funded a secularized anti-Semitism which were used for political purposes, by anti-Christian regimes, such as Nazi Germany.[45]

For the purposes of this book, while Ruether acknowledges that the Nazis were not Christians, she asserts "...the Church must bear a substantial responsibility for a tragic history of the Jew in Christendom which was the foundation upon which political anti-Semitism and the Nazi use of it was erected."[46] In this manner, it is very similar to Tillich's views as expressed in the *Judenfrage* lectures: "Anti-Judaism has occurred in all of church history and represents the tragic guilt of the church."[47]

42 Hawk Dissertation, 54; cf. Ruether, *Faith and Fratricide*, 186. Also, "the Christian emperors do not legislate as secular rulers. Nor do they act simply as tools of the Church...[s]till less are they simply cynical exploiters of the situation for political or economic advantage...the emperors speak here as exponents of the Christian theological view of the Jews, acting in their own right as priest-kings of the Christian theocratic empire." *Faith and Fratricide*, 195; cf. Hawk Dissertation, 54–55.

43 For example, Ruether, *Faith and Fratricide*, 232, 234, 238.

44 Hawk Dissertation, 56–57.

45 This three point summary is taken from the Hawk Dissertation, 58.

46 Ruether, *Faith and Fratricide*, 184; see Hawk Dissertation, 53.

47 Tillich, *Judenfrage* lectures, 428.

Transcending Historic, Metaphysical Dualisms

In the prior chapters, especially in the Bampton Lectures, it was shown that Tillich's dialectical history of religion possesses a unitive and inclusive aspect, which enables any religion that responds both critically (prophetically) and creatively to "the present situation" will endure and not die off. Both Tillich and Ruether essentially agree that Christian theology provided an ideological basis for the growth and flourishing of political anti-Semitism. Yet, the inclusive and dynamic aspects of Tillich's history of religion enable his thought to provide a fruitful contrast to the essentializing aspects of the anti-Jewish tradition within Christianity, as characterized by Ruether. Granted, there are limitations to addressing the problem of Christian anti-Judaism from a philosophical standpoint, as opposed to an exegetical standpoint, but that is the strength that Tillich's view brings to bear on these issues. Ruether identifies three "schisms", or dualisms, that manifest the "Christian anti-Judaic myth," and that will require a fundamental reconstruction of Christian theology.[48] The three schisms are judgment versus promise, particularism versus universalism, and letter versus spirit.[49] While not a perfect point-by-point response, Tillich's view addresses two of these three dualisms, in an "anti, anti-Jewish" manner. Due to the limits of space, only the first schism will be discussed, between judgment and promise, with similar reasoning applying to the third schism, between letter and spirit.

Judgment and Promise

According to Ruether, the schism of judgment and promise in the exegesis of the historical and prophetic books of the Old Testament was fundamental to the anti-Judaic argument. The Church Fathers interpreted the Jewish Scriptures to say that the world contains "two peoples," the sinful Jews who are condemned, and the Church, which is the true heir of the promises of God. Any instance of sin or rebellion became attributed to Jews, as "prophetic judgment," whether or not Jews were the subjects of the action in the text. Ruether observes that in the *adversus Judaeos* tradition, in the Psalms the "enemies" of the Davidic king are frequently interpreted to be "the Jews," such as in Augustine's reading of Psalm 58:12, "My God shall let me see over my enemies; slay them not, lest at any time they forget they law. Scatter them by thy power."[50] Following the same rea-

48 Ruether, *Faith and Fratricide*, 226.

49 Judgment and Promise 228–232; Particularism and Universalism 233–239; Letter and Spirit 239–245; *Faith and Fratricide.*

50 Augustine, *adversus Judaeos* 7 (9); cf. Ruether, *Faith and Fratricide*, 132. Also, in note 60, 272, for a list of patristic references. A magisterial treatment of Augustine's "witness doctrine"

soning, *any* instance of blessing or faithfulness is attributed to the Church, or "messianic hope," avoiding the historical fact that nothing in the Old Testament could possibly have had its *original referent* to be anything that had to do with the Christian Church. Not only did this interpretive pattern violate the historical/literal sense of the text, but when applied to the prophets, it denied them their original role of internal or self-criticism:

> By applying prophetic judgment to "the Jews" and messianic hope to "the Church," Christianity deprived Jews of their future. They also denied the Jews the record of their greatest moral accomplishment, the breakthrough from ideological religion to self-critical faith. By the same token, the Church deprived itself of the tradition of prophetic self-criticism.[51]

It has been shown above that Tillich avoids the interpretive error described by Ruether, in particular depriving Jews of their own prophetic history. He does engage in his own form of symbolic exegesis, for lack of a better term. His prototypical prophet Amos is a figure of world-historical significance. Not only does Amos serve as a pattern of self-criticism and critique of idolatry, especially the idolatry of religious nationalism, he makes possible, for the first time in world history, "something new," which can transcend the cycle of birth, growth, development, and death.[52] Tillich's interpretation of Amos is the basis for the most significant dimension of his spirit of Judaism, which will be discussed in the final section below.

7.4 The Conflict Between Historical Spirits: Amos versus Anaximander

For Tillich, Amos and Anaximander serve as exemplars of two competing views of history. In *The Socialist Decision*, Anaximander is the progenitor of the law of cyclical motion that fundamentally characterizes the pagan, polytheistic and Gnostic world view. This is the cycle of birth, growth and development, and death, which results in a conservative world-view when applied to the political sphere, referred to as political romanticism. Tillich quotes Anaximander twice, first to establish the law of circular motion: "It is necessary that things should

appears in Paula Fredriksen's *Augustine and the Jews: A Christian Defense of Jews and Judaism* (New York: Doubleday, 2008).

51 Ruether, *Faith and Fratricide*, 230.

52 See 4.5.5. above; cf. Tillich, *Judenfrage* lectures, 467–468.

pass away into that from which they are born."[53] Second, a culture that is governed by an "unbroken myth of origin," in which there is continuous struggle, exhibits the tragic character of life: "the rising and perishing of forces that 'pay one another the penalty and compensation for their injustice according to the ordinance of time.' "[54] This was written in 1932, and published in 1933.

In the *Judenfrage* lectures from 1952, Tillich elevated Amos, over and above Abraham and Moses, to be the progenitor of the Jewish prophetic world view. Abraham's role was to be the prototypical first person to break the law of cyclical motion by permitting himself to be "called out" of his native land, to a far country, to something new.[55] In addition, this established a pattern to be repeated in Israel's history of Exodus, Exile and *diaspora.*[56] Yet, this role was limited as it constituted a distinct, particular, people. Moses's role as the giver of the law was limited to delivering the demands of divine justice, which were to be universally applicable, although they were also limited to the people of Israel at the time. One aspect of the idolatry of the Jewish monarchy was that it failed to make the law of Moses universally available. In the *Judenfrage* lectures, Tillich argued that it was one of the greatest moments in the history of humanity when Amos threatened Israel with destruction and destroyed the connection between divine election and ethnocentrism and nationalism, signaling divine judgment on "every sacrally consecrated injustice."[57] The importance of Amos and Anaximander were contrasted at the same time, in an obscure, unpublished essay by Tillich from the early- to mid-1930s.

7.4.1 Ideology and the Roots of Anti-Semitism

For Tillich, anti-Semitism is the recurring response to not only nationalism, but "all forms of reaction:" "Anti-Semitism is the most visible symbol of all forms of reac-

---

53 Cf. Werner Jaeger's *Paideia: The Ideals of Greek Culture*, trans. Gilbert Highet (Oxford: Oxford University Press, 1945), vol. 1, 159. Also, "1. The Non-Limited is the original material of existing things; further, the source from which existing things derive their existence is also that to which they return at their destruction, according to necessity; for they give justice and make reparation to one another for their injustice, according to the arrangement of Time." Anaximander of Miletus, *Ancilla to the Pre-Socratic Philosophers: A complete translation of the Fragments in Diels, Fragmente der Vorsokratiker,* Kathleen Freeman (Cambridge, MA: Harvard University Press, 1978), 19.

54 Tillich, *The Socialist Decision*, 6.

55 Tillich, *Judenfrage* lectures, 464–465.

56 Ibid., 465.

57 Chapter Four, 4.5.5. Amos: The Broken Covenant, Exile and the Righteous Remnant; *Judenfrage* lectures, 467–468.

tion. Ultimately it is reaction against the God who has liberated mankind from the servitude under its origins and opened the path towards the new mankind and the new creature."[58] This recurring problem is explained in a brief unpublished article written by Tillich in 1933, titled "Two Types of Historical Vision."[59] This article, despite its peculiar provenance, is important because Tillich articulates the philosophical and theological presuppositions of anti-Semitism.

In attempting to identify these presuppositions, Tillich seeks to isolate them from the ideological overlay that is the ostensible cause for marginalization and persecution. For Tillich, the ideology varies, but the goal is the same, to marginalize Jews and/or to stigmatize Judaism. He gives three examples of anti-Jewish

---

58 Tillich, *Two Types of Historical Vision*, 11.

59 This document includes a cover page and an eleven-page essay. There is shared content between the cover page and the essay, although it seems that they are standalone documents, and I am left to wonder if the cover page is mis-filed with the essay. The Harvard Tillich Archive document number is bMS 649/ 87 (5). The cover page is titled: "The Religious and Philosophical Presuppotion (sic) of the National Socialistic (sic) Attack on Judaism," publ. 1936, with an additional title, "Two Types of Historical Vision." In this analysis, I will refer to this piece as "*Two Types of Historical Vision*," although in the Bibliography I will use the title it is currently identified by in the archive. There is also an explanatory paragraph on the cover page which reads as follows: "The following article is the (free) translation of two chapters of my German book: "Die Sozialistische Entscheidung," (The Socialistic Decision), that just appeared in the moment in which Hitler came to power and consequently, has been destroyed by the Nazi authorities. The book tried to analyze the religious and philosophical implications of fascism, liberalism and socialism, and to give a solution of (sic) the political problem of our period in terms of the Religious-Socialist Movement of Germany. The first chapter is translated in my English book *The Interpretation of History*, Scribner's, 1936, as Part III, chapter 2: "The Two Roots of Political Thinking." The other parts are not translated. The two following chapters contain the fundamental ideas of the first part and, to a certain extent, of the whole book." Tillich, *Two Types of Historical Vision*, cover page.

There are several peculiarities to this document. First, the cover page says that the accompanying eleven page essay is a translation of two chapters in Tillich's *Die Sozialistische Entscheidung*. While there is some overlap in content, they clearly are not the same. The book's first two full chapters have different titles, and even the first two sub-chapters are different. Second, there are numerous mis-spellings (such as "origine" for "origin"), which could reflect Tillich's ongoing difficulty with English, beginning when he emigrated in 1933. Third, the article has eleven pages of typescript, but it has three numbered sections, number 1 on page 2, number 5 on page 3, and number 11 on page 7, with no other numbered sections to complete the sequence from 1 through 11. For these reasons, I think the cover page may be incorrectly associated with the eleven page essay, and that the latter document is a standalone document. The dating is uncertain, as Tillich only arrived in the U.S. in November of 1933, and only began to learn English on the trans-Atlantic crossing, so the translation is likely a bit later. I am assuming that the vivid content and numerous misspellings would place the document in the 1933–1936 time frame. I have not been able to locate the German original.

ideology, similar to his discussion in the *Judenfrage* lectures: in ancient Rome Jews were seen as a subversive threat to Roman state religion; in 19th century Europe, the lower bourgeoisie reacted to the superior critical spirit of the Jewish intelligentsia; and in National Socialist Germany, Jews were feared because they were seen as an alien influence threatening the integrity of German racial purity ("blood") and territorial integrity ("soil").[60]

The next step for Tillich is to uncover what is common to each of these, indeed to all, instances of anti-Semitism, the assumption being that there is a common source for each:

> Even if one would say that this is only ideology, produced in order to hide the real economic motives of Anti-Semitism it must be explained why this ideology could become so successful and could find so innumerable believers. Ideology cannot simply be invented. It always needs a kernel of truth, as lie (sic) always lives from the element of truth, used and distorted by it. Therefore it is worthwhile and necessary for the understanding of Anti-Semitism to discover the non-ideological element in the anti-Semitic ideologies. For there is a real contrast between the original and unique spirit of Judaism and the spirit of national groups amongst which the Jews are living. In order to find the difference of spirit some basic philosophical and religious considerations must be made.[61]

For Tillich, these two "spirits" are manifest in two competing views of history, the circular view from ancient Greece, and the Jewish prophetic view, which provides the possibility of transcending the pagan cycle of birth, growth and development, and death, through something truly "new."

7.4.2 Anaximander and Striving for Self-Destruction

The circular view of history *is the basis for* the tragic character of life. In a discussion of the power of "blood," or ancestry, one of the three powers of origin, Tillich warns that war results from idolatry, and represents the self-destructive nature of the pagan worldview, which embodies a "striving toward self-destruction."

> The glorification of war for the sake of war, of sacrifice of life for the sake of sacrifice of life, is rooted in the myth of origins, especially in the myth of blood. The deification of groups and heroes does not mean the valuation of creative progress but it means the praise of just the opposite, the striving back to the powers of origin. The tragic character of life is not only recognized but also affirmed and glorified. The necessity for everything to return to the

60 Tillich also mentions that Jews were restricted socially by the medieval feudal system, but does not say why. Tillich, *Two Types of Historical Vision*, 1.
61 Ibid., 1–2.

> abyss from which it comes, as expressed in the first fragment of Greek philosophy (in the words of Anaximander) is realized as ecstatic self-destruction. This is the reason why, despite of all economic and political inhibitions, the present war was unavoidable.[62]

In a fashion similar to *The Socialist Decision*, Tillich argues that the idolatry of space results in a self-destructive cult of death:

> The law of self-destruction is unescapable (sic) in the realm of space. The tragic self-destruction of the national units even in our period reveals on the one hand the power of the origin. It reveals on the other hand the tragic character of this power. The myth of origin is pagan and polytheistic and consequently in all its greatness, power and glory it is doomed to mutual self-destruction.[63]

7.4.3 Amos and Creative Destruction

For Tillich, the prophetic view of history breaks the unending circularity through a *transformation* of the powers of origin. Something qualitatively new arises, analogous to creation itself:

> In the prophetic interpretation of history time has a direction. It runs toward something which did not exist but will come into existence. The expectation of a new heaven and a new earth is the expectation of a being which is not subject to the power of original being which is free from the origin. There will be something new in history and by this the origin itself is transformed. It gets the character of a beginning, of a start to which we are not supposed to return. Prophetism transforms the original (sic) in the beginning of an historical process. This is the idea of creation.[64]

The destruction of Israel in the exile opened up the possibility of making the law of Moses, the prototype of justice, universal. Tillich elevates Amos to be the exemplar of prophetic judgment, if justice is not maintained among the people of Israel: "The prophetic message as for example in Amos pronounces God's threat against his own nation to cut the bond between itself and his elected nation if justice is suppressed. There is no more decisive step in all history of religion than these words of the great Jewish prophets."[65]

For Tillich, Judaism had to be replaced by Christianity, for two reasons. First, because Judaism failed to transcend its religious nationalism, a recurring theme

62 Ibid., 4.
63 Ibid., 7.
64 Ibid., 9.
65 Ibid., 7–8.

in the primary source analyses presented in prior chapters. The second reason reiterates his reasoning from *The Socialist Decision*, arguing that the powers of origin need to be transformed, not destroyed: "prophetic criticism has entirely dissolved the powers of origin which must be preserved, and *transformed*, not destroyed.[66] Transformation, not destruction, is required to maintain ontological continuity between the created order and subsequent historical manifestations: "The prophetic message of the Old Testament is the world historical criticism of the myth of origin. It does not deny it entirely. It maintains those elements in it which are essential for being itself and for human nature."[67]

Tillich's understanding of the ongoing struggle between the powers of origin and the prophetic spirit assigns them quasi-personal qualities:

> The words of vocation to Abraham, the command to leave Egypt, the exile, the destruction of Jerusalem, all these events are considered by Prophetism not as defeats of a God of space but as a final victory of the God of time and justice. In this interpretation of history the myth of soil is destroyed forever. Its ultimate power is taken although it arises again and again and has arisen in Judaism and Christianity. And whenever it arises it hates the prophetic spirit by which its original power was destroyed. That is the reason why nationalism hates and must always hate Judaism and prophetic Christianity.[68]

Given the increasing militarism and strident anti-Semitism of Germany in the 1930s, Tillich's imagery seems especially appropriate. More importantly, the enduring importance of his argument is that he identified the destructive power of German National Socialism, when and where he did.

---

66 The two reasons are embodied in this quote: "Judaism has the tragic fate that on the one hand his religious nationalism never has been overcome completely and therefore that it had to be replaced by Christianity and that on the other hand prophetic criticism has netirely (sic) dissolved the powers of origine (sic) which are justified and necessary in their place." Ibid., 11.
67 "The prophetic message of the Old Testament is the world historical criticism of the myth of origin. It does not deny it entirely. It maintains those elements in it which are essential for being itself and for human nature. It does not even deprive the origin of the holiness but it subjects the holiness of what is to the holiness of what ought to be. Prophetism denies that a soil, a holy land, an elected nation is holy by its very being. It is holy only if it realizes truth and justice." Ibid., 7.
68 Ibid., 8.

Select Bibliography

Paul Tillich Primary Sources

Books

Against the Third Reich: Paul Tillich's Wartime Radio Broadcasts into Nazi Germany. Translated by Matthew Lon Weaver. Edited by Ronald H. Stone and Matthew Lon Weaver. Louisville, KY: Westminster John Knox Press, 1998.

A History of Christian Thought: From its Judaic and Hellenistic Origins to Existentialism. Edited by Carl E. Braaten. New York: Simon & Schuster Touchstone, 1967.

Berliner Vorlesungen (1919–1920). Ergänzungs- und Nachlaßbände zu den Gesammelten Werken, Band XII; ed. Erdmann Sturm. Berlin: De Gruyter, 2001.

Biblical Religion and the Search for Ultimate Reality. Chicago: University of Chicago Press, 1955.

Christianity and the Encounter of the World Religions. Bampton Lectures in America 14, Columbia University, 1961. New York: Columbia University Press, 1963.

The Construction of the History of Religion in Schelling's Positive Philosophy: Its Presuppositions and Principles. Translated with an introduction and notes by Victor Nuovo. Lewisburg, PA: Bucknell University Press, 1974.

Dynamics of Faith. New York: Harper & Row, 1957.

The Eternal Now. New York: Charles Scribner's Sons, 1963.

Frühe Predigten (1909–1918). Ergänzungs- und Nachlaßbände zu den Gesammelten Werken VII; ed. Erdmann Sturm. Berlin: De Gruyter, 1994.

The Interpretation of History. Translated by N. A. Rasetzki and Elsa L. Talmey. New York: Charles Scribner's Sons, 1936.

Love, Power and Justice: Ontological Analyses and Ethical Applications. New York: Oxford University Press, 1954.

Mysticism and Guilt-Consciousness in Schelling's Philosophical Development. Translated with an introduction and notes by Victor Nuovo. Lewisburg, PA: Bucknell University Press, 1974.

The New Being. New York: Charles Scribner's Sons, 1955.

On the Boundary: An Autobiographical Sketch. Translated by N. A. Rasetzki and Elsa L. Talmey. New York: Charles Scribner's Sons, 1966.

Political Expectation. Edited by James Luther Adams. New York: University Press of America, 1971.

The Protestant Era. Translated by James Luther Adams. Chicago: University of Chicago Press, 1948.

Religion, Kultur, Gesellschaft: unveröffentliche Texte aus der deutschen Zeit (1908–1933). Zweiter Teil. Ergänzungs- und Nachlaßbände zu den Gesammelten Werken, Band XI; ed. Erdmann Sturm. Berlin: De Gruyter, 1999.

The Religious Situation. 1932. Translated by H. Richard Niebuhr. New York: Meridian Books, 1956.

The Shaking of the Foundations. New York: Charles Scribner's Sons, 1948.

The Socialist Decision. Translated by Franklin Sherman with an introduction by John R. Stumme. Washington, D.C.: University Press of America, 1977. Originally published as *Die Sozialistische Entscheidung*. Potsdam: Alfred Protte Verlag, 1933.
Systematic Theology. 3 volumes. Chicago: University of Chicago Press, 1951, 1957 and 1963.
Theology of Culture. Edited by Robert C. Kimball. Oxford: Oxford University Press, 1972.
Theology of Peace. Edited by Ronald H. Stone. Louisville, KY: Westminster John Knox Press, 1990.

Articles

"Anti-Semitism and the Christian Church." Handwritten in German, no date; bMS 649/28 (11).
"Can the Jew Return to Germany?." Handwritten, no date; bMS 649/62 (5).
"Catholicism and Anti-Judaism." Early 1940s. bMS 649/62 (6).
'The Concept of Faith in the Jewish-Christian Tradition." Article, handwritten, no date; bMS 649/46 (3).
"An Evaluation of Martin Buber: Protestant and Jewish Thought." In *Theology of Culture*, 188–199. Oxford: Oxford University Press, 1972. First published as "Martin Buber and Christian Thought: His Threefold Contribution to Protestantism", *Commentary* (New York) 5/6 (June 1948): 515–521.
"'Faith' in the Jewish-Christian Tradition." *Christendom* (New York) 7/4 (Autumn 1942): 518–526.
"Historical and Nonhistorical Interpretations of History: A Comparison." Address at the annual meeting of the American Theological Society, Eastern Branch, 14 April 1939. *Protestant Era* (1948): 16–31.
"I Am an American." *Protestant Digest* 3/12 (June–July): 24–26.
"Is There a Judeo-Christian Religion?" (the document title appears to be misnamed as the document itself is titled "Is There a Judeo-Christian Tradition?"). Three versions of a presentation at the Jewish Theological Seminary of America; handwritten and typescript; dated 10 December 1947; bMS 649/81 (5).
"Is There a Judeo-Christian Tradition?." *Judaism* 1/2 (April 1952): 106–109.
"Jewish Influences on Contemporary Christian Theology." *Cross Currents* (New York) 2/3 (Spring 1952): 35–42. Transcript of a lecture given as one of the Milton Steinberg Lectures in Jewish Theology, given at the Park Avenue Synagogue in New York City.
"The Jewish Question." 31 March 1942. *Voice of America* broadcast. Originally published as *An meine deutschen Freunde*. Stuttgart: Evangelisches Verlagswerk, 1973. Also in *Against the Third Reich: Paul Tillich"s Wartime Radio Broadcasts into Nazi Germany. 1942–1944*. Translated by Matthew Lon Weaver. Louisville, KY: Westminster John Knox Press, 1998.
"The Jewish Question: A Christian and a German Problem." Four lectures delivered at Der Deutschen Hochschule für Politik, summer 1952. First published in *Schriftenreihe der Deutschen Hochschule für Politik*. Berlin: Gebruder Weiss, 1953. Subsequently published in *Gesammelte Werke*, volume III, ed. Renate Albrecht, *Das Religiöse Fundament des Moralischen Handelns: Schriften zur Ethik und zum Menschenbild*, 128–170. Stuttgart: Evangelisches Verlagswerk, 1965. Translated into English by Marion Pauck, *North*

American Paul Tillich Society Bulletin 30/3 (Summer 2004): 3–24; and by Glenn David Earley, Earley Dissertation, 418–491.
"Man and Society in Religious Socialism." Paper presented at the Philosophy Group, "Week of Work." National Council on Religion in Higher Education. *Christianity and Society* (New York) 8/4 (Fall 1943).
"The Meaning of Anti-Semitism." *Radical Religion* (New York) 4/1 (Winter 1938): 34–36. Originally delivered on 21 November 1938 in Madison Square Garden, in response to the *Kristallnacht* pogrom in Germany on 9–10 November 1938. See Stone, *Tillich"s Radical Thought*, p. 96.
"My Changing Thoughts on Zionism." From the Christian–Jewish Colloquy "Israel"s Rebirth in the Middle East" (Chicago, IL). Includes programme, handwritten typescript, 21 January 1959; bMS 649/45 (4).
"Nation of Time, Nation of Space." *Land Reborn* 8/1 (1959): 4–5.
"Philosophy and Theology." Address at Union Theological Seminary upon Tillich"s election as Professor of Philosophical Theology. *Religion and Life* 10/ 1 (New York, 1941): 21–30.
"Protestantism and Anti-Semitism." Early 1940s. Handwritten, no date; bMS 649/62 (7).
"The Relevance of Judaism and Christianity in Face of the Secular Systems of Life." Handwritten, no date; bMS 649/45 (2).
"The Religious and Philosophical Presuppotion (sic) of the National Socialistic (sic) Attack on Judaism." Published 1936. Typescript; bMS 649/87 (5). In Chapter Seven, referred to as "Two Types of Historical Vision."
"The Religious Relation Between Christianity and Judaism in the Future." Handwritten and typescript; no date; bMS 649/62 (8).
"The Role of Judaism in Post-War World Reconstruction." Typescript, no date; bMS 649/45 (11).
"The Search for Truth and Unity in the Judaic-Christian Tradition." Cooper Union University, New York, handwritten, 14 February 1955; bMS 649/45 (3).
"Tillich–Thomas Mann Letter", 23 May 1943. *The Intellectual Legacy of Paul Tillich*. Edited by James R. Lyons, 99–107. Detroit, MI: Wayne State University Press, 1969.
"Victory in Defeat: The Meaning of History in the Light of Christian Prophetism." *Interpretation* 6/1 (January 1952): 17–26.
"What is Wrong with the "Dialectic" Theology?" In Mark Kline Taylor, *Paul Tillich: Theologian of the Boundaries*, Making of Modern Theology: 19th and 20th Century Texts series, ed. John W. de Gruchy, 104–116. San Francisco: Collins Liturgical Publications, 1987.

Secondary Sources

Adams, James Luther. *Paul Tillich's Philosophy of Culture, Science and Religion*. New York: Harper & Row, 1965.
Adams, James Luther. "Paul Tillich on Luther." *Interpreters of Luther: Essays in Honor of Wilhelm Pauck*. Edited by Jaroslav Pelikan. Philadelphia: Fortress Press, 1968.
Adams, James Luther, Pauck, Wilhelm, and Shinn, Roger, eds. *The Thought of Paul Tillich*. San Francisco: Harper & Row, 1985.
Arendt, Hannah. *For the Love of the World*. Second edition. Edited by Elisabeth Young-Bruehl. New Haven, CT: Yale University Press, 2004.

Arendt, Hannah. "Organized Guilt and Universal Responsibility." In *The Portable Hannah Arendt*, 146–156. Edited and with an introduction by Peter Baehr. New York: Penguin Classics, 2003. Originally published as "German Guilt," in *Jewish Frontier* 12 (January 1945).

Baeck, Leo. *Judaism and Christianity: Essays by Leo Baeck.* Translated by Walter Kaufman. Philadelphia: Jewish Publication Society of America, 1968.

Barnes, Kenneth C. *Nazism, Liberalism and Christianity: Protestant Social Thought in Germany and Great Britain, 1925–1937.* Lexington, KY: University Press of Kentucky, 1991.

Bergen, Doris L. *Twisted Cross: The German Christian Movement in the Third Reich.* Chapel Hill, NC: University of North Carolina Press, 1996.

Bernet-Strahm, Anton. *Die Vermittlung des Christlichen. Eine theologiegeschichtliche Untersuchung zu Paul Tillichs Anfängen des Theologiesierens und seiner christologischen Auseinandersetzung mit philosophischen Einsichten des deutschen Idealismus.* Frankfurt-on-Main: Peter Lang, 1982.

Bonhoeffer, Dietrich. *Works*, volume XII, *Berlin: 1932–1933.* Edited by Larry L. Rasmussen, translation Isabel Best and David Higgins. Minneapolis, MN: Fortress Press, 2009.

Bowie, Andrew. *Schelling and Modern European Philosophy. An Introduction.* London: Routledge, 1993.

Bowie, Andrew. "Schelling." In *Routledge Encyclopedia of Philosophy*, vol. VIII, 509–520. Ten volumes, edited by Edward Craig. London: Routledge, 1998.

Bracken, Joseph, "Schelling's Positive Philosophy." *Review of the History of Philosophy* 5 (1977): 324–330.

Brown, D. Mackenzie, ed. *Ultimate Concern: Tillich in Dialogue.* New York: Harper Colophon Books, 1965.

Carey, John J., ed. *"Kairos" and "Logos": Studies in the Roots and Implications of Tillich's Theology.* Cambridge, MA: North American Paul Tillich Society, 1978.

Clayton, John Powell. *The Concept of Correlation: Paul Tillich and the Possibility of a Mediating Theology.* New York: Walter De Gruyter, 1980.

Cooper, John Charles. *The "Spiritual Presence" in the Theology of Paul Tillich: Tillich's Use of St Paul.* Macon, GA: Mercer University Press, 1997.

Coser, Lewis A. *Masters of Sociological Thought: Ideas in Historical and Social Context* (New York: Harcourt Brace Jovanovich; 1971).

Crossman, Richard C. *Paul Tillich: A Comprehensive Bibliography and Keyword Index of Primary and Secondary Writings in English.* Metuchen, NJ: Scarecrow Press, 1983.

Crary, Stephen T. "Idealistic Elements in Tillich's Thought." Doctoral dissertation, Yale University, 1955.

Danz, Christian. *Die philosophische Christologie F.W.J. Schellings.* Stuttgart: Fromann-Holzboog, 1996.

Davies, Alan T. *Antisemitism and the Christian Mind.* New York: Herder & Herder, 1969.

Davies, Alan T. "Paul Tillich on Judaism and Martin Buber on Christianity." *Studies in Religion* 5/1 , 68.

Dillenberger, John. *God Hidden and Revealed.* Philadelphia: Muhlenberg Press, 1953.

Donnelly, Brian. *The Socialist Émigré: Marxism and the Later Tillich.* Macon, GA: Mercer University Press, 2003.

Doi, Masatoshi. "Paul Tillich's Religious Socialism." S.T.M. thesis, Hartford Seminary, May 1952.

Earley, Glenn D. "Tillich and Judaism: Analysis of the "Jewish Question"." In *Theonomy and Autonomy: Studies in Paul Tillich's Engagement with Modern Culture*, edited by John J. Carey, 213–241. Macon, GA: Mercer University Press, 1982.

Edgcomb, Gabrielle Simon. *From Swastika to Jim Crow: Refugee Scholars at Black Colleges.* Malabar, FL: Krieger, 1993.

Encyclopedia Judaica. Second edition, 22 volumes. General editor Fred S. Kolnik. New York: MacMillan/Thomson/Gale, 2007.

Ericksen, Robert P. *Theologians under Hitler: Gerhard Kittel, Paul Althaus and Emanuel Hirsch.* New Haven, CT: Yale University Press, 1985.

Ericksen, Robert P., and Heschel, Susannah, eds. *Betrayal: German Churches and the Holocaust.* Minneapolis, MN: Fortress Press, 1999.

Even-Chen, Alexander. "Faith and the Courage to Be: Heschel and Tillich." In Marcel Poorthuis et al., eds., *Interaction between Judaism and Christianity in History, Religion, Art and Literature*, 337–355. Jewish and Christian Perspectives 17. Boston, MA: Brill, 2009.

Fackenheim, Emil, "Schelling's Conception of Positive Philosophy." *Review of Metaphysics* 7 (1954): 563–582.

Feige, Franz G. M. *The Varieties of Protestantism in Nazi Germany: Five Theopolitical Positions.* Toronto Studies in Theology 50. Lewiston, N.Y.: Edwin Mellen Press, 1990.

Fiorenza, Elisabeth Schüssler and Nasrallah, Laura. *Prejudice and Christian Beginnings: Investigating Race, Gender and Ethnicity in Early Christian Studies.* Minneapolis, MN: Fortress Press, 2009.

Forstman, Jack. *Christian Faith in Dark Times: Theological Conflicts in the Shadow of Hitler.* Louisville, KY: Westminster John Knox Press, 1992.

Franz, Albert. *Philosophische Religion. Eine Auseinandersetzung mit den Grundlegungsproblem der Spätphilosophie F. W. J. Schellings.* Amsterdam: Editions Rodopi B.V., 1992.

Fredriksen, Paula. *Augustine and the Jews: A Christian Defense of Jews and Judaism.* New York: Doubleday, 2008.

Freeman, Kathleen. *Ancilla to the Pre-Socratic Philosophers: A complete translation of the Fragments in Diels, Fragmente der Vorsokratiker.* Cambridge, MA: Harvard University Press, 1978.

Frei, Hans. *The Eclipse of Biblical Narrative: A Study in Eighteenth- and Nineteenth-Century Hermeneutics.* New Haven, CT: Yale University Press, 1974.

Friedlander, Albert H. *Leo Baeck–Teacher of Theresienstadt.* New York: Holt, Rinehart & Winston, 1968.

Gerlach, Wolfgang. *And the Witnesses Were Silent: The Confessing Church and the Persecution of the Jews.* Translated and edited by Victoria J. Barnett. Lincoln, NE: University of Nebraska Press, 2000.

Graf, Friedrich Wilhelm, and Alf Christopherson, eds. "Die Korrespondenz zwischen Fritz Medicus und Paul Tillich." *Zeitschrift für neuere Theologiegeschichte* 11 (2004): 126–147.

Graf, Friedrich Wilhelm. ""Politische Romantik" und "Sozialistische Entscheidung." Eine freundschaftliche Annonce für Heinrich Meier zum 8. April 2013." *Zeitschrift für neuere Theologiegeschichte,* 2012, 19 (2): 247–268.

Hammond, G. "Tillich, Adorno and the Debate About Existentialism." *Laval Theologique et Philosophie* 47/3 (1991): 343–355.

Heidegger, Martin. *Schelling's Treatise on the Essence of Human Freedom (1936 Lecture).* Translated by Joan Stambaugh. Athens, OH: Ohio University Press, 1985.

Hegel, G. W. F. *The Difference Between Fichte's and Schelling's System of Philosophy. An English translation of G. W. F. Hegel's Differenz des Fichte'schen und Schelling'schen Systems der Philosophie.* Prepared and edited by H. S. Harris and Walter Cerf. Albany, New York: SUNY Press, 1977.

Hegel, G. W. F. *The Spirit of Christianity and its Fate.* Translated by T. J. Knox. In *Early Theological Writings.* Chicago: University of Chicago Press, 1948; reprint Philadelphia: University of Pennsylvania Press, 1971.

Heschel, Susannah. "Race as Incarnational Theology: Affinities Between German Protestantism and Racial Theory." In Fiorenza, Nasrallah, *Prejudice and Christian Beginnings*, 211–234.

Heschel, Susannah. *The Aryan Jesus: Christian Theologians and the Bible in Nazi Germany.* Princeton, NJ: Princeton University Press, 2008.

Hesslein, Kayko Driedger. "The (Dis)Integration of Judaism in Tillich's Theology of Universal Salvation." *North American Paul Tillich Society Newsletter* 36/ 3 (Summer 2010): 32–36.

Hirsch, Emanuel. *Das Alte Testament und die Predigt des Evangeliums.* Tübingen: J.C.B. Mohr (Paul Siebeck), 1936.

Hooper, David H. *Tillich: A Theological Portrait.* New York: J. B. Lippincott, 1968.

Howard, Thomas Albert. *Protestant Theology and the Making of the Modern German University.* Oxford: Oxford University Press, 2006.

Howard, Thomas Albert. *Religion and the Rise of Historicism: W. M. L. de Wette, Jacob Burckhardt, and the Theological Origins of Nineteenth-Century Historical Consciousness.* Cambridge: Cambridge University Press, 2000.

Hsia, R. Po Chia. *The Myth of Ritual Murder: Jews and Magic in Reformation Germany.* New Haven, CT: Yale University Press, 1988.

Jantzen, Kyle T. Review of Susannah Heschel's *The Aryan Jesus: Christian Theologians and the Bible in Nazi Germany. Church History* 79/4 (December 2010): 968–971.

Kegley, Charles W., and Bretall, Robert W., eds. *The Theology of Paul Tillich.* New York: Macmillan, 1952.

Kelly, J.N.D. *Early Christian Doctrine.* Revised edition. San Francisco; Harper & Row, 1978.

Kelly, Shawn. *Racializing Jesus: Race, Ideology and the Formation of Modern Biblical Scholarship.* New York: Routledge, 2002.

Kelsey, David H. *The Fabric of Paul Tillich's Theology.* New Haven, CT: Yale University Press, 1967.

Kitagawa, Joseph M. "Tillich, Kraemer and the Encounter of Religions." In James Luther Adams, ed., *The Thought of Paul Tillich*, 197–217. San Francisco: Harper & Row, 1985.

Kitagawa, Joseph M., ed. *The History of Religions: Retrospect and Prospect.* A collection of original essays by Mircea Eliade, Paul Ricoeur, Michael Meslin, Ugo Bianchi, Ninian Smart, Charles H. Long, Kurt Rudolph, and Joseph M. Kitagawa. Afterword Gregory D. Alles and the editor. London and New York: Collier Macmillan, 1985.

Klein, Charlotte. *Anti-Judaism in Christian Theology.* Translated by Edward Quinn. Philadelphia: Fortress Press, 1978.

Kline Taylor, Mark. *Paul Tillich: Theologian of the Boundaries.* Edited by John W. De Gruchy. The Making of Modern Theology: 19th and 20th Century Texts. San Francisco: Collins Liturgical Publications, 1987.

Krieg, Robert A. *Catholic Theologians in Nazi Germany.* New York: Continuum, 2004.

Levenson, Alan T. *Between Philosemitism and Antisemitism: Defenses of Jews and Judaism in Germany, 1871–1932.* Lincoln, NE: University of Nebraska Press, 2004.
Lewis, Thomas A. *Religion, Modernity and Politics in Hegel.* Oxford: Oxford University Press, 2011.
Livingston, James C. *Modern Christian Thought: From the Enlightenment to Vatican II.* New York: Macmillan, 1971.
Loncar, Samuel. "Marcion's Child: Friedrich Schleiermacher, Anti-Judaism, and the Birth of Protestant Liberalism." Unpublished paper.
Lyons, James R. editor. *The Intellectual Legacy of Paul Tillich.* Detroit, MI: Wayne State University Press, 1969.
Maccoby, Hyam. *Judaism on Trial: Jewish-Christian Disputations in the Middle Ages.* London: Littman Library of Jewish Civilization, 1996.
Mack, Michael. *German Idealism and the Jew: The Inner Anti-Semitism of Philosophy and German Jewish Responses.* Chicago, IL: University of Chicago Press, 1992.
Madigan, Kevin. Review of Susannah Heschel's *The Aryan Jesus: Christian Theologians and the Bible in Nazi Germany. Journal of the American Academy of Religion* 77/3 (2009): 742–748.
Mann, Erika. *School for Barbarians: Education Under the Nazis.* Introduction by Thomas Mann. Mineola, New York: Dover Publications, Inc., 2014. First published by Modern Age Books, 1938.
Marchand, Suzanne L. *German Orientalism in the Age of Empire: Religion, Race and Scholarship.* Washington, DC and New York: German Historical Institute and Cambridge University Press, 2009.
Martin, Bernard. *The Existential Theology of Paul Tillich.* New York: Bookman Associates, 1963.
Marx, Werner. *The Philosophy of F. W. J. Schelling. History, System and Freedom.* Translated by Thomas Nenon. Bloomington: Indiana University Press, 1984.
Mazzenga, Maria, ed. *American Religious Responses to Kristallnacht.* New York: Palgrave, Macmillan, 2009.
Meditz, Robert E. "The Dialectic of the Holy: The Evolution of Paul Tillich's Understanding of Judaism." *North American Paul Tillich Society Newsletter* 37/3 (Summer 2011): 26–42.
Mendes-Flohr, Paul and Jehuda Reinharz, editors. *The Jew in the Modern World: A Documentary History.* Second edition. New York: Oxford University Press, 1995.
Meyer, Michael A. Review of Susannah Heschel's *The Aryan Jesus: Christian Theologians and the Bible in Nazi Germany. Modern Judaism* 30/1 (February 2010): 120–122.
Mokrosch, Reinhold. *Theologische Freiheitsphilosophie. Metaphysik, Freihiet und Ethik in der philosophischen Entwicklung Schellings und in den Anfängen Tillichs.* Frankfurt-on-Main: Vittorio Klosterman, 1976.
Nauen, Franz Gabriel. *Revolution, Idealism and Human Freedom: Schelling, Hölderlin and Hegel and the Crisis of Early German Idealism.* International Archives for the History of Ideas 45. The Hague: Martinus Nijhoff, 1971.
Neugebauer, Georg. *Tillichs frühe Christologie: Eine Untersuchung zu Offenbarung und Geschichte bei Tillich vor dem Hintergrund seiner Schellingrezeption.* New York: Walter de Gruyter, 2007.
Nirenberg, David. *Anti-Judaism: The Western Tradition.* New York: W. W. Norton, 2013.
Norman, Judith, and Welchman, Alistair. *The New Schelling.* New York: Continuum, 2004.

Nuovo, Victor David. "The Early/Late Tillich and the History of Religion." *Philosophy of Religion and Theology: 1973 Proceedings*, compiled by D. Griffin, 213 – 219. Missoula, MT: Scholars Press for the American Academy of Religion, 1973.

Oberman, Heiko A. *The Roots of Anti-Semitism in the Age of Renaissance and Reformation.* Translated by James I. Porter. Philadelphia: Fortress Press, 1984.

O'Hanlon, Daniel J., S.J. *The Influence of Schelling on the Philosophy of Paul Tillich.* Rome: Pontifica Universitas Gregoriana, 1958.

O'Keefe, Terrence M. "Between Critical Theory and New Being: Paul Tillich's Concept of the Proletariat." Unpublished essay, University of Ulster, 1988.

O'Keefe, Terrence M. "Ideology and the Protestant Principle." *Journal of the American Academy of Religion* 52/2 (1983): 283 – 305.

O'Keefe, Terrence M. "Paul Tillich and the Frankfurt School." In John J. Carey, ed., *Theonomy and Autonomy: Studies in Paul Tillich's Engagement with Modern Culture*, 67 – 82. Macon, GA: Mercer University Press, 1982.

O'Keefe, Terrence M. "Paul Tillich's Marxism." *Social Research* 48/3 (1981): 472 – 499.

Olender, Maurice. *The Languages of Paradise: Race, Religion and Philology in the Nineteenth Century.* Translated by Arthur Goldhammer. Cambridge, MA: Harvard University Press, 1992.

O'Meara, O.P., Thomas F. "'Christianity is the Future of Paganism': Schelling's Philosophy of Religion." In Leroy S. Rouner, ed., *Meaning, Truth and God.* Notre Dame: University of Notre Dame Press, 1982.

O'Neill, Andrew. *Tillich: A Guide for the Perplexed.* New York: T&T Clark/Continuum, 2008.

Otto, Rudolf. *The Idea of the Holy: An Inquiry into the non-rational factor in the idea of the divine and its relation to the rational.* Translated by John W. Harvey. Oxford: Oxford University Press, 1958.

Pauck, Wilhelm. *From Luther to Tillich: The Reformers and their Heirs.* Edited by Marion Pauck. New York: Harper & Row, 1984.

Pauck, Wilhelm and Marion. *Paul Tillich: His Life and Thought.* New York: Harper & Row, 1976.

Pelikan, Jaroslav. *The Emergence of the Catholic Tradition (100 – 600).* Volume One in *The Christian Tradition: A History of the Development of Doctrine.* Chicago: The University of Chicago Press, 1971.

Pfau, Thomas. "Critical Introduction." In Thomas Pfau, ed. and trans., *Idealism and the Endgame of Theory. Three Essays by F.W.J. Schelling.* Albany, NY: SUNY Press, 1994.

Price, David. *Johannes Reuchlin and the Campaign to Destroy Jewish Books.* New York: Oxford University Press, 2010.

Re Manning, Russell. *Theology at the End of Culture: Paul Tillich's Theology of Culture and Art (Studies in Philosophical Theology).* Dudley, MA: Peeters, 2005.

Reimer, A. James. *The Emanuel Hirsch and Paul Tillich Debate: A Study in the Political Ramifications of Theology.* Lewiston, NY: Edwin Mellen Press, 1989.

Richard, Jean. "An Ontologisation of History in Tillich's Systematic Theology?" *North American Paul Tillich Society Bulletin* 39/1 (Winter 2013): 16 – 22.

Ruether, Rosemary Radford. *Faith and Fratricide: The Theological Roots of Anti-Semitism.* Minneapolis, MN: Seabury Press, 1974.

Ruether, Rosemary Radford. "The *Adversus Judaeos* Tradition in the Church Fathers: The Exegesis of Christian Anti-Judaism," in *Essential Papers on Judaism and Christianity in Conflict*, ed. Jeremy Cohen (New York: New York University Press, 1991), 174 – 189.

Runyon, Theodore. “Tillich’s Understanding of Revolution.” In John J. Carey, ed., *Theonomy and Autonomy: Studies in Paul Tillich’s Engagement with Modern Culture*, 267 – 280. Macon, GA: Mercer University Press, 1982.

Said, Edward W. *Orientalism*. New York: Vintage Books, 1979.

Scharf, Uwe Carsten. *The Paradoxical Breakthrough of Revelation. Interpreting the Divine–Human Interplay in Paul Tillich’s Work 1913 – 1964*. Berlin: De Gruyter, 1999. (Contains an English translation of Tillich’s 1913 *Systematic Theology*.)

Schelling, F. W. J. *Sämtliche Werke*. Edited by von K. F. A. Schelling. Fourteen volumes. Stuttgart and Augsburg: J. M. Cotta Verlag, 1856 – 1861.

Schelling, F. W. J. *Historical-Critical Introduction to the Philosophy of Mythology*. Translated by Mason Richey and Markus Zisselberger. Albany, NY: SUNY Press, 2007.

Schelling, F. W. J. *On Human Freedom*. Translated by James Gutman. Chicago, IL: Open Court, 1936.

Schelling, F. W. J. *The Philosophy of Art*. Translated by Douglas W. Stott. Minneapolis: University of Minnesota Press, 1989.

Schelling, F. W. J. *Philosophy and Religion (1804)*. Translated by Klaus Ottmann. Putnam, CT: Spring Publications, 2010.

Schelling, F. W. J. *The Unconditioned in Human Knowledge: Four Early Essays (1794 – 1796)*. Translated with a commentary by Fritz Marti. Lewisburg, PA: Bucknell University Press, 1980.

Schmitt, Carl. *Politische Romantik*. München und Leipzig: Duncker & Humblot, 1919.

Scholder, Klaus. *The Churches and the Third Reich*. Volume I, *Preliminary History and the Time of Illusions 1918 – 1934*. London: SCM Press, 1987.

Scholder, Klaus. *A Requiem for Hitler and Other New Perspectives on the German Church Struggle*. Eugene, OR: Wipf & Stock, 2008.

Schüßler, Werner. *Paul Tillich*. Beck“sche Reihe “Denker.” München: C. H. Beck, 1997.

Sifton, Elisabeth and Hans von Dohnanyi. *No Ordinary Men: Dietrich Bonhoeffer and Hans von Dohnanyi – Resisters Against Hitler in Church and State*. New York: New York Review of Books, 2013.

Smart, Ninian, Clayton, John, Katz, Steven T., and Sherry, Patrick, eds. *Nineteenth-Century Religious Thought in the West*. Three volumes. Cambridge: Cambridge University Press, 1985.

Smith, Helmut Walser. *The Continuities of German History: Nation, Religion, and Race Across the Long Nineteenth Century*. Cambridge: Cambridge University Press, 2008.

Sommer, Günther. “The Significance of the Late Philosophy of Schelling for the Formation and Interpretation of the Thought of Paul Tillich.” Doctoral dissertation, Duke University, 1960.

Steigmann-Gall, Richard. *The Holy Reich: Nazi Conceptions of Christianity, 1919 – 1945*. Cambridge: Cambridge University Press, 2003.

Steinacker, Peter. “Die Bedeutung der Philosophie Schellings für die Theologie Paul Tillichs.” In Hermann Fischer, ed., *Paul Tillich: Studien zu einer Theologie der Moderne*, 37 – 61. Frankfurt-on-Main: Athenäum Verlag, 1989.

Stone, Jerome A. “Tillich and Schelling’s Later Philosophy.” In Carey, Kairos *and* Logos, 11 – 44.

Stone, Ronald H. “Paul Tillich: On the Boundary between Protestantism and Marxism.” *Laval Theologique et Philosophie* 45 (October 1989): 393 – 417.

Stone, Ronald H. *Paul Tillich’s Radical Social Thought*. Atlanta, GA: John Knox Press, 1980.

Stone, Ronald H. *Politics and Faith: Reinhold Niebuhr and Paul Tillich at Union Seminary in New York.* Macon, GA: Mercer University Press, 2012.
Stone, Ronald H. "Tillich's Critical Use of Marx and Freud in the Social Context of the Frankfurt School." *Union Seminary Quarterly Review* 32/1 (1977): 3–9.
Stumme, John R. *Socialism in Theological Perspective: A Study of Paul Tillich, 1918–1933.* Missoula, MT: Scholars Press, 1978.
Sturm, Erdmann. "Between Apologetics and Pastoral Care: Paul Tillich's Early Sermons (1908–1918)." *North American Paul Tillich Society Newsletter* 26/1 (Winter 2000): 7–20.
Sturm, Erdmann. ""Holy Love Claims Life and Limb": Paul Tillich's War Theology (1914–1918)." *Zeitschrift für neuere Theologiegeschichte* 2/1 (1995): 60–54.
Tal, Uriel. *Christians and Jews in Germany: Religions, Politics, and Ideology in the Second Reich, 1870–1914.* Translated by Noah Jonathan Jacobs. Ithaca, NY: Cornell University Press, 1975.
"A Theology for Protestants." *Time*, March 16, 1959.
Thomas, John Heywood. "J. G. Fichte and F. W. J. Schelling." In Smart, et al., *Nineteenth-Century Religious Thought in the West*, vol. I, 41–79.
Thomas, John Heywood. *Paul Tillich: An Appraisal.* London: SCM Press, 1963.
Thomas, John Heywood. "Philosophical Influences on Tillich's Development of a Theology of Culture." In Carey, Kairos *and* Logos, 11–44.
Thomas, John Heywood. *Tillich.* New York: Continuum, 2000.
Tillich, Hannah. *From Time to Time.* New York: Stein & Day, 1973.
Weaver, Matthew Lon. *Religious Internationalism: War and Peace in the Thought of Paul Tillich.* Macon, GA: Mercer University Press, 2010.
Weber, Max. *Ancient Judaism.* Translated and edited by Hans H. Gerth and Don Martindale. Glencoe, Illinois: The Free Press, 1952.
Weber, Max. *The Methodology of the Social Sciences.* Translated and edited by Edward A. Shils and Henry A. Finch. New York: The Free Press, 1949.
Weisskopf, Walter A. "Tillich and the Crisis of the West." In James Luther Adams, Wilhelm Pauck and Roger Shinn, eds., *The Thought of Paul Tillich*, 63–80. San Francisco: Harper & Row, 1985.
Welch, Claude. *Protestant Thought in the Nineteenth Century*, volume I, *1799–1870*, and volume II, *1870–1914.* New Haven: Yale University Press, 1972 and 1985.
Wheat, Leonard F. *Paul Tillich's Dialectical Humanism: Unmasking the God above God.* Baltimore, MD: Johns Hopkins Press, 1970.
Wilder, Courtney S. "Existentialism and Exegesis: Being and the Bible in Tillich and Bultmann." Doctoral dissertation, University of Chicago, 2008.
Wistrich, Robert S. *A Lethal Obsession: Anti-Semitism from Antiquity to the Global Jihad.* New York: Random House, 2010.
Yovel, Yirmiyahu. *Dark Riddle: Hegel, Nietzsche and the Jews.* University Park, PA; Pennsylvania State University Press, 1998.
Zeitlow, Harold Howard. *The Living God: The Existential Systems of F. W. J. Schelling and Paul Tillich.* Chicago, IL: University of Chicago Press, 1961
Ziolkowski, Theodore. *Clio the Romantic Muse: Historicizing the Faculties in Germany.* Ithaca, NY: Cornell University Press, 2004.

Subject index

11/15